SPANISH
FOR EVERYONE
JUNIOR
5 WORDS A DAY

FREE AUDIO
website and app

www.dk5words.com/us

SPANISH
FOR EVERYONE
JUNIOR

5 WORDS A DAY

FREE AUDIO
website and app

www.dk5words.com/us

DK

For the curious

DK LONDON
Project Editors Sophie Adam, Elizabeth Blakemore
Project Art Editor Anna Scully
Designer Annabel Schick
Illustrators Amy Child, Gus Scott
Managing Editor Christine Stroyan
Managing Art Editor Anna Hall
Production Editor Kavita Varma
Production Controller Samantha Cross
Senior Jacket Designer Suhita Dharamjit
Jacket Design Development Manager Sophia MTT
Publisher Andrew Macintyre
Art Director Karen Self
Publishing Director Jonathan Metcalf

Translation Andiamo! Language Services Ltd

DK INDIA
Pre-Production Manager Sunil Sharma
DTP Designers Manish Chandra Upreti,
Umesh Singh Rawat

First American Edition, 2021
Published in the United States by DK Publishing
1745 Broadway, 20th Floor, New York NY 10019

Copyright © 2021 Dorling Kindersley Limited
DK, a Division of Penguin Random House LLC
22 23 24 25 10 9 8 7 6 5 4
007–322377–Jul/2021

A catalog record for this book
is available from the Library of Congress.
ISBN: 978-0-7440-3676-3
DK books are available at special discounts
when purchased in bulk for sales promotions, premiums,
fund-raising, or educational use. For details, contact: DK
Publishing Special Markets,
1745 Broadway, 20th Floor, New York NY 10019
SpecialSales@dk.com

Printed and bound in China

For the curious
www.dk.com

This book was made with Forest
Stewardship Council ™ certified
paper – one small step in DK's
commitment to a sustainable future.
For more information go to
www.dk.com/our-green-pledge

Contents

How to use this book

Spanish for Everyone Junior: 5 Words a Day is a vocabulary book
for children that teaches and tests more than 1,000 Spanish words.
Words are taught in weekly units of 5 days.

Learning new vocabulary

On Days 1–4, the child will be presented with 20 new words, which
are taught 5 words at a time through colorful illustrations.

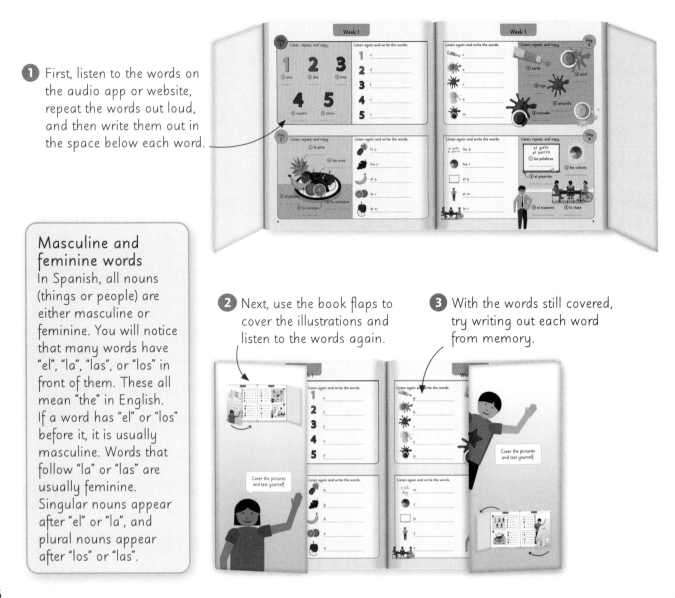

1 First, listen to the words on
the audio app or website,
repeat the words out loud,
and then write them out in
the space below each word.

Masculine and feminine words
In Spanish, all nouns
(things or people) are
either masculine or
feminine. You will notice
that many words have
"el", "la", "las", or "los" in
front of them. These all
mean "the" in English.
If a word has "el" or "los"
before it, it is usually
masculine. Words that
follow "la" or "las" are
usually feminine.
Singular nouns appear
after "el" or "la", and
plural nouns appear
after "los" or "las".

2 Next, use the book flaps to
cover the illustrations and
listen to the words again.

3 With the words still covered,
try writing out each word
from memory.

Testing new vocabulary

On Day 5, the child can practice the 20 new words and reinforce their learning through fun exercises.

A variety of exercises are used to test all 20 words.

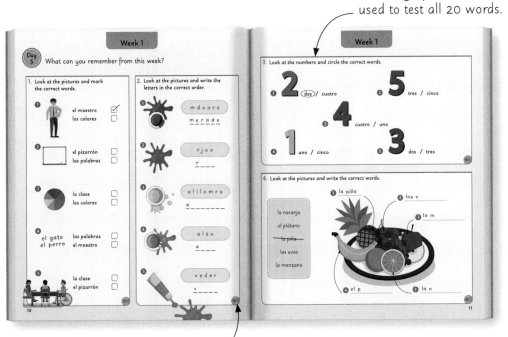

Once you have finished an exercise, listen to the words again on the app or website.

Answers to all the questions are given at the back of the book.

Audio

Pronunciation is an important aspect of learning a new language. Audio for all the words in this book is available on the **DK 5 Words** website and app. You should encourage your child to listen to the audio and repeat the words out loud.

Access the audio recordings for free at **www.dk5words.com/us** or download the **DK 5 Words** app from the App Store or Google Play.

FREE AUDIO
website and app

www.dk5words.com/us

Day 1

Listen, repeat, and copy.

1

2

3

① uno

② dos

③ tres

4

5

④ cuatro

⑤ cinco

Listen again and write the words.

1 u

2 d

3 t

4 c

5 c

Day 2

Listen, repeat, and copy.

① la piña

② las uvas

③ el plátano

④ la naranja

⑤ la manzana

Listen again and write the words.

la p

las u

el p

la n

la m

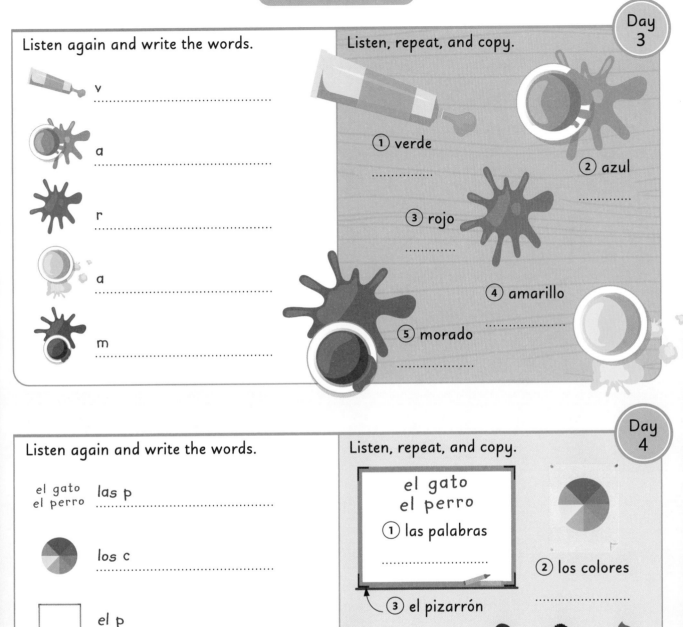

Day 3

Listen again and write the words.

v ....

a ....

r ....

a ....

m ....

Listen, repeat, and copy.

① verde
....

② azul
....

③ rojo
....

④ amarillo
....

⑤ morado
....

Day 4

Listen again and write the words.

el gato
el perro   las p ....

los c ....

el p ....

el m ....

la c ....

Listen, repeat, and copy.

el gato
el perro
① las palabras
....

② los colores
....

③ el pizarrón
....

④ el maestro
....

⑤ la clase
....

Week 1

What can you remember from this week?

1. Look at the pictures and mark the correct words.

① el maestro ☑
   los colores ☐

② el pizarrón ☐
   las palabras ☐

③ la clase ☐
   los colores ☐

④ el gato
   el perro
   las palabras ☐
   el maestro ☐

⑤ la clase ☐
   el pizarrón ☐

2. Look at the pictures and write the letters in the correct order.

① m d o a r o
m o r a d o
_ _ _ _ _ _

② r j o o
r _ _ _ _

③ a l i l o m r a
a _ _ _ _ _ _ _ _

④ a l z u
a _ _ _ _

⑤ v e d e r
v _ _ _ _ _

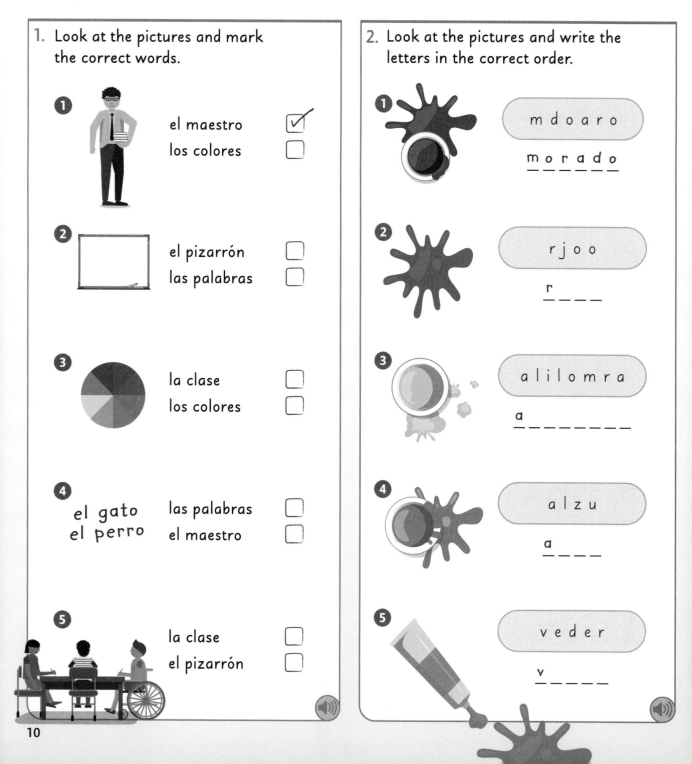

3. Look at the numbers and circle the correct words.

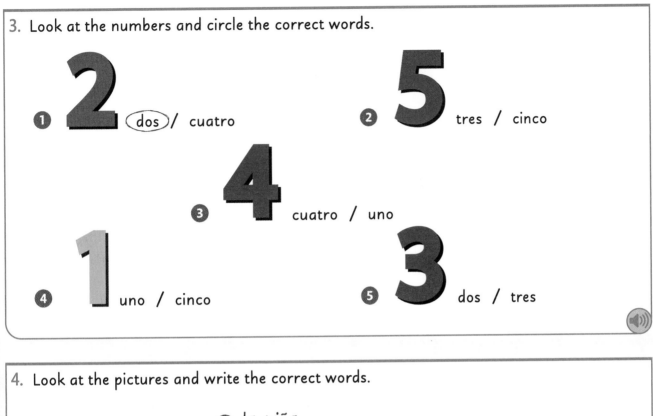

❶ (dos) / cuatro

❷ tres / cinco

❸ cuatro / uno

❹ uno / cinco

❺ dos / tres

4. Look at the pictures and write the correct words.

la naranja

el plátano

~~la piña~~

las uvas

la manzana

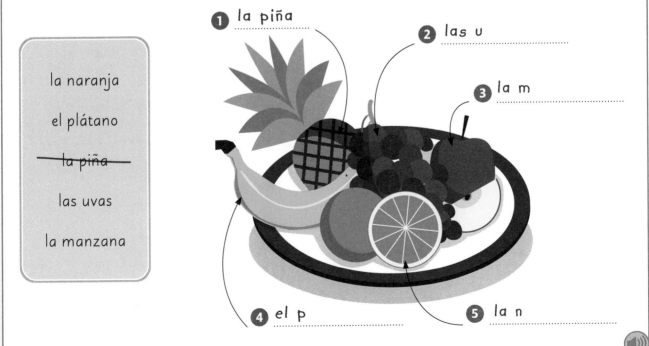

❶ la piña

❷ las u

❸ la m

❹ el p

❺ la n

Day 1

Listen, repeat, and copy.

6 ① seis

7 ② siete

8 ③ ocho

9 ④ nueve

10 ⑤ diez

Listen again and write the words.

6 s ....

7 s ....

8 o ....

9 n ....

10 d ....

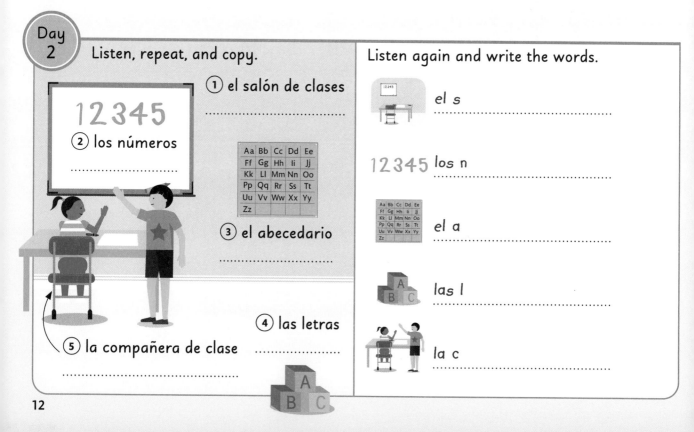

Day 2

Listen, repeat, and copy.

① el salón de clases ....

12345 ② los números ....

③ el abecedario ....

④ las letras ....

⑤ la compañera de clase ....

Listen again and write the words.

el s ....

los n ....

el a ....

las l ....

la c ....

Week 2

Listen again and write the words.

la m ....

la f ....

el o ....

el j ....

la m ....

Listen, repeat, and copy.

① la marioneta
....

② la figura de acción
....

③ el osito
....

④ el juego de mesa
....

⑤ la muñeca
....

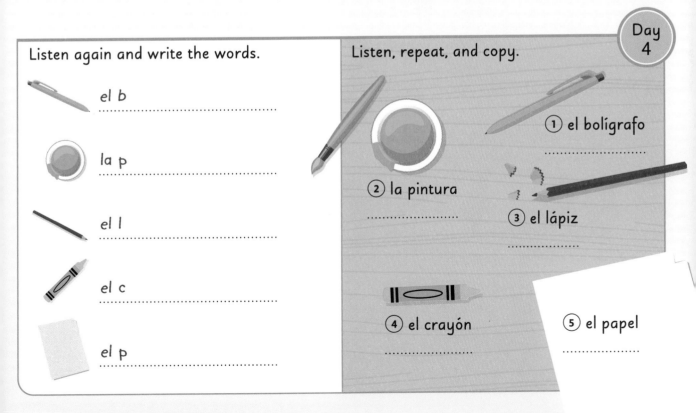

Listen again and write the words.

el b ....

la p ....

el l ....

el c ....

el p ....

Listen, repeat, and copy.

① el bolígrafo
....

② la pintura
....

③ el lápiz
....

④ el crayón
....

⑤ el papel
....

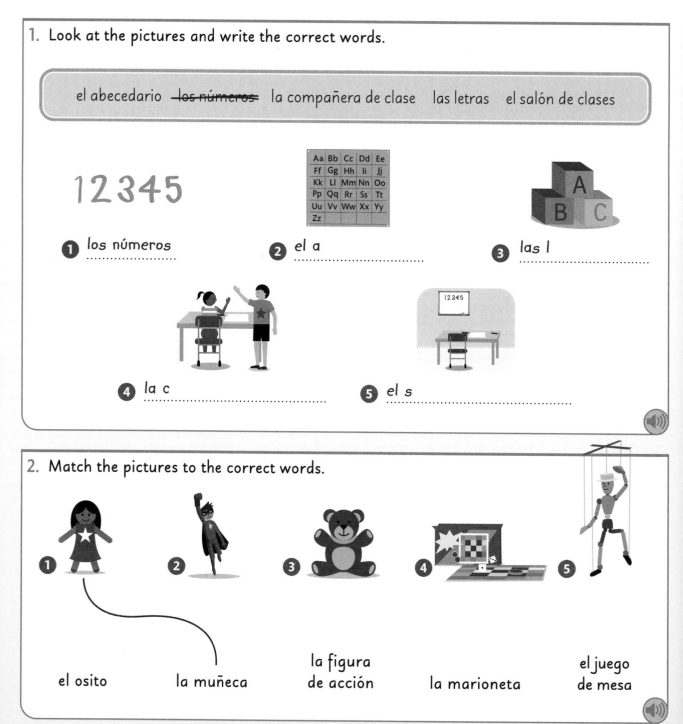

Day 5

What can you remember from this week?

1. Look at the pictures and write the correct words.

el abecedario   ~~los números~~   la compañera de clase   las letras   el salón de clases

1 2 3 4 5

Aa	Bb	Cc	Dd	Ee
Ff	Gg	Hh	Ii	Jj
Kk	Ll	Mm	Nn	Oo
Pp	Qq	Rr	Ss	Tt
Uu	Vv	Ww	Xx	Yy
Zz				

A
B C

1 los números

2 el a

3 las l

4 la c

5 el s

2. Match the pictures to the correct words.

1   **2**   **3**   **4**   **5**

el osito   la muñeca   la figura de acción   la marioneta   el juego de mesa

3. Read the words and mark the correct pictures.

1 el bolígrafo   A ☐   B ☑

2 el crayón   A ☐   B ☐

3 el papel   A ☐   B ☐

4 la pintura   A ☐   B ☐

5 el lápiz   A ☐   B ☐

4. Look at the numbers and fill in the missing letters.

1 8   o c h o

2 6   _ _ e _ s

3 9   n _ e _ e

4 7   s _ e _ e

5 10   _ _ i _ z

Day 1

Listen, repeat, and copy.

11 ① once

12 ② doce

13 ③ trece

14 ④ catorce

15 ⑤ quince

Listen again and write the words.

11 o ....

12 d ....

13 t ....

14 c ....

15 q ....

Day 2

Listen, repeat, and copy.

① la escuela

② la casa

③ la calle

④ el parque

⑤ el parque infantil

Listen again and write the words.

la e ....

la c ....

la c ....

el p ....

el p ....

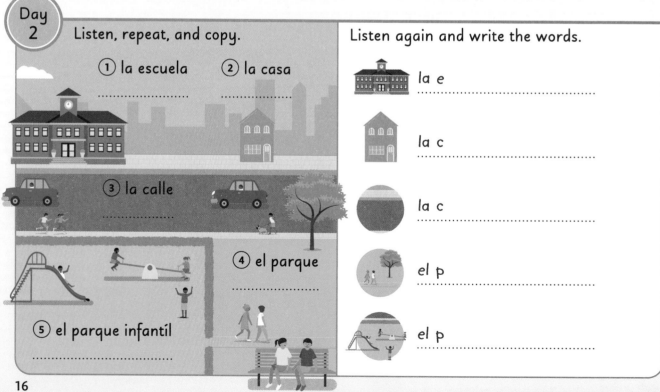

16

Day 3

Listen again and write the words.

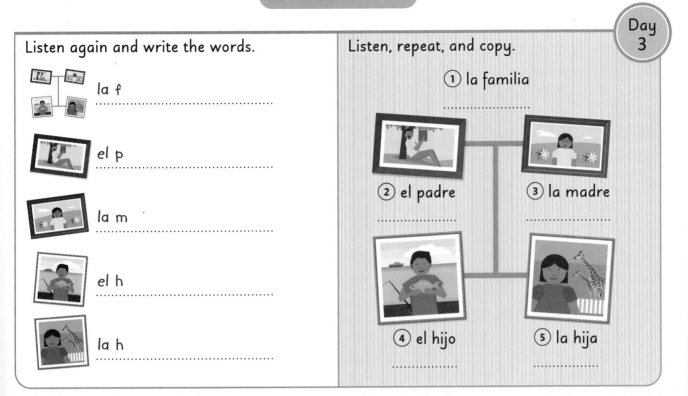

la f ....

el p ....

la m ....

el h ....

la h ....

Listen, repeat, and copy.

① la familia
....

② el padre ....

③ la madre ....

④ el hijo ....

⑤ la hija ....

Day 4

Listen again and write the words.

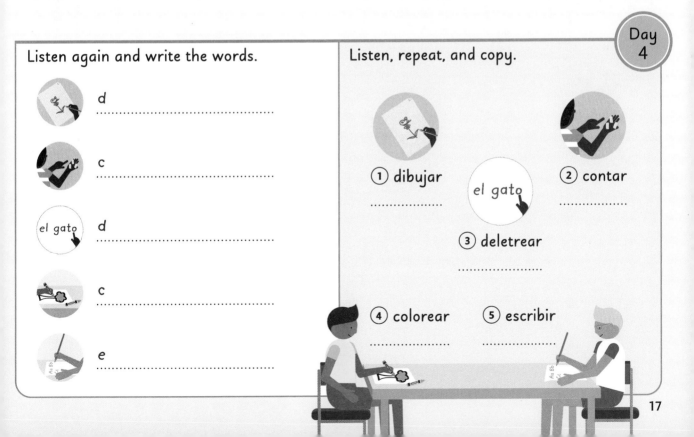

d ....

c ....

d ....

c ....

e ....

Listen, repeat, and copy.

① dibujar ....

el gato

② contar ....

③ deletrear

....

④ colorear ....

⑤ escribir ....

17

What can you remember from this week?

1. Look at the pictures and mark the correct words.

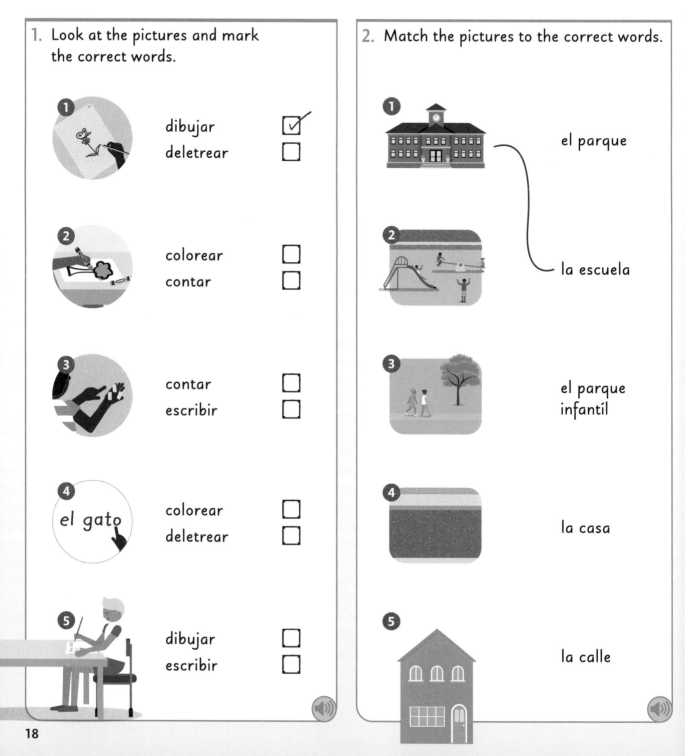

1. dibujar ☑
   deletrear ☐

2. colorear ☐
   contar ☐

3. contar ☐
   escribir ☐

4. el gato   colorear ☐
   deletrear ☐

5. dibujar ☐
   escribir ☐

2. Match the pictures to the correct words.

1. el parque

2. la escuela

3. el parque infantil

4. la casa

5. la calle

3. Look at the numbers and write the correct words.

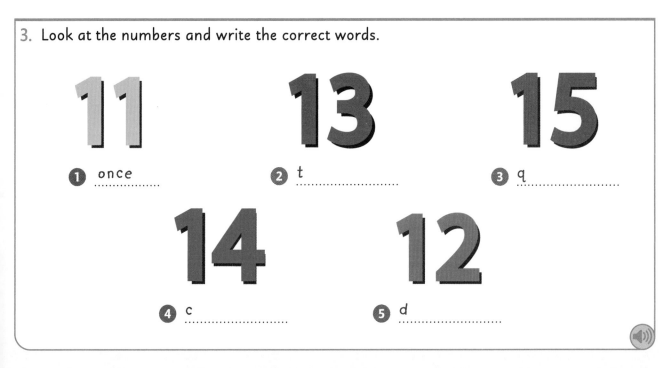

11

❶ once ....

13

❷ t ....

15

❸ q ....

14

❹ c ....

12

❺ d ....

4. Look at the pictures and write the correct words.

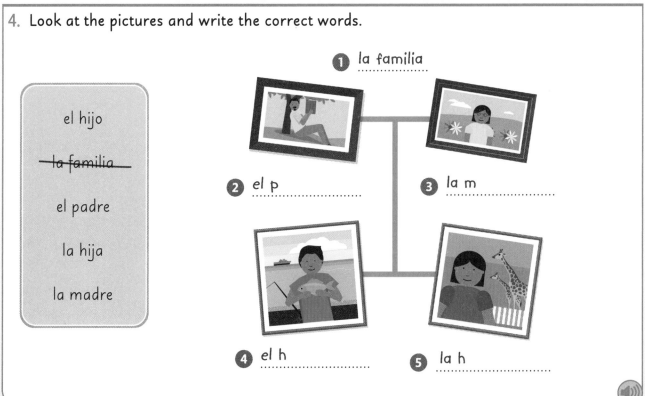

el hijo

~~la familia~~

el padre

la hija

la madre

❶ la familia ....

❷ el p ....

❸ la m ....

❹ el h ....

❺ la h ....

Day 1

Listen, repeat, and copy.

16 ① dieciséis

17 ② diecisiete

18 ③ dieciocho

19 ④ diecinueve

20 ⑤ veinte

Listen again and write the words.

16 d ....

17 d ....

18 d ....

19 d ....

20 v ....

Day 2

Listen, repeat, and copy.

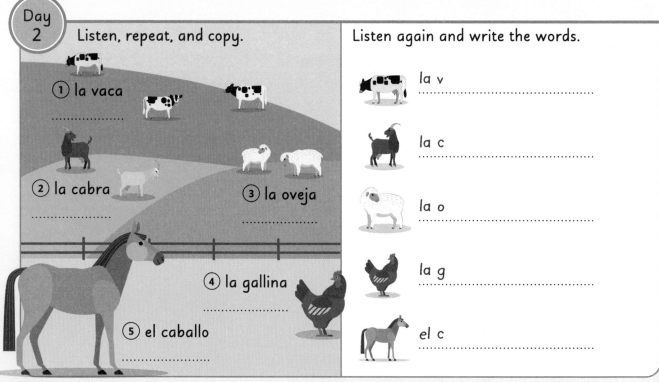

① la vaca

② la cabra

③ la oveja

④ la gallina

⑤ el caballo

Listen again and write the words.

la v ....

la c ....

la o ....

la g ....

el c ....

Week 4

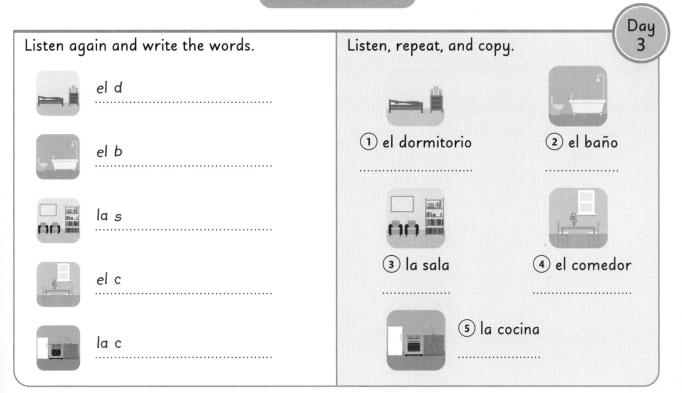

Listen again and write the words.

el d ....

el b ....

la s ....

el c ....

la c ....

Listen, repeat, and copy.

① el dormitorio ....

② el baño ....

③ la sala ....

④ el comedor ....

⑤ la cocina ....

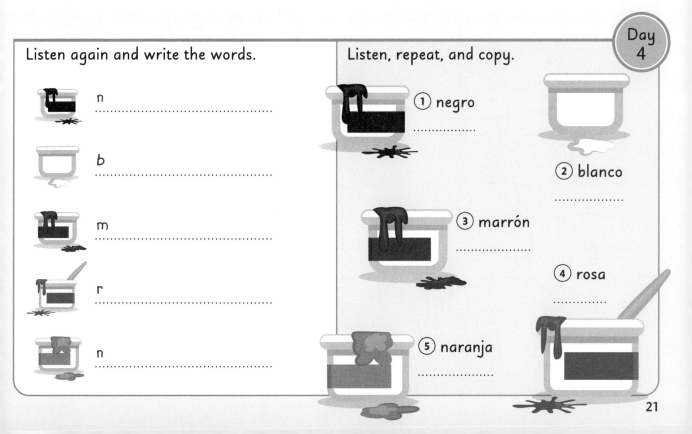

Listen again and write the words.

n ....

b ....

m ....

r ....

n ....

Listen, repeat, and copy.

① negro ....

② blanco ....

③ marrón ....

④ rosa ....

⑤ naranja ....

Day 5

What can you remember from this week?

1. Look at the pictures and fill in the missing letters.

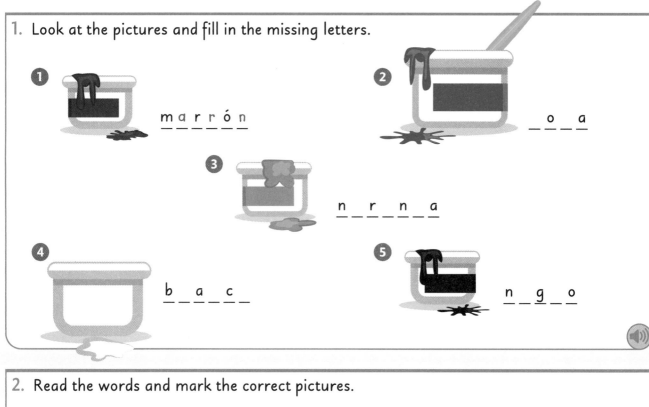

① m a r r ó n

② _ o _ a

③ n _ r _ n _ a

④ b _ a _ c _

⑤ n _ g _ o

2. Read the words and mark the correct pictures.

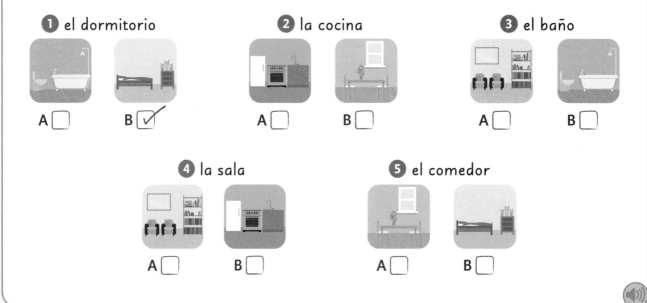

① el dormitorio

A ☐   B ☑

② la cocina

A ☐   B ☐

③ el baño

A ☐   B ☐

④ la sala

A ☐   B ☐

⑤ el comedor

A ☐   B ☐

3. Look at the pictures and mark the correct words.

1. la vaca ☐
   la gallina ✓
   la oveja ☐

2. la gallina ☐
   la cabra ☐
   el caballo ☐

3. la oveja ☐
   la vaca ☐
   el caballo ☐

4. la cabra ☐
   la gallina ☐
   la vaca ☐

5. el caballo ☐
   la oveja ☐
   la cabra ☐

4. Look at the numbers and write the letters in the correct order.

1. **17**
   d e e t i s i c i e
   d i e c i s i e t e

2. **20**
   v n e t e i
   v _ _ _ _ _ _

3. **18**
   d o c i h e c i o
   d _ _ _ _ _ _ _ _ _

4. **16**
   d s i i e c s é i
   d _ _ _ _ _ _ _ _ _

5. **19**
   d n u i e v e c i e
   d _ _ _ _ _ _ _ _ _

23

Day 1

Listen, repeat, and copy.

① la cebra

② la jirafa

③ el león

④ el hipopótamo

⑤ el elefante

Listen again and write the words.

la c
....

la j
....

el l
....

el h
....

el e
....

Day 2

Listen, repeat, and copy.

① el borrador

② las tijeras

③ la regla

④ el libro

⑤ la mochila

Listen again and write the words.

el b
....

las t
....

la r
....

el l
....

la m
....

24

Week 5

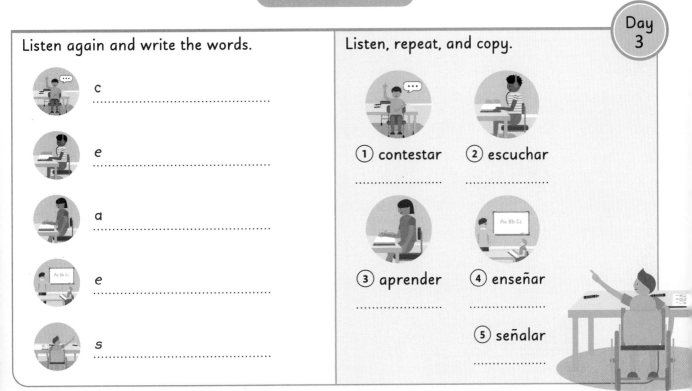

Day 3

Listen again and write the words.

c ....

e ....

a ....

e ....

s ....

Listen, repeat, and copy.

① contestar ....

② escuchar ....

③ aprender ....

④ enseñar ....

⑤ señalar ....

Day 4

Listen again and write the words.

el m ....

la p ....

el k ....

la s ....

el c ....

Listen, repeat, and copy.

① el mango ....

② la pera ....

③ el kiwi ....

④ la sandía ....

⑤ el coco ....

Day 5 What can you remember from this week?

1. Match the pictures to the correct words.

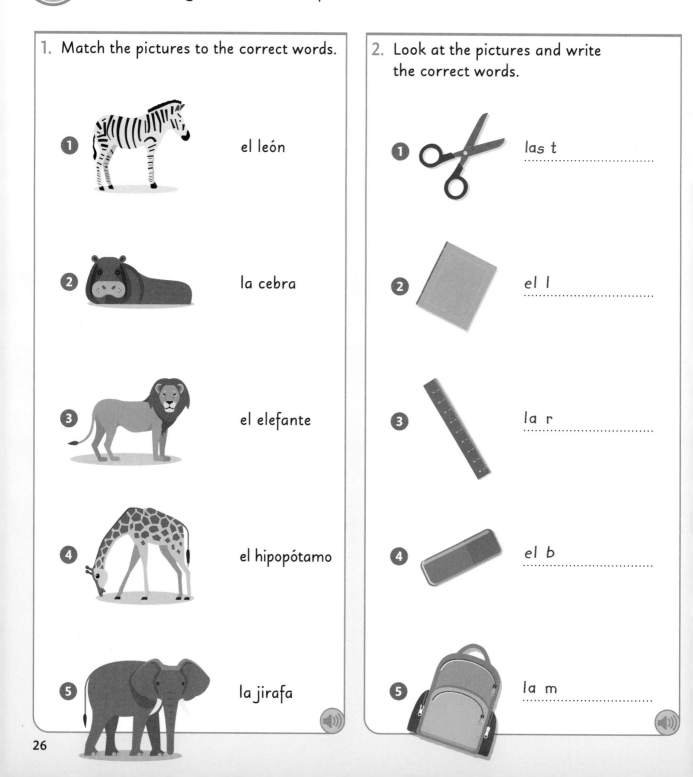

1   el león

2   la cebra

3   el elefante

4   el hipopótamo

5   la jirafa

2. Look at the pictures and write the correct words.

1   las t ....

2   el l ....

3   la r ....

4   el b ....

5   la m ....

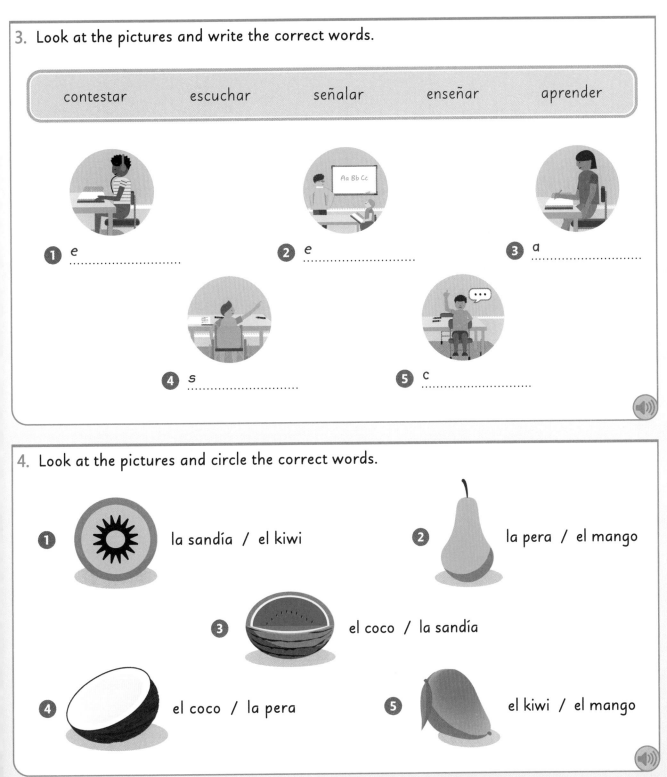

3. Look at the pictures and write the correct words.

| contestar | escuchar | señalar | enseñar | aprender |

1 e ....

2 e ....

3 a ....

4 s ....

5 c ....

4. Look at the pictures and circle the correct words.

1 la sandía / el kiwi

2 la pera / el mango

3 el coco / la sandía

4 el coco / la pera

5 el kiwi / el mango

Day 1

Listen, repeat, and copy.

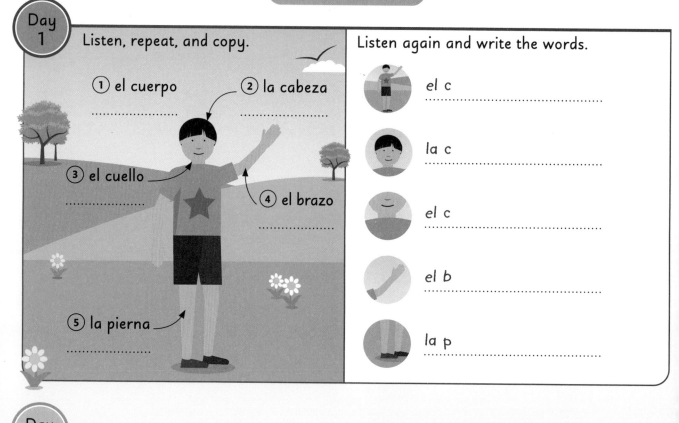

① el cuerpo ② la cabeza

③ el cuello

④ el brazo

⑤ la pierna

Listen again and write the words.

el c ....

la c ....

el c ....

el b ....

la p ....

Day 2

Listen, repeat, and copy.

① el tenis ② el béisbol

③ el hockey

④ el bádminton ⑤ el baloncesto

Listen again and write the words.

el t ....

el b ....

el h ....

el b ....

el b ....

Week 6

Listen again and write the words.

la g ....

la c ....

el b ....

el m ....

la p ....

Listen, repeat, and copy.

① la gaviota
....

② la cometa
....

③ el barco
....

④ el mar
....

⑤ la pelota
....

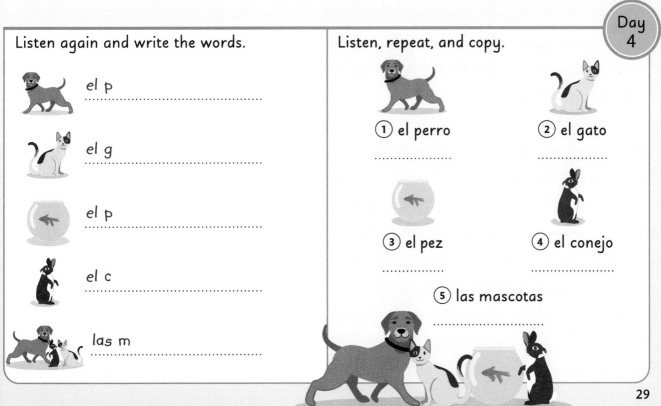

Listen again and write the words.

el p ....

el g ....

el p ....

el c ....

las m ....

Listen, repeat, and copy.

① el perro
....

② el gato
....

③ el pez
....

④ el conejo
....

⑤ las mascotas
....

What can you remember from this week?

1. Read the words and mark the correct pictures.

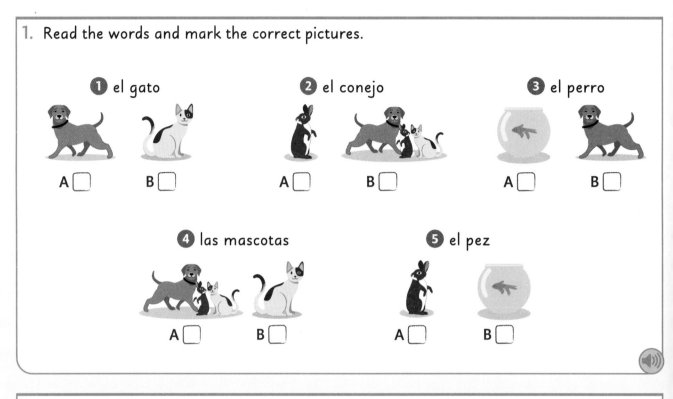

❶ el gato

A ☐   B ☐

❷ el conejo

A ☐   B ☐

❸ el perro

A ☐   B ☐

❹ las mascotas

A ☐   B ☐

❺ el pez

A ☐   B ☐

2. Look at the pictures and fill in the missing letters.

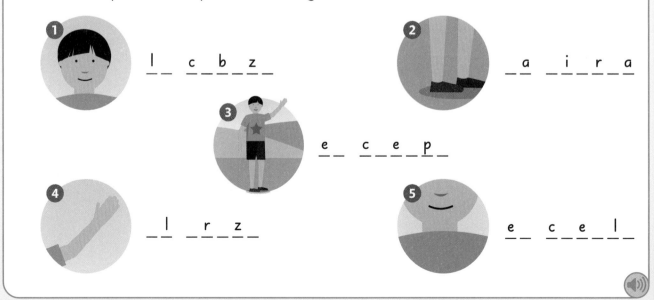

1 | l   c   b   z
__ __   __ __ __ __

2 | a   i   r   a
__ __   __ __ __ __ __

3 | e   c   e   p
__ __   __ __ __ __ __

4 | l   r   z
__ __   __ __ __ __

5 | e   c   e   l
__ __   __ __ __ __

3. Look at the pictures and mark the correct words.

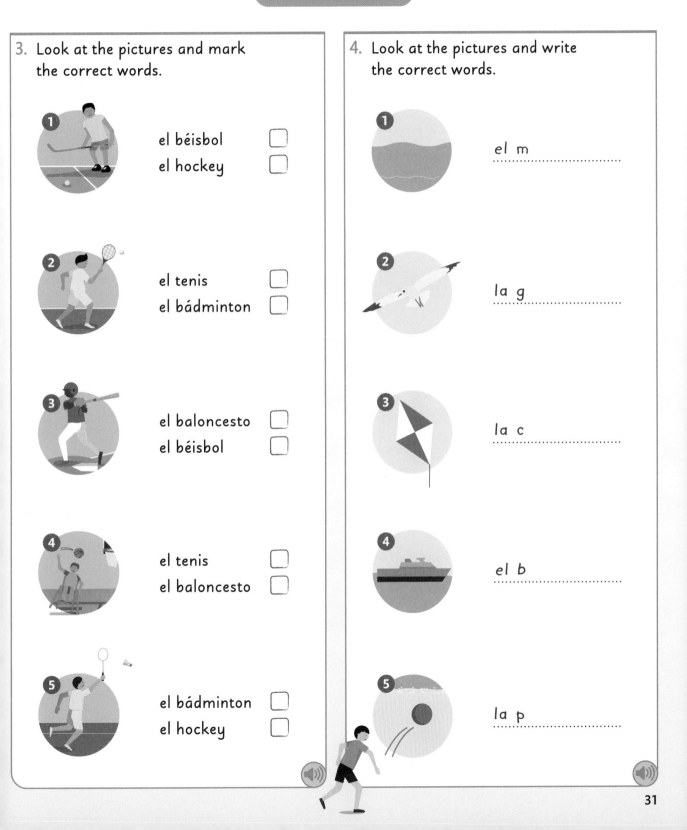

1. el béisbol ☐
   el hockey ☐

2. el tenis ☐
   el bádminton ☐

3. el baloncesto ☐
   el béisbol ☐

4. el tenis ☐
   el baloncesto ☐

5. el bádminton ☐
   el hockey ☐

4. Look at the pictures and write the correct words.

1. el m ....

2. la g ....

3. la c ....

4. el b ....

5. la p ....

Day 1

Listen, repeat, and copy.

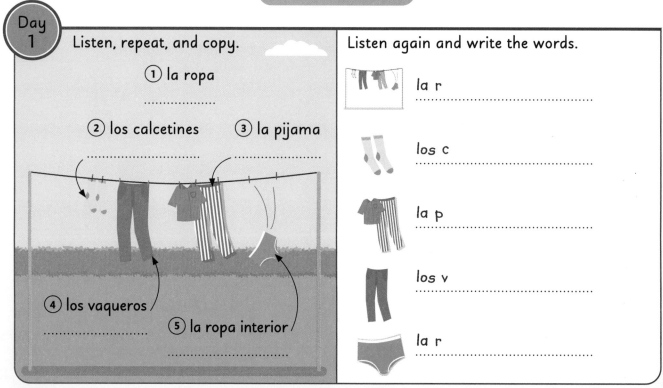

① la ropa

....

② los calcetines ③ la pijama

....

④ los vaqueros

....

⑤ la ropa interior

....

Listen again and write the words.

la r ....

los c ....

la p ....

los v ....

la r ....

Day 2

Listen, repeat, and copy.

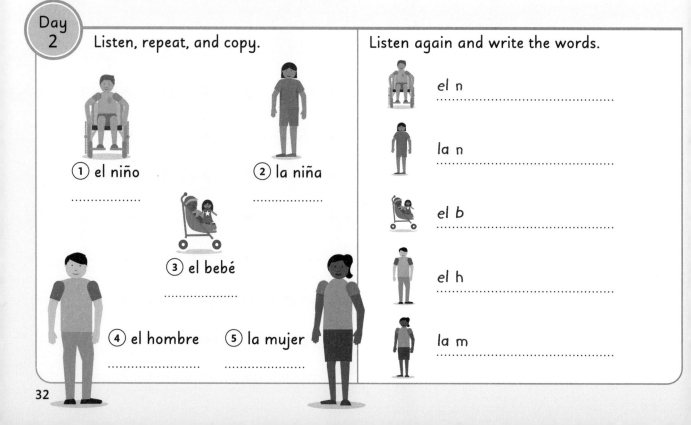

① el niño

....

② la niña

....

③ el bebé

....

④ el hombre ⑤ la mujer

....

Listen again and write the words.

el n ....

la n ....

el b ....

el h ....

la m ....

Day 3

Listen again and write the words.

la h ....

la p ....

el p ....

las p ....

los f ....

Listen, repeat, and copy.

① la hamburguesa ....

② la pizza ....

③ el pollo ....

④ las papas fritas ....

⑤ los fideos ....

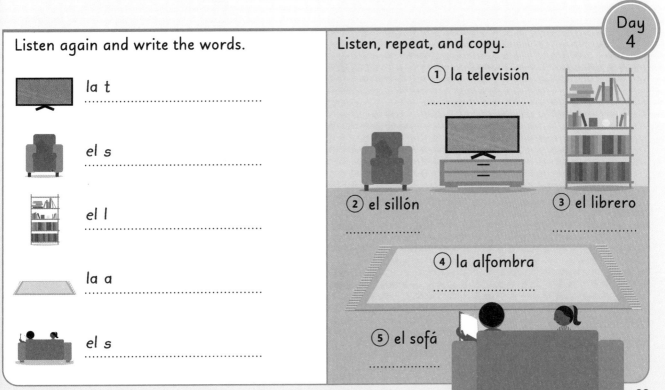

Day 4

Listen again and write the words.

la t ....

el s ....

el l ....

la a ....

el s ....

Listen, repeat, and copy.

① la televisión ....

② el sillón ....

③ el librero ....

④ la alfombra ....

⑤ el sofá ....

33

Day 5

What can you remember from this week?

1. Look at the pictures and fill in the missing letters.

① l_ _ n _ ñ _

② _ _ l _ _ o _ b _ e

③ e _ _ n _ _ ñ _

④ _ _ l _ _ e _ é

⑤ l _ _ m _ _ j _ r

2. Read the words and mark the correct pictures.

① los vaqueros   A ☐   B ☐

② la ropa interior   A ☐   B ☐

③ la pijama   A ☐   B ☐

④ los calcetines   A ☐   B ☐

⑤ la ropa   A ☐   B ☐

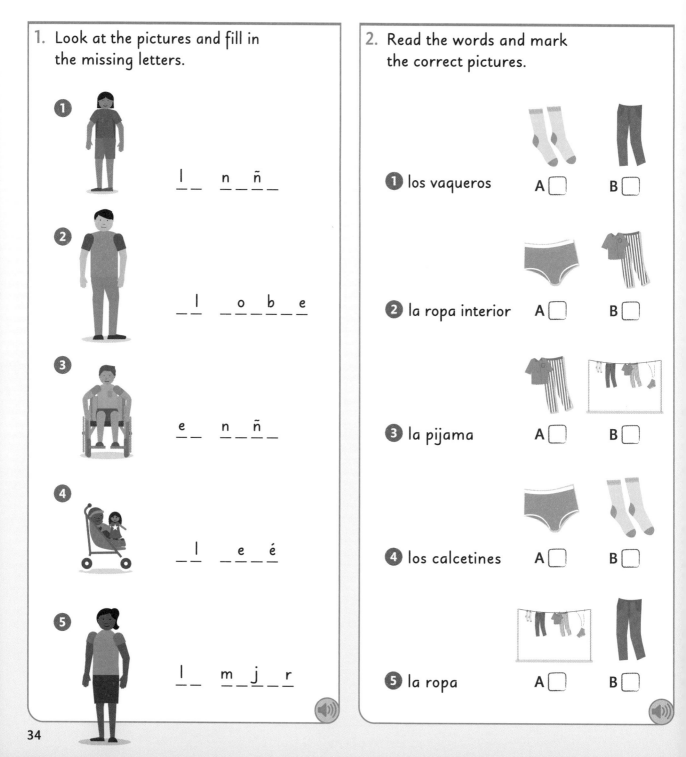

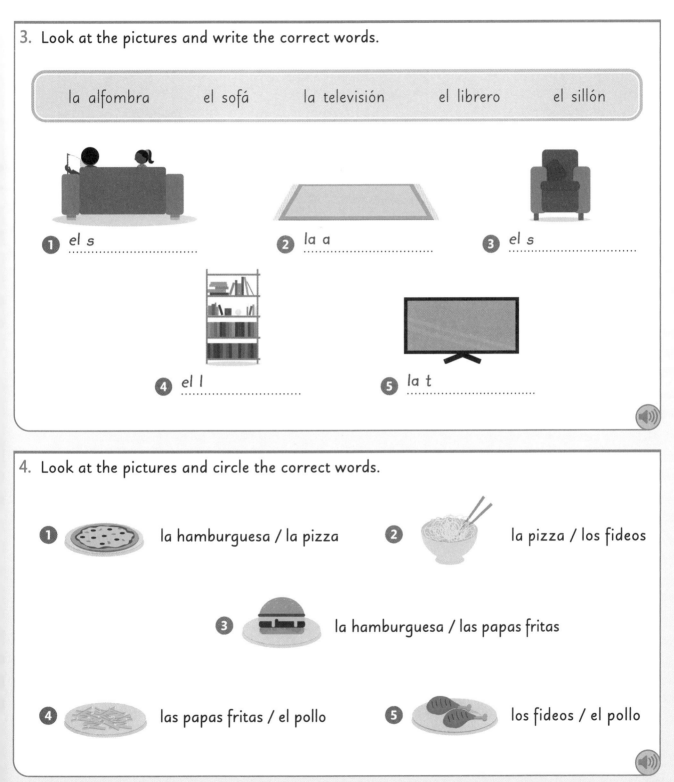

3. Look at the pictures and write the correct words.

la alfombra   el sofá   la televisión   el librero   el sillón

1 el s ....

2 la a ....

3 el s ....

4 el l ....

5 la t ....

4. Look at the pictures and circle the correct words.

1 la hamburguesa / la pizza

2 la pizza / los fideos

3 la hamburguesa / las papas fritas

4 las papas fritas / el pollo

5 los fideos / el pollo

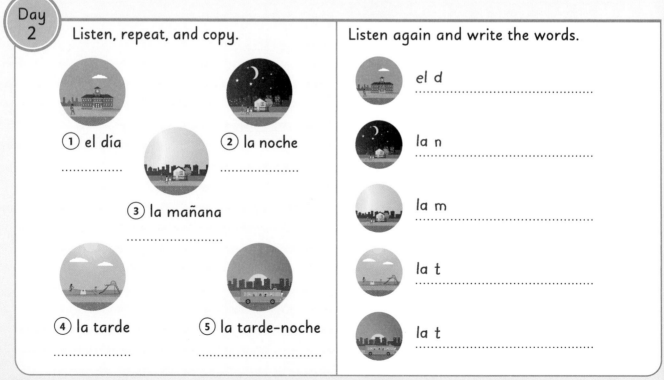

Day 1

Listen, repeat, and copy.

① el calendario

② el póster

③ la cama

④ los juguetes

⑤ el juguetero

Listen again and write the words.

el c

el p

la c

los j

el j

Day 2

Listen, repeat, and copy.

① el día

② la noche

③ la mañana

④ la tarde

⑤ la tarde-noche

Listen again and write the words.

el d

la n

la m

la t

la t

Week 8

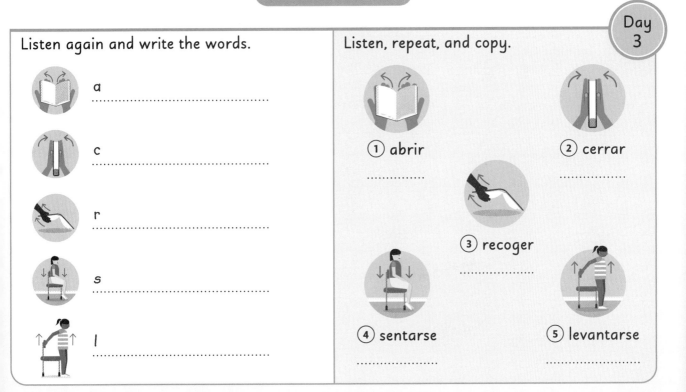

Listen again and write the words.

a ....

c ....

r ....

s ....

l ....

Listen, repeat, and copy.

① abrir ....

② cerrar ....

③ recoger ....

④ sentarse ....

⑤ levantarse ....

Listen again and write the words.

la s ....

el m ....

el t ....

el o ....

la r ....

Listen, repeat, and copy.

① la selva ....

② el mono ....

③ el tigre ....

④ el oso ....

⑤ la rana ....

Day 5

What can you remember from this week?

1. Look at the pictures and write the correct words.

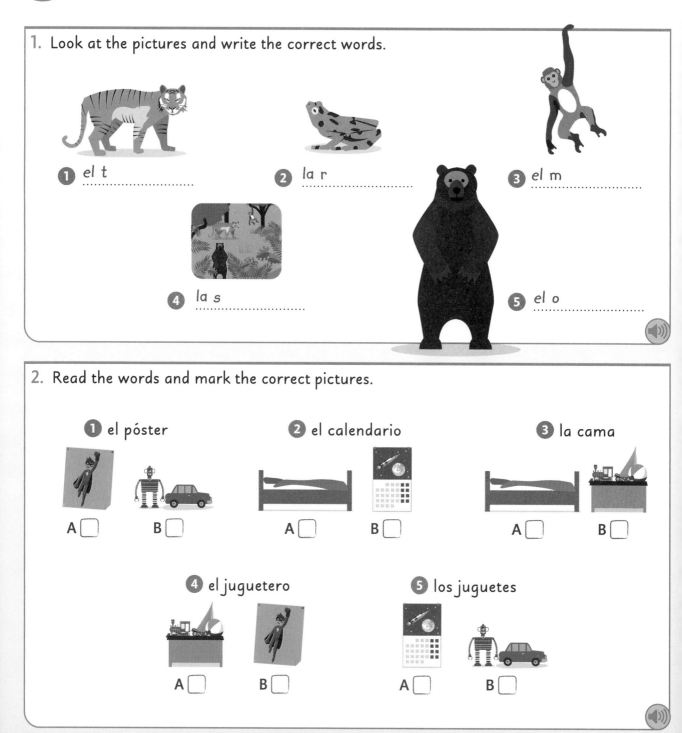

1 el t ....

2 la r ....

3 el m ....

4 la s ....

5 el o ....

2. Read the words and mark the correct pictures.

1 el póster

A ☐   B ☐

2 el calendario

A ☐   B ☐

3 la cama

A ☐   B ☐

4 el juguetero

A ☐   B ☐

5 los juguetes

A ☐   B ☐

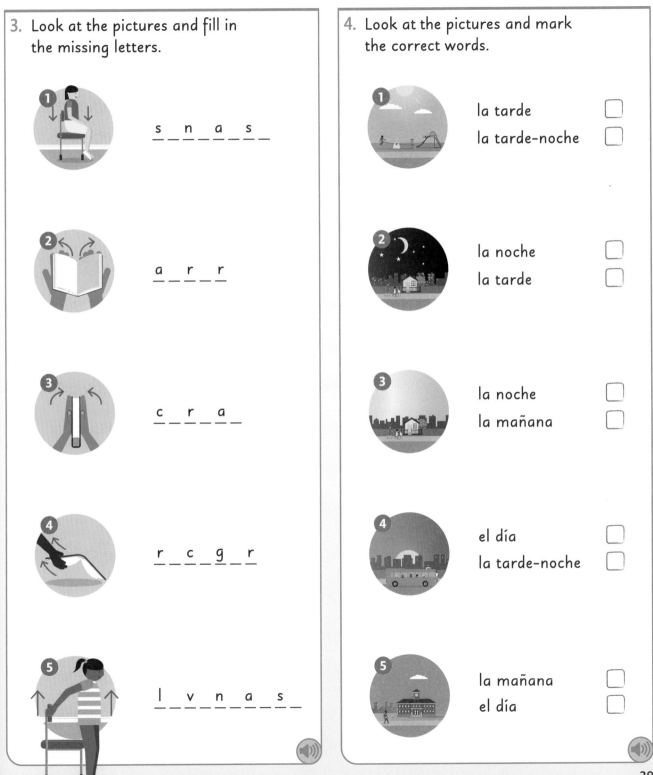

3. Look at the pictures and fill in the missing letters.

1. s _ n _ a _ s _

2. a _ r _ r _

3. c _ r _ a _

4. r _ c _ g _ r _

5. l _ v _ n _ a _ s _

4. Look at the pictures and mark the correct words.

1. la tarde ☐
   la tarde-noche ☐

2. la noche ☐
   la tarde ☐

3. la noche ☐
   la mañana ☐

4. el día ☐
   la tarde-noche ☐

5. la mañana ☐
   el día ☐

Week 9

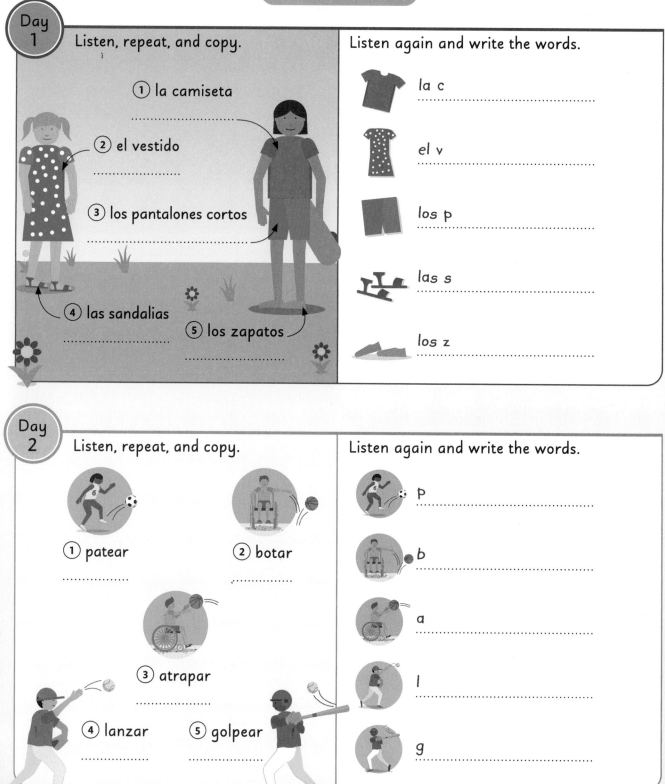

Day 1

Listen, repeat, and copy.

1. la camiseta
2. el vestido
3. los pantalones cortos
4. las sandalias
5. los zapatos

Listen again and write the words.

la c ....

el v ....

los p ....

las s ....

los z ....

Day 2

Listen, repeat, and copy.

1. patear
2. botar
3. atrapar
4. lanzar
5. golpear

Listen again and write the words.

p ....

b ....

a ....

l ....

g ....

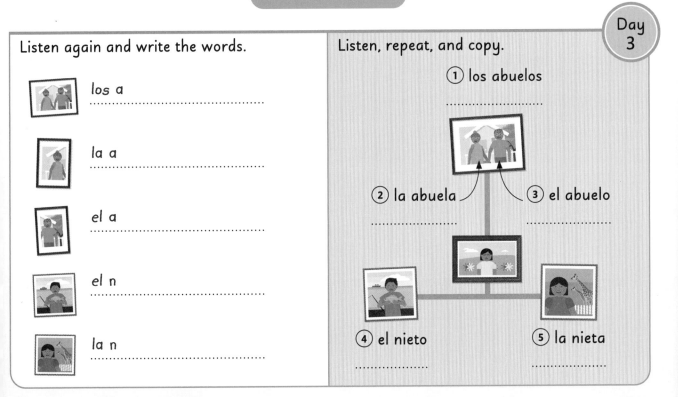

Day 3

Listen again and write the words.

los a
....

la a
....

el a
....

el n
....

la n
....

Listen, repeat, and copy.

① los abuelos
....

② la abuela
....

③ el abuelo
....

④ el nieto
....

⑤ la nieta
....

Day 4

Listen again and write the words.

b
....

j
....

v
....

a
....

g
....

Listen, repeat, and copy.

① bonito
....

② joven
....

③ viejo
....

④ agradable
....

⑤ gruñón
....

What can you remember from this week?

1. Look at the pictures and write the correct words.

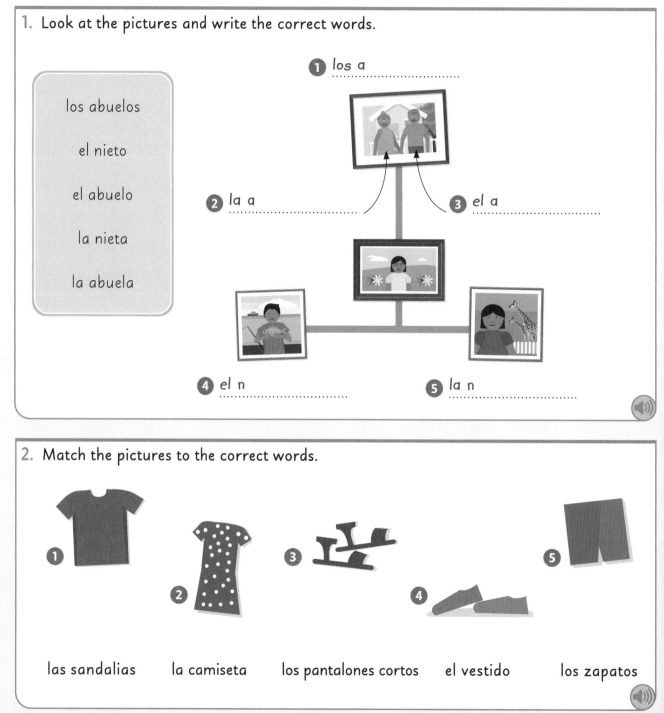

1 los a ....

los abuelos

el nieto

el abuelo

la nieta

la abuela

2 la a ....

3 el a ....

4 el n ....

5 la n ....

2. Match the pictures to the correct words.

1   2   3   4   5

las sandalias   la camiseta   los pantalones cortos   el vestido   los zapatos

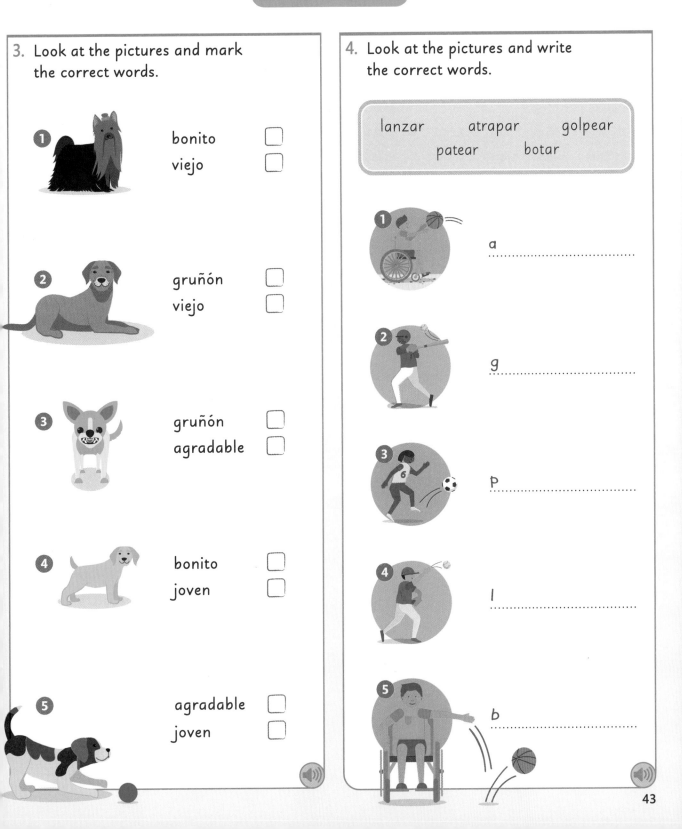

3. Look at the pictures and mark the correct words.

1. bonito ☐
   viejo ☐

2. gruñón ☐
   viejo ☐

3. gruñón ☐
   agradable ☐

4. bonito ☐
   joven ☐

5. agradable ☐
   joven ☐

4. Look at the pictures and write the correct words.

| lanzar | atrapar | golpear |
| patear | botar |

1. a ....

2. g ....

3. p ....

4. l ....

5. b ....

43

Day 1

Listen, repeat, and copy.

① la granja
....

② el tractor
....

③ los animales
....

④ el campo
....

⑤ el granero
....

Listen again and write the words.

la g ....

el t ....

los a ....

el c ....

el g ....

Day 2

Listen, repeat, and copy.

① el monstruo
....

② el dinosaurio
....

③ el robot
....

④ el monopatín
....

⑤ el videojuego
....

Listen again and write the words.

el m ....

el d ....

el r ....

el m ....

el v ....

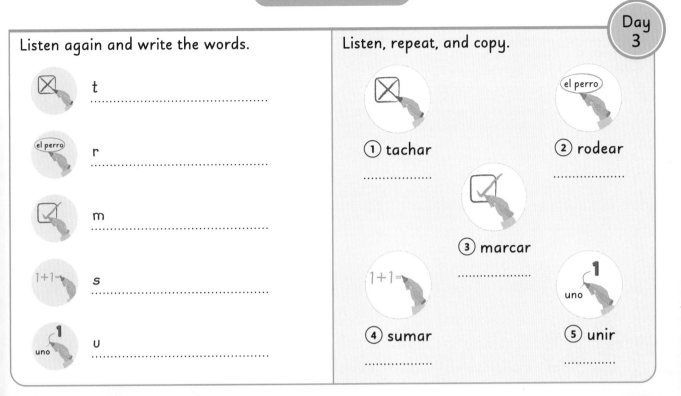

Listen again and write the words.

t ....

r ....

m ....

s ....

u ....

Listen, repeat, and copy.

① tachar
....

② rodear
....

③ marcar
....

④ sumar
....

⑤ unir
....

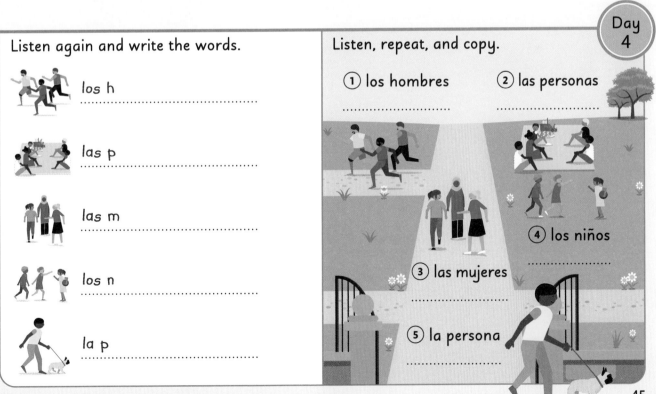

Listen again and write the words.

los h ....

las p ....

las m ....

los n ....

la p ....

Listen, repeat, and copy.

① los hombres
....

② las personas
....

③ las mujeres
....

④ los niños
....

⑤ la persona
....

Day 5

What can you remember from this week?

1. Look at the pictures and write the letters in the correct order.

1. la praseon

   la p ....

2. las mjeusre

   las m ....

3. los noñis

   los n ....

4. las psonesra

   las p ....

5. los hbrsome

   los h ....

2. Read the words and mark the correct pictures.

1. tachar   A ☐   B ☐

2. sumar   A ☐   B ☐

3. marcar   A ☐   B ☐

4. rodear   A ☐   B ☐

5. unir   A ☐   B ☐

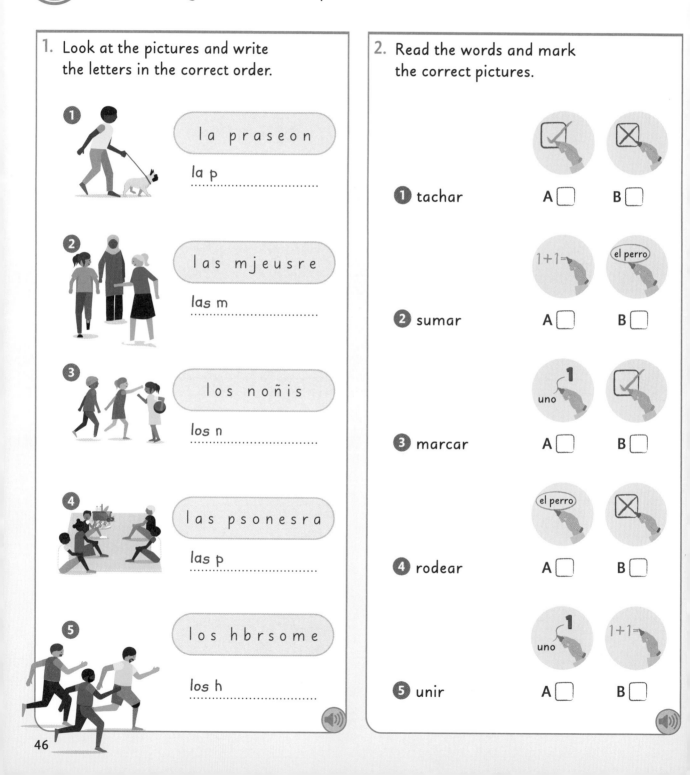

Week 10

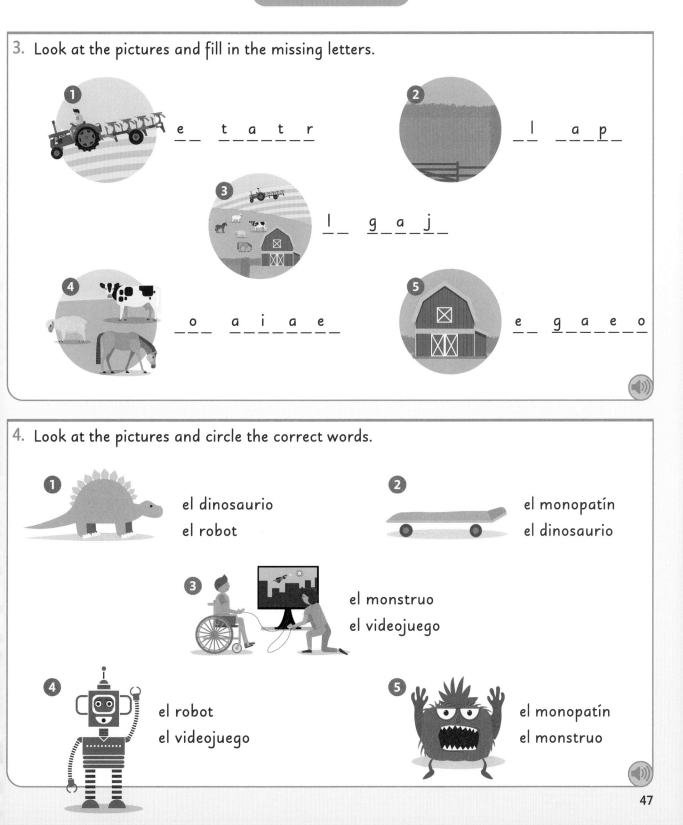

3. Look at the pictures and fill in the missing letters.

1. e _   _ t _ a _ t _ r

2. _ l   _ _ a p _

3. l _   g _ a _ j _

4. _ _ o   _ a _ i _ a _ e

5. e _   g _ a _ e _ o

4. Look at the pictures and circle the correct words.

1. el dinosaurio / el robot

2. el monopatín / el dinosaurio

3. el monstruo / el videojuego

4. el robot / el videojuego

5. el monopatín / el monstruo

Day 1

Listen, repeat, and copy.

① cantar

....

② bailar

....

③ tocar el piano

....

④ tocar la guitarra

....

⑤ tomar una foto

....

Listen again and write the words.

c ....

b ....

t ....

t ....

t ....

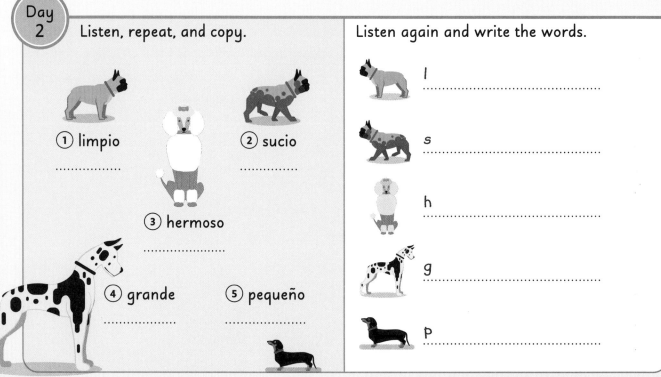

Day 2

Listen, repeat, and copy.

① limpio

....

② sucio

....

③ hermoso

....

④ grande

....

⑤ pequeño

....

Listen again and write the words.

l ....

s ....

h ....

g ....

p ....

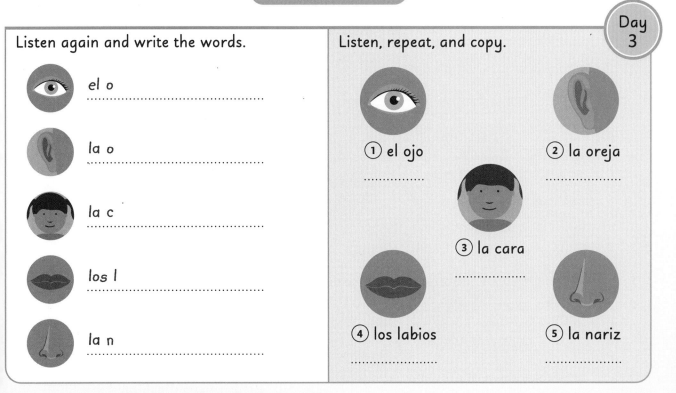

Listen again and write the words.

el o ....

la o ....

la c ....

los l ....

la n ....

Listen, repeat, and copy.

1 el ojo ....

2 la oreja ....

3 la cara ....

4 los labios ....

5 la nariz ....

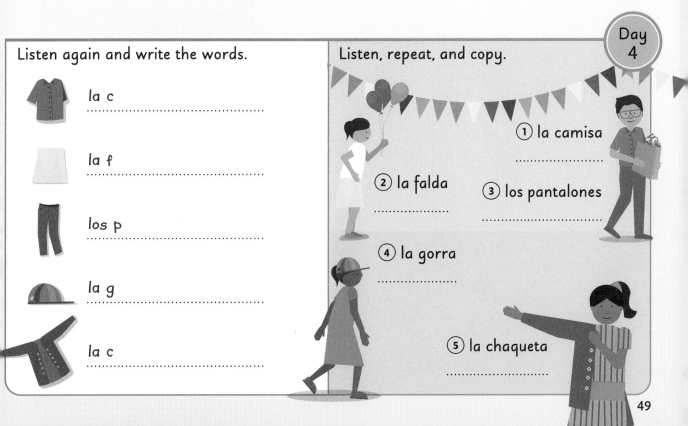

Listen again and write the words.

la c ....

la f ....

los p ....

la g ....

la c ....

Listen, repeat, and copy.

1 la camisa ....

2 la falda ....

3 los pantalones ....

4 la gorra ....

5 la chaqueta ....

Day 5

What can you remember from this week?

1. Look at the pictures and write the correct words.

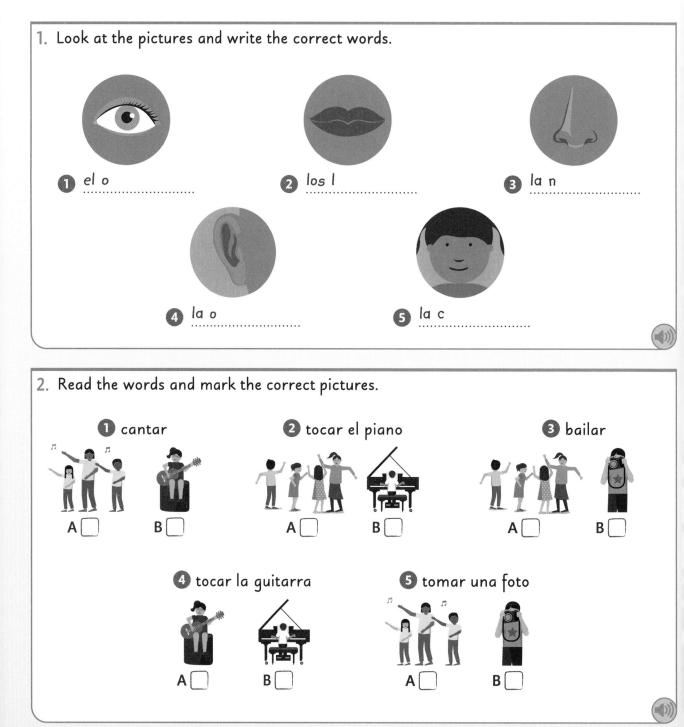

1 el o ....

2 los l ....

3 la n ....

4 la o ....

5 la c ....

2. Read the words and mark the correct pictures.

1 cantar   A ☐   B ☐

2 tocar el piano   A ☐   B ☐

3 bailar   A ☐   B ☐

4 tocar la guitarra   A ☐   B ☐

5 tomar una foto   A ☐   B ☐

3. Look at the pictures and write the letters in the correct order.

1 h m s o o e r

h ....

2 l p i i m o

l ....

3 p o q e u e ñ

p ....

4 s i o u c

s ....

5 g d a n r e

g ....

4. Match the pictures to the correct words.

1 la falda

2 la camisa

3 la gorra

4 la chaqueta

5 los pantalones

Day 1

Listen, repeat, and copy.

1. el desayuno
....
2. el huevo
....
3. el cereal
....
4. la salchicha
....
5. el pastelito
....

Listen again and write the words.

el d ....

el h ....

el c ....

la s ....

el p ....

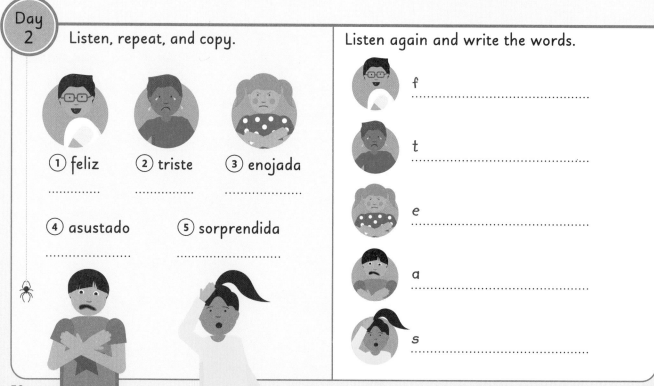

Day 2

Listen, repeat, and copy.

1. feliz
....
2. triste
....
3. enojada
....
4. asustado
....
5. sorprendida
....

Listen again and write the words.

f ....

t ....

e ....

a ....

s ....

Week 12

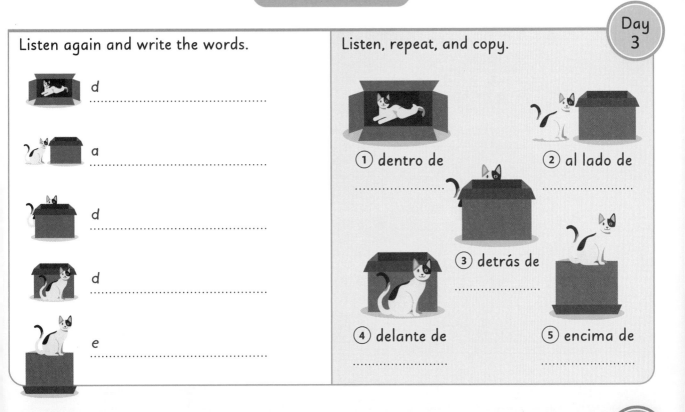

Day 3

Listen again and write the words.

d ....

a ....

d ....

d ....

e ....

Listen, repeat, and copy.

① dentro de

② al lado de

....

③ detrás de

....

④ delante de   ⑤ encima de

....

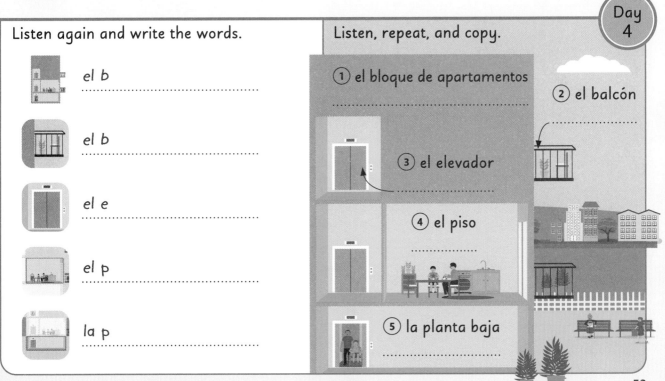

Day 4

Listen again and write the words.

el b ....

el b ....

el e ....

el p ....

la p ....

Listen, repeat, and copy.

① el bloque de apartamentos

....

② el balcón

....

③ el elevador

....

④ el piso

....

⑤ la planta baja

....

53

Day 5

What can you remember from this week?

1. Look at the pictures and write the correct words.

> dentro de   detrás de   encima de
> delante de   al lado de

① d ....

② d ....

③ d ....

④ a ....

⑤ e ....

2. Look at the pictures and mark the correct words.

①
el cereal ☐
el huevo ☐

②
el pastelito ☐
el desayuno ☐

③
el huevo ☐
la salchicha ☐

④
el pastelito ☐
el cereal ☐

⑤
el desayuno ☐
la salchicha ☐

3. Look at the pictures and circle the correct words.

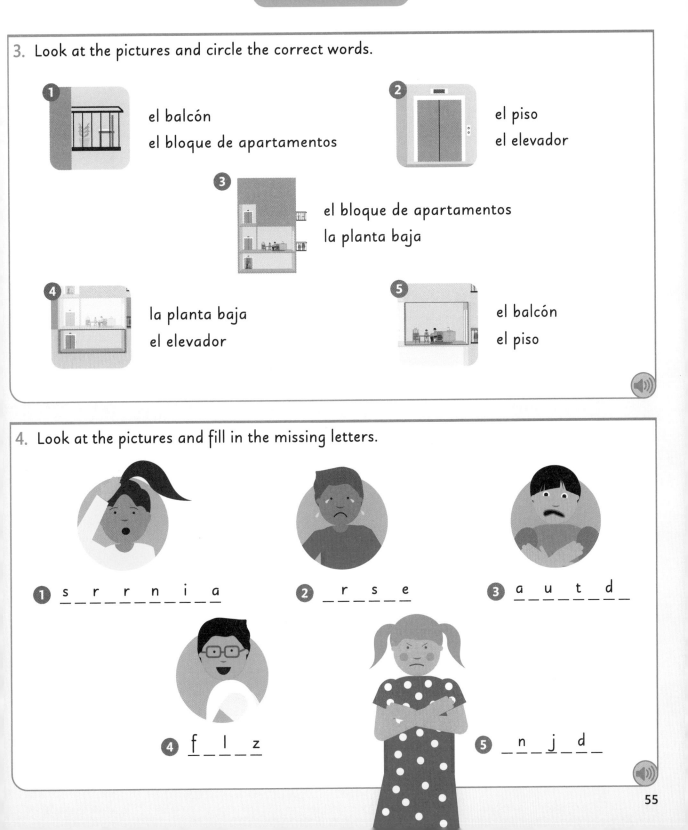

1. el balcón
   el bloque de apartamentos

2. el piso
   el elevador

3. el bloque de apartamentos
   la planta baja

4. la planta baja
   el elevador

5. el balcón
   el piso

4. Look at the pictures and fill in the missing letters.

1. s _ r _ r _ n _ i _ a

2. _ r _ s _ e

3. a _ u _ t _ d _

4. f _ l _ z

5. _ n _ j _ d _

Day 1

Listen, repeat, and copy.

① el almuerzo

② el emparedado ③ el refrigerio

④ el yogurt ⑤ la fruta

Listen again and write the words.

el a ....

el e ....

el r ....

el y ....

la f ....

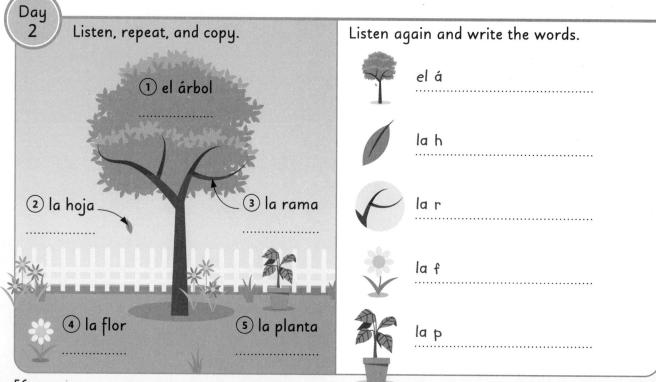

Day 2

Listen, repeat, and copy.

① el árbol

② la hoja ③ la rama

④ la flor ⑤ la planta

Listen again and write the words.

el á ....

la h ....

la r ....

la f ....

la p ....

Week 13

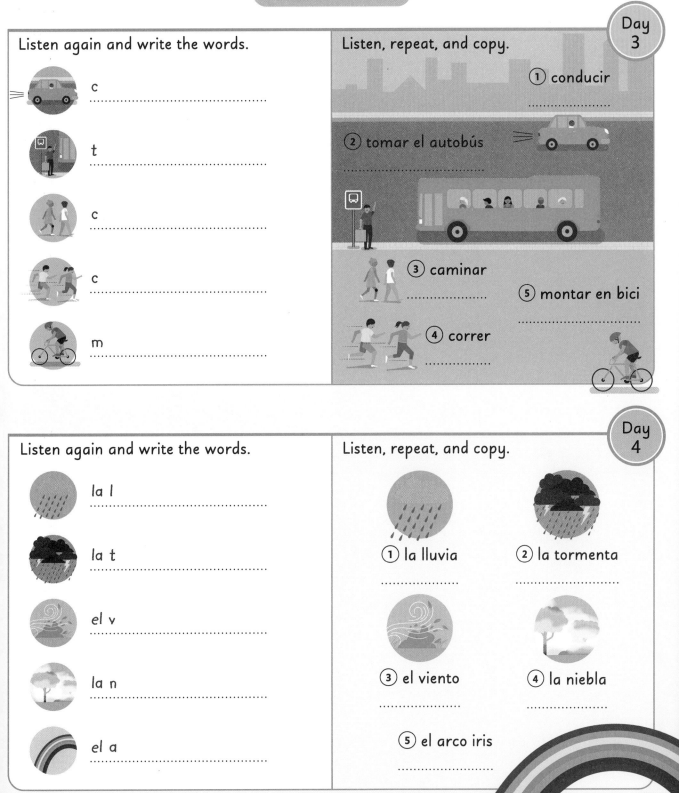

Listen again and write the words.

c ....

t ....

c ....

c ....

m ....

Listen, repeat, and copy.

1 conducir
....

2 tomar el autobús
....

3 caminar
....

4 correr
....

5 montar en bici
....

Listen again and write the words.

la l ....

la t ....

el v ....

la n ....

el a ....

Listen, repeat, and copy.

1 la lluvia
....

2 la tormenta
....

3 el viento
....

4 la niebla
....

5 el arco iris
....

What can you remember from this week?

1. Read the words and mark the correct pictures.

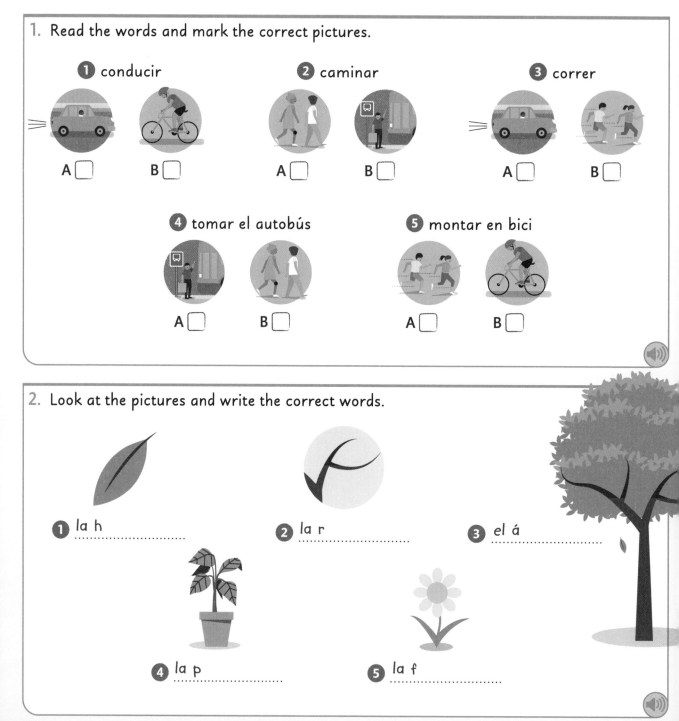

1 conducir

A ☐   B ☐

2 caminar

A ☐   B ☐

3 correr

A ☐   B ☐

4 tomar el autobús

A ☐   B ☐

5 montar en bici

A ☐   B ☐

2. Look at the pictures and write the correct words.

1 la h ....

2 la r ....

3 el á ....

4 la p ....

5 la f ....

3. Look at the pictures and write the correct words.

la lluvia   la tormenta   el viento
el arco iris   la niebla

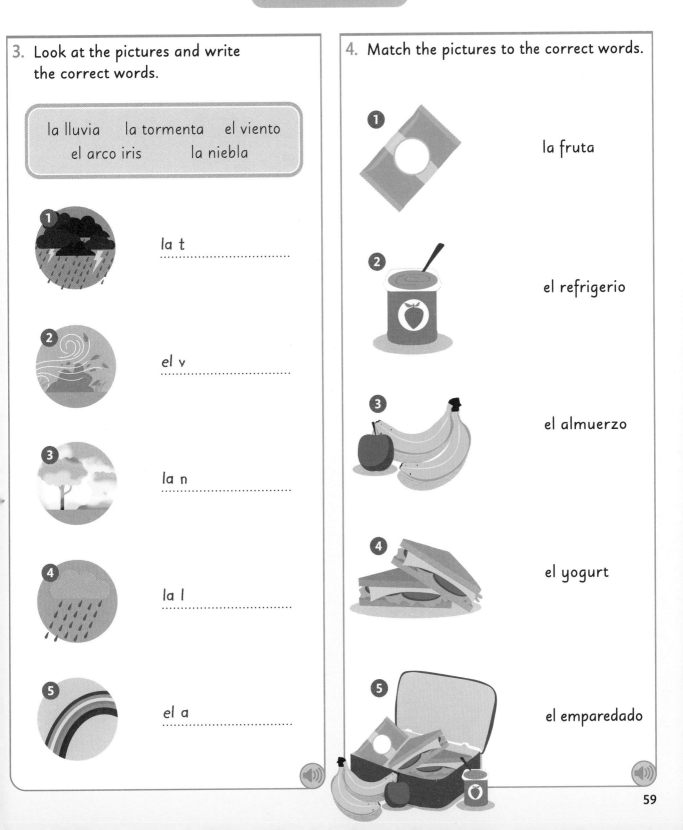

1. la t _____

2. el v _____

3. la n _____

4. la l _____

5. el a _____

4. Match the pictures to the correct words.

1

la fruta

2

el refrigerio

3

el almuerzo

4

el yogurt

5

el emparedado

Day 1

Listen, repeat, and copy.

① la cena

....

② la pasta

....

③ la salsa

....

④ el pan

....

⑤ las albóndigas

....

Listen again and write the words.

la c ....

la p ....

la s ....

el p ....

las a ....

Day 2

Listen, repeat, and copy.

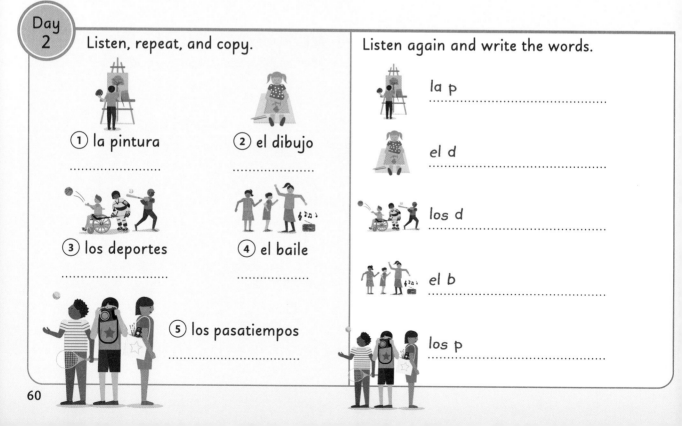

① la pintura

....

② el dibujo

....

③ los deportes

....

④ el baile

....

⑤ los pasatiempos

....

Listen again and write the words.

la p ....

el d ....

los d ....

el b ....

los p ....

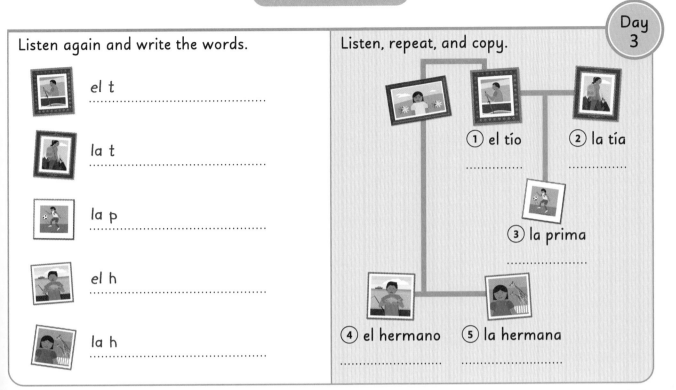

Day 3

Listen again and write the words.

el t ....

la t ....

la p ....

el h ....

la h ....

Listen, repeat, and copy.

① el tío   ....

② la tía   ....

③ la prima   ....

④ el hermano   ....

⑤ la hermana   ....

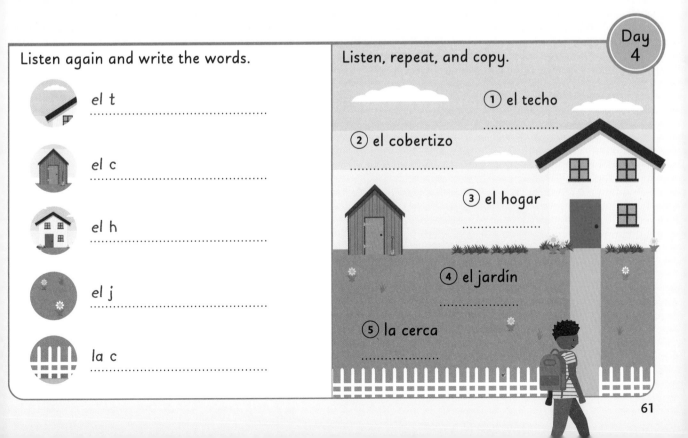

Day 4

Listen again and write the words.

el t ....

el c ....

el h ....

el j ....

la c ....

Listen, repeat, and copy.

① el techo   ....

② el cobertizo   ....

③ el hogar   ....

④ el jardín   ....

⑤ la cerca   ....

Day 5

What can you remember from this week?

1. Look at the pictures and circle the correct words.

1. el techo / el jardín

2. el cobertizo / la cerca

3. el jardín / el hogar

4. el techo / el cobertizo

5. el hogar / la cerca

2. Look at the pictures and write the letters in the correct order.

1. el duijbo

el d ....

2. el blaie

el b ....

3. la purtina

la p ....

4. los dortepes

los d ....

5. los papsasotiem

los p ....

3. Look at the pictures and write the correct words.

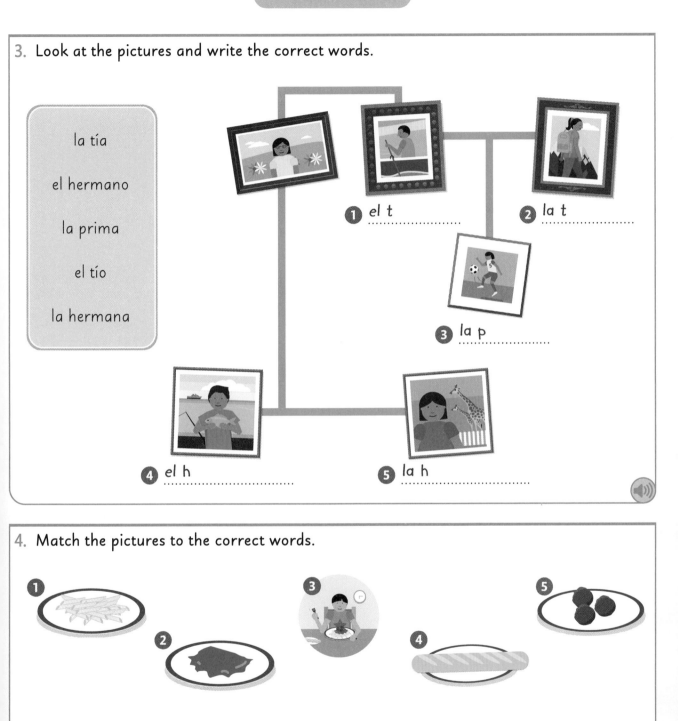

la tía

el hermano

la prima

el tío

la hermana

① el t ....

② la t ....

③ la p ....

④ el h ....

⑤ la h ....

4. Match the pictures to the correct words.

la cena   la pasta   las albóndigas   la salsa   el pan

Day 1

Listen, repeat, and copy.

① jugar

② trepar

③ correr

④ saltar

⑤ saltar a la soga

Listen again and write the words.

j ....

t ....

c ....

s ....

s ....

Day 2

Listen, repeat, and copy.

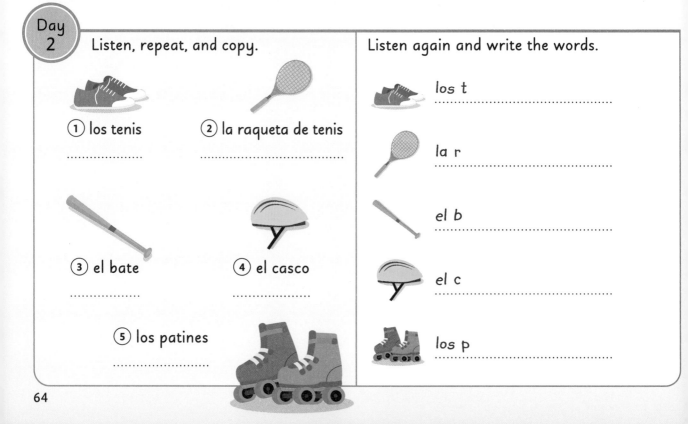

① los tenis

② la raqueta de tenis

③ el bate

④ el casco

⑤ los patines

Listen again and write the words.

los t ....

la r ....

el b ....

el c ....

los p ....

Listen again and write the words.

la o
....

el m
....

la i
....

la a
....

la p
....

Listen, repeat, and copy.

① la ola
....

② el mar
....

③ la isla
....

④ la arena
....

⑤ la playa
....

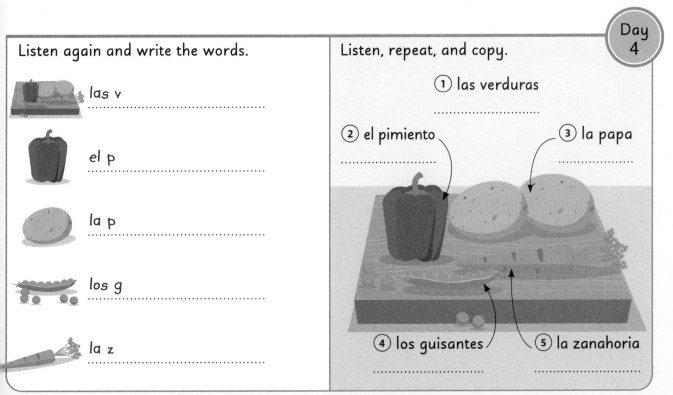

Listen again and write the words.

las v
....

el p
....

la p
....

los g
....

la z
....

Listen, repeat, and copy.

① las verduras
....

② el pimiento
....

③ la papa
....

④ los guisantes
....

⑤ la zanahoria
....

Day 5

What can you remember from this week?

1. Look at the pictures and mark the correct words.

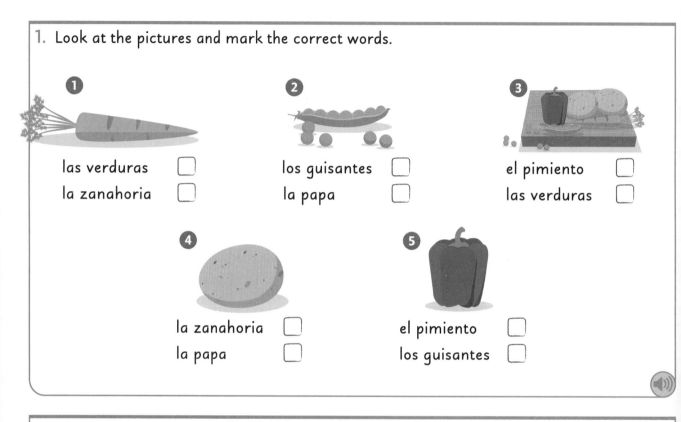

1

las verduras ☐
la zanahoria ☐

2

los guisantes ☐
la papa ☐

3

el pimiento ☐
las verduras ☐

4

la zanahoria ☐
la papa ☐

5

el pimiento ☐
los guisantes ☐

2. Look at the pictures and fill in the missing letters.

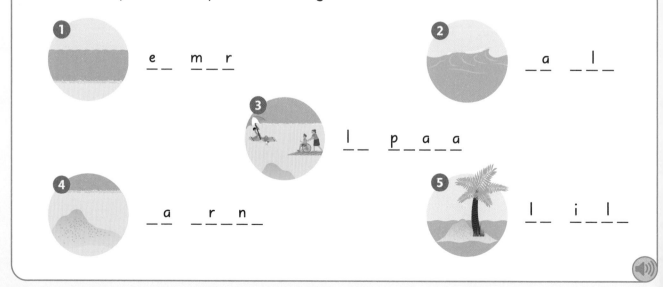

1 e _ _ m _ r

2 _ _ a _ _ _ l _

3 l _ _ p _ a _ a

4 _ _ a _ r _ _ n _

5 l _ _ i _ l _

3. Match the pictures to the correct words.

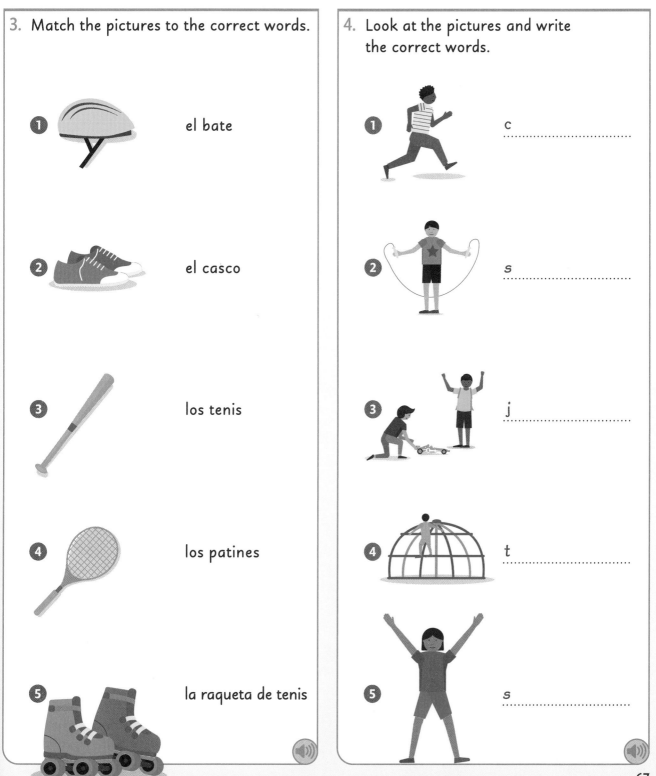

①   el bate

②   el casco

③   los tenis

④   los patines

⑤   la raqueta de tenis

4. Look at the pictures and write the correct words.

①   c ....

②   s ....

③   j ....

④   t ....

⑤   s ....

Day 1

Listen, repeat, and copy.

① el reloj

....

② el teléfono

....

③ la lámpara

....

④ el escritorio

....

⑤ la silla

....

Listen again and write the words.

el r ....

el t ....

la l ....

el e ....

la s ....

Day 2

Listen, repeat, and copy.

① el perro

....

② el cachorro

....

③ el gato

....

④ el gatito

....

⑤ el ratón

....

Listen again and write the words.

el p ....

el c ....

el g ....

el g ....

el r ....

Week 16

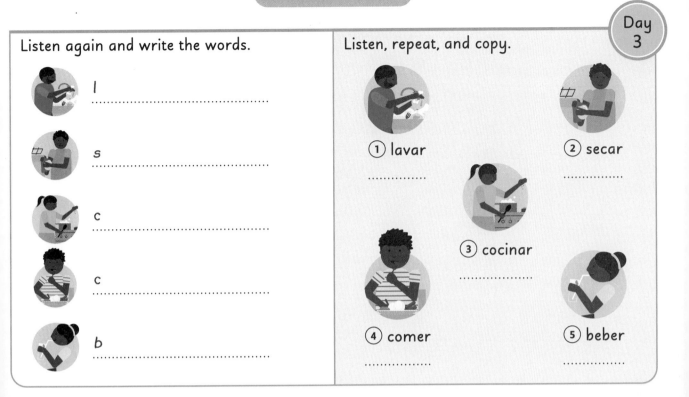

Listen again and write the words.

l ....

s ....

c ....

c ....

b ....

Listen, repeat, and copy.

1 lavar ....

2 secar ....

3 cocinar ....

4 comer ....

5 beber ....

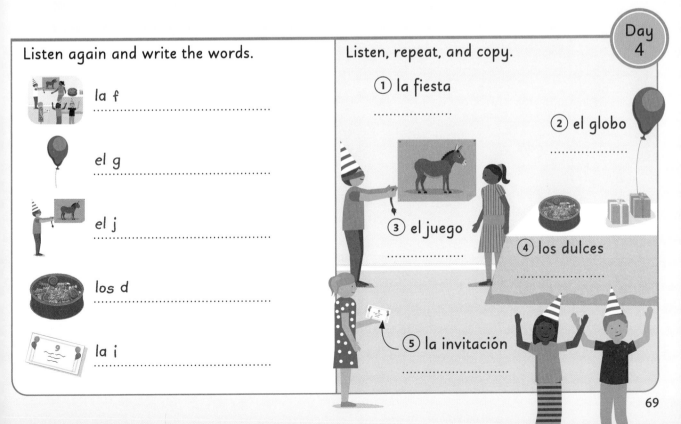

Listen again and write the words.

la f ....

el g ....

el j ....

los d ....

la i ....

Listen, repeat, and copy.

1 la fiesta ....

2 el globo ....

3 el juego ....

4 los dulces ....

5 la invitación ....

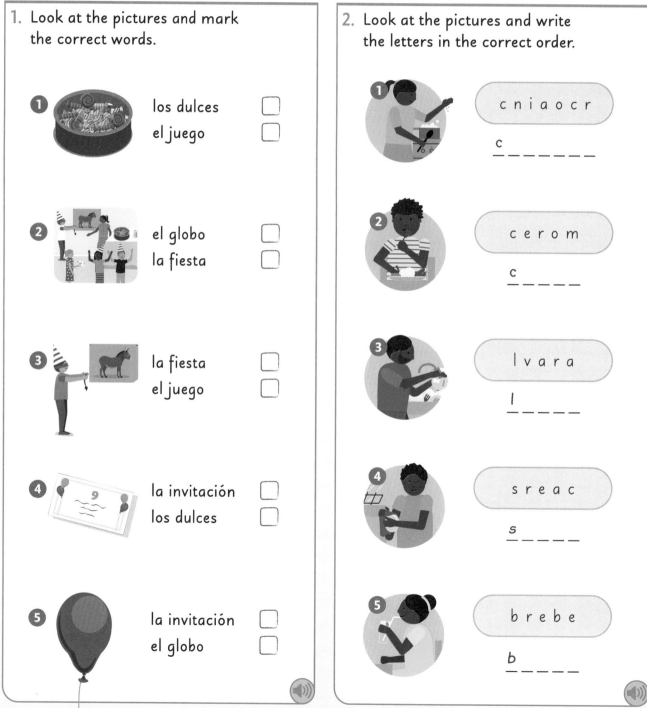

Week 16

Day 5

What can you remember from this week?

1. Look at the pictures and mark the correct words.

① los dulces ☐
el juego ☐

② el globo ☐
la fiesta ☐

③ la fiesta ☐
el juego ☐

④ la invitación ☐
los dulces ☐

⑤ la invitación ☐
el globo ☐

2. Look at the pictures and write the letters in the correct order.

① c n i a o c r

c _ _ _ _ _ _

② c e r o m

c _ _ _ _

③ l v a r a

l _ _ _ _

④ s r e a c

s _ _ _ _

⑤ b r e b e

b _ _ _ _

70

3. Look at the pictures and write the correct words.

el perro   el ratón   el gato   el cachorro   el gatito

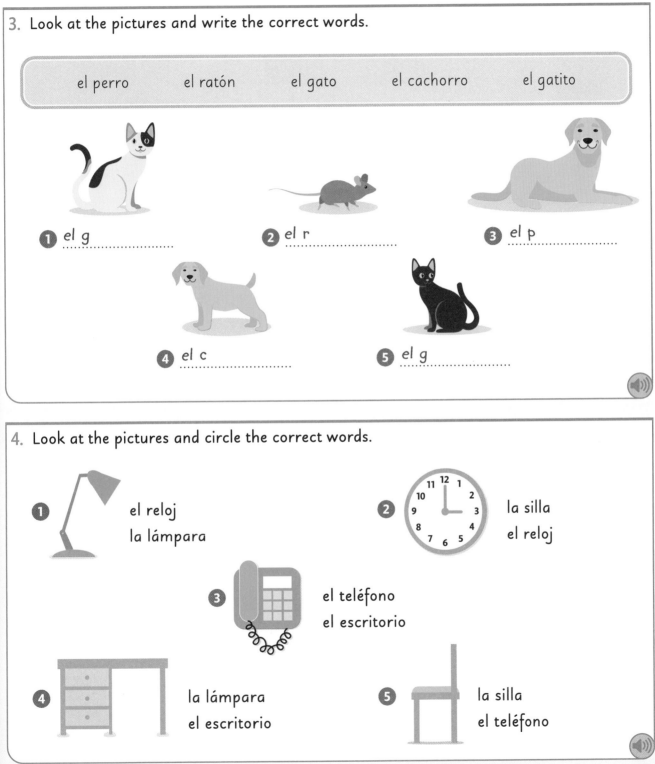

1 el g _____

2 el r _____

3 el p _____

4 el c _____

5 el g _____

4. Look at the pictures and circle the correct words.

1 el reloj
la lámpara

2 la silla
el reloj

3 el teléfono
el escritorio

4 la lámpara
el escritorio

5 la silla
el teléfono

Day 1

Listen, repeat, and copy.

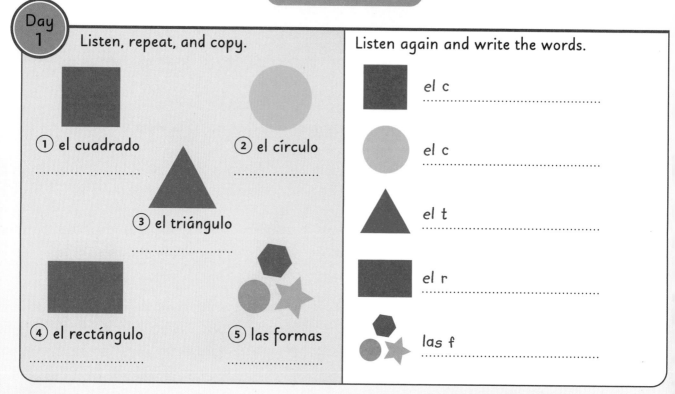

① el cuadrado

② el círculo

③ el triángulo

④ el rectángulo

⑤ las formas

Listen again and write the words.

el c ....

el c ....

el t ....

el r ....

las f ....

Day 2

Listen, repeat, and copy.

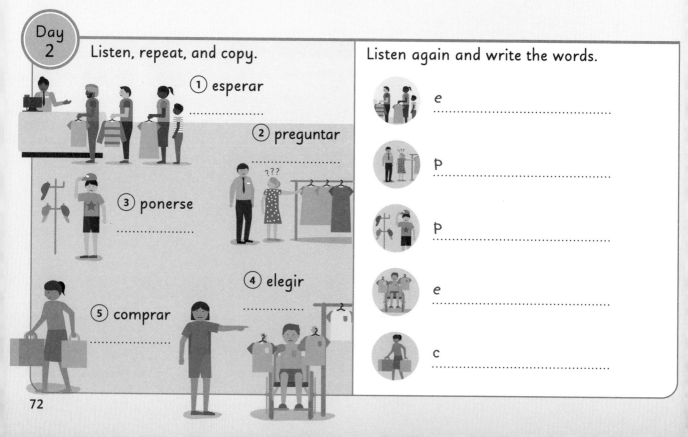

① esperar

② preguntar

③ ponerse

④ elegir

⑤ comprar

Listen again and write the words.

e ....

p ....

p ....

e ....

c ....

Week 17

Listen again and write the words.

la l ....

la o ....

la a ....

la m ....

la h ....

Listen, repeat, and copy.

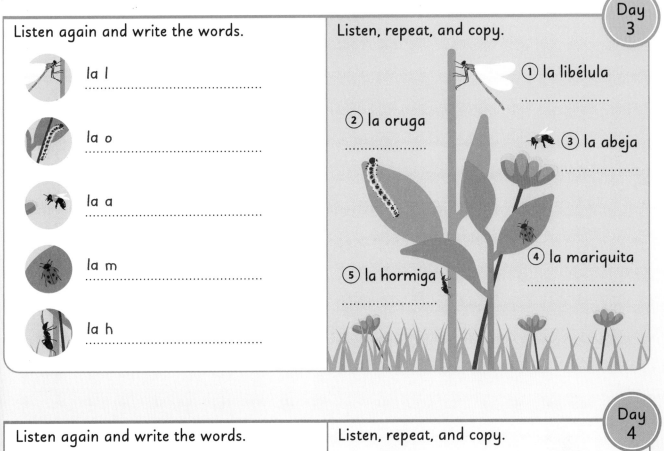

① la libélula ....

② la oruga ....

③ la abeja ....

④ la mariquita ....

⑤ la hormiga ....

Listen again and write the words.

el a ....

el j ....

la l ....

el l ....

las b ....

Listen, repeat, and copy.

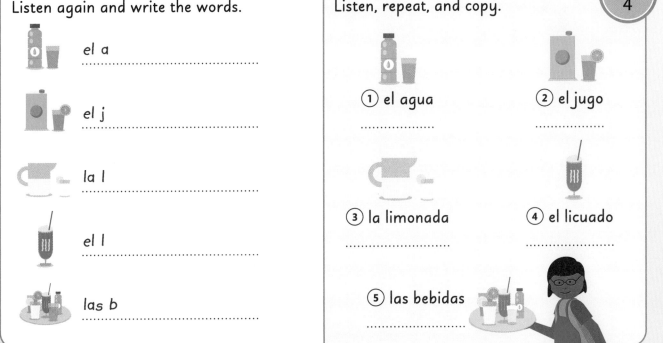

① el agua ....

② el jugo ....

③ la limonada ....

④ el licuado ....

⑤ las bebidas ....

Day
5

What can you remember from this week?

1. Match the pictures to the correct words.

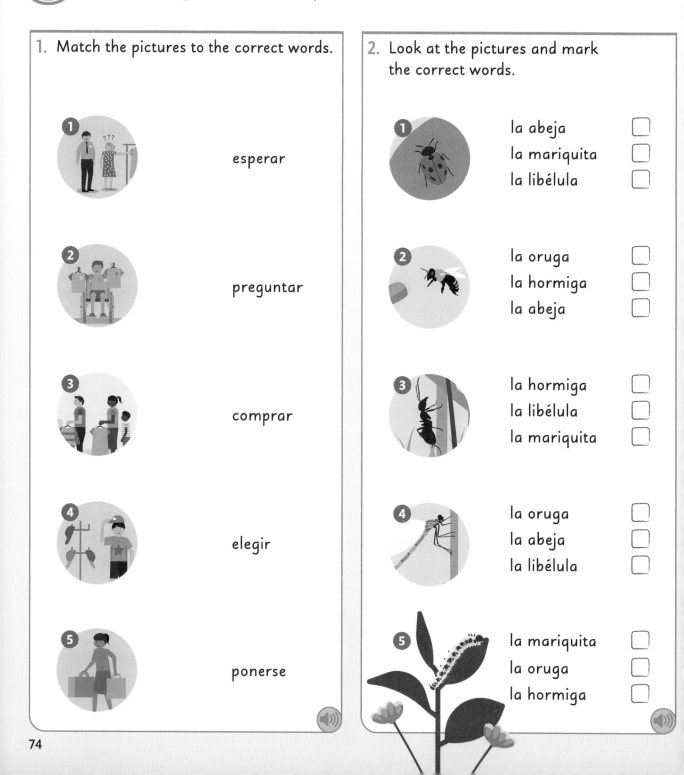

esperar

preguntar

comprar

elegir

ponerse

2. Look at the pictures and mark the correct words.

1
la abeja ☐
la mariquita ☐
la libélula ☐

2
la oruga ☐
la hormiga ☐
la abeja ☐

3
la hormiga ☐
la libélula ☐
la mariquita ☐

4
la oruga ☐
la abeja ☐
la libélula ☐

5
la mariquita ☐
la oruga ☐
la hormiga ☐

3. Look at the pictures and write the correct words.

el agua   el jugo   las bebidas   el licuado   la limonada

1 el j ....

2 las b ....

3 el a ....

4 la l ....

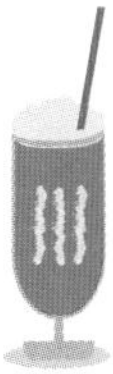

5 el l ....

4. Look at the pictures and fill in the missing letters.

1 e _ _ t _ _ i _ n _ u _ o

2 _ _ l _ _ í _ c _ l _

3 e _ _ r _ c _ _ á _ g _ l _

4 _ _ l _ _ u _ d _ a _ o

5 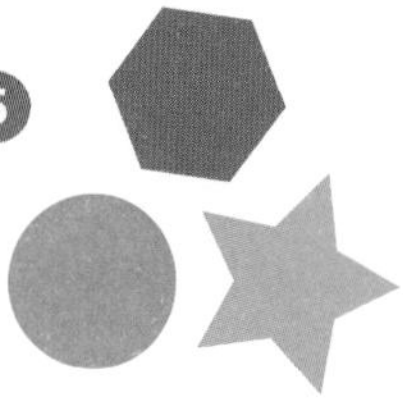 l _ _ s _ _ o _ m _ s

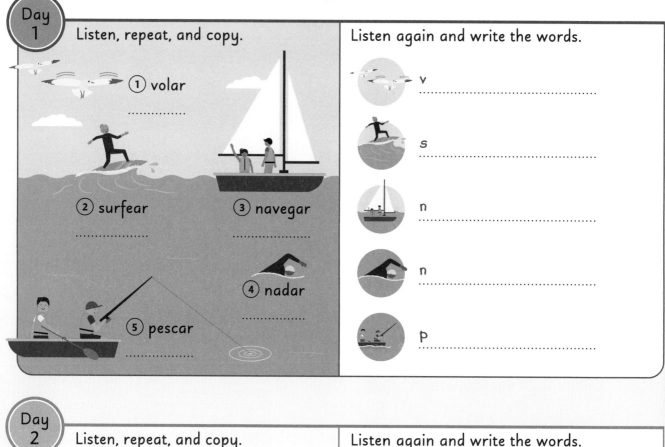

Day 1

Listen, repeat, and copy.

① volar
....

② surfear
....

③ navegar
....

④ nadar
....

⑤ pescar
....

Listen again and write the words.

v ....

s ....

n ....

n ....

p ....

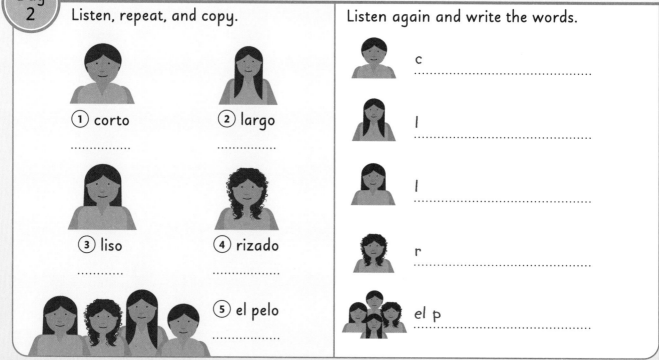

Day 2

Listen, repeat, and copy.

① corto
....

② largo
....

③ liso
....

④ rizado
....

⑤ el pelo
....

Listen again and write the words.

c ....

l ....

l ....

r ....

el p ....

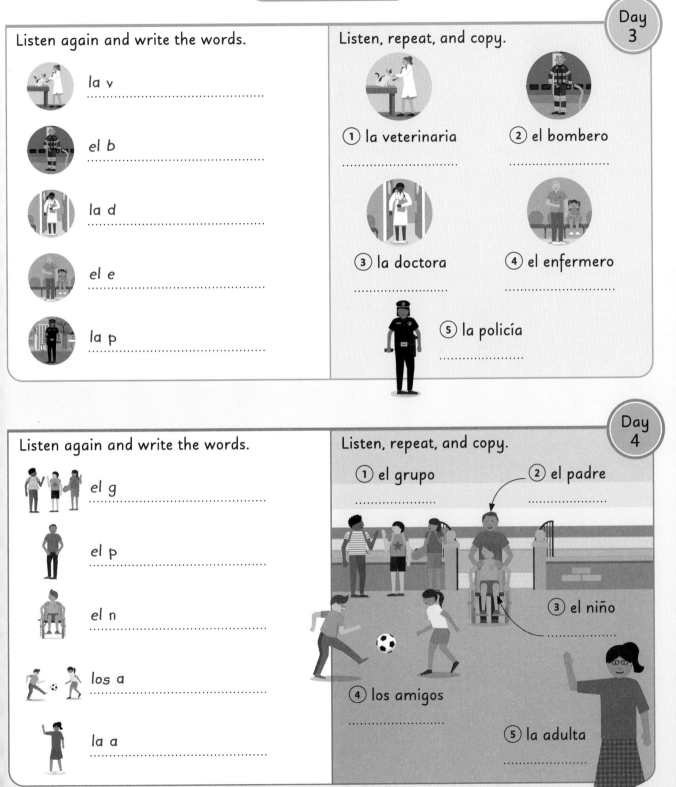

Day 3

Listen again and write the words.

la v ....

el b ....

la d ....

el e ....

la p ....

Listen, repeat, and copy.

① la veterinaria ....

② el bombero ....

③ la doctora ....

④ el enfermero ....

⑤ la policía ....

Day 4

Listen again and write the words.

el g ....

el p ....

el n ....

los a ....

la a ....

Listen, repeat, and copy.

① el grupo ....

② el padre ....

③ el niño ....

④ los amigos ....

⑤ la adulta ....

Day 5

What can you remember from this week?

1. Read the words and mark the correct pictures.

① la veterinaria   ② el bombero   ③ la doctora

A ☐   B ☐   A ☐   B ☐   A ☐   B ☐

④ la policía   ⑤ el enfermero

A ☐   B ☐   A ☐   B ☐

2. Look at the picture and write the correct words.

largo

rizado

el pelo

corto

liso

① el p ....

② c ....

③ l ....

④ l ....

⑤ r ....

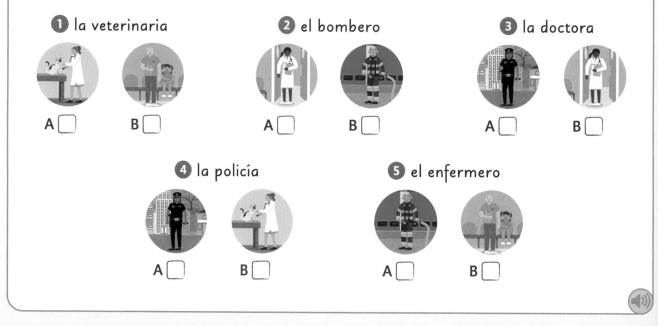

3. Look at the pictures and write the letters in the correct order.

1.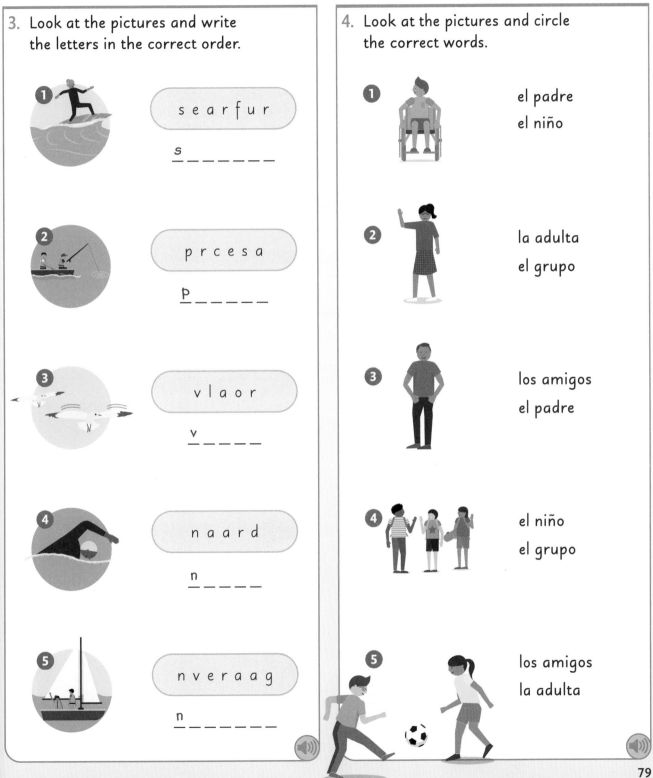
   s e a r f u r

   s _ _ _ _ _ _ _

2. p r c e s a

   p _ _ _ _ _ _

3. v l a o r

   v _ _ _ _ _

4. n a a r d

   n _ _ _ _ _

5. n v e r a a g

   n _ _ _ _ _ _ _

4. Look at the pictures and circle the correct words.

1. el padre
   el niño

2. la adulta
   el grupo

3. los amigos
   el padre

4. el niño
   el grupo

5. los amigos
   la adulta

Day 1

Listen, repeat, and copy.

① las luces

② el cojín   ③ la mesa

④ la silla   ⑤ la alfombra

Listen again and write the words.

las l

el c

la m

la s

la a

Day 2

Listen, repeat, and copy.

① el pájaro

② el burro   ③ el cerdo

④ el agricultor

⑤ el establo

Listen again and write the words.

el p

el b

el c

el a

el e

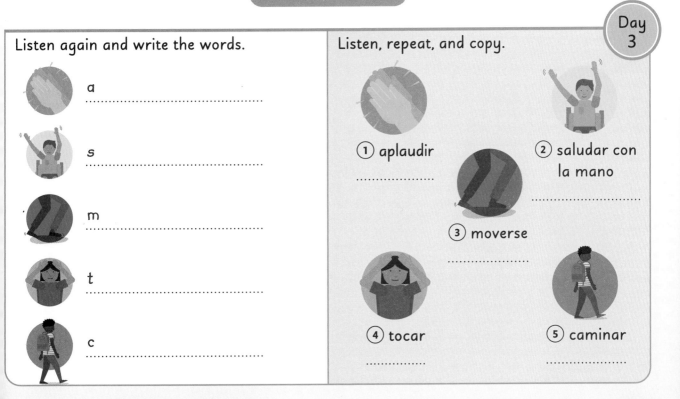

Listen again and write the words.

a ....

s ....

m ....

t ....

c ....

Listen, repeat, and copy.

① aplaudir
....

② saludar con la mano
....

③ moverse
....

④ tocar
....

⑤ caminar
....

Listen again and write the words.

la f ....

el r ....

la v ....

la t ....

el p ....

Listen, repeat, and copy.

① la fiesta de cumpleaños
....

② el regalo
....

③ la vela
....

④ la tarjeta
....

⑤ el pastel
....

Day 5

What can you remember from this week?

1. Match the pictures to the correct words.

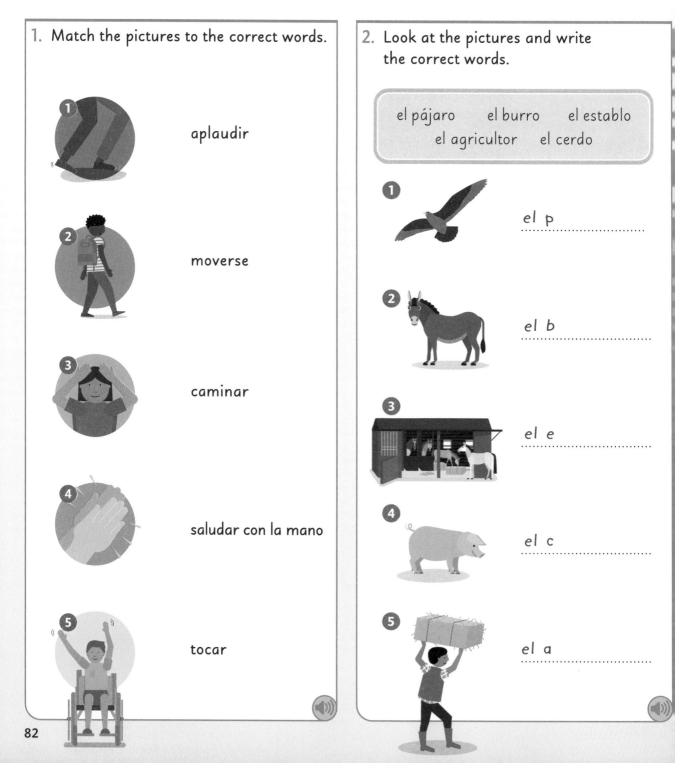

1   aplaudir

2   moverse

3   caminar

4   saludar con la mano

5   tocar

2. Look at the pictures and write the correct words.

el pájaro   el burro   el establo
el agricultor   el cerdo

1   el p ....

2   el b ....

3   el e ....

4   el c ....

5   el a ....

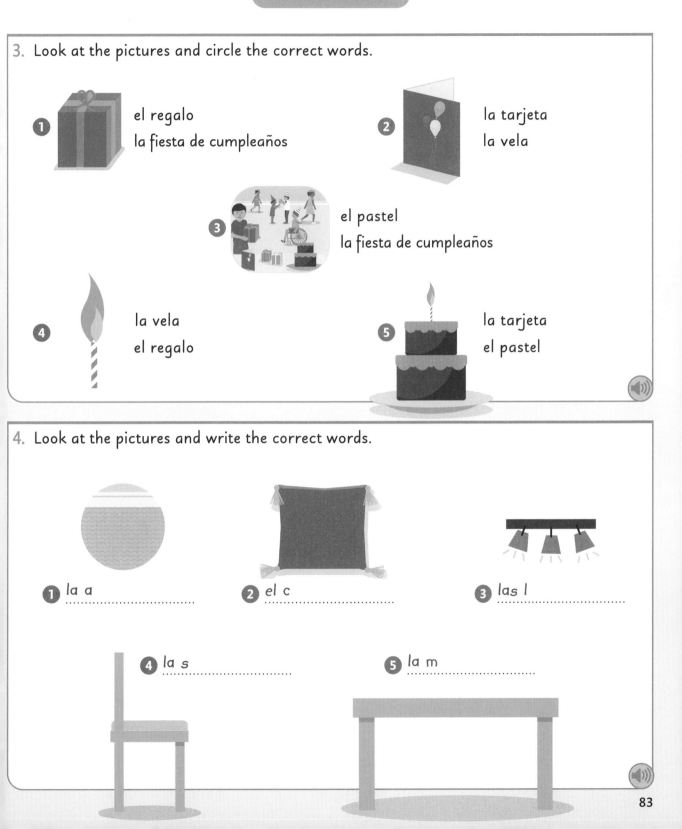

3. Look at the pictures and circle the correct words.

1. el regalo
   la fiesta de cumpleaños

2. la tarjeta
   la vela

3. el pastel
   la fiesta de cumpleaños

4. la vela
   el regalo

5. la tarjeta
   el pastel

4. Look at the pictures and write the correct words.

1. la a ....

2. el c ....

3. las l ....

4. la s ....

5. la m ....

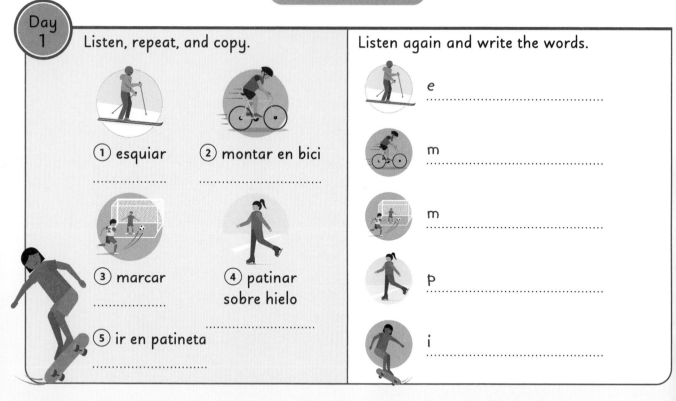

Day 1

Listen, repeat, and copy.

① esquiar

② montar en bici

③ marcar

④ patinar sobre hielo

⑤ ir en patineta

Listen again and write the words.

e ....

m ....

m ....

p ....

i ....

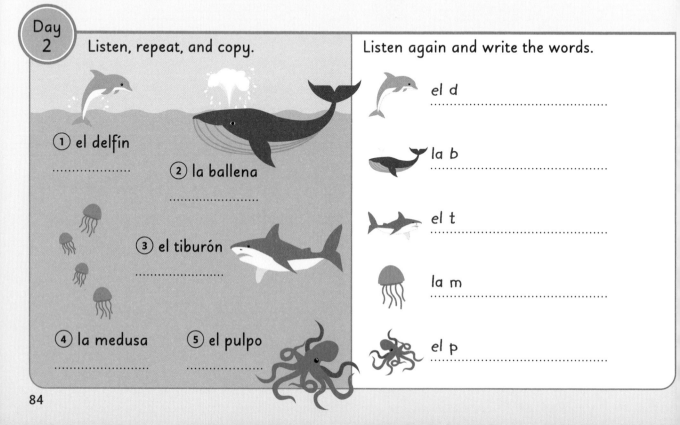

Day 2

Listen, repeat, and copy.

① el delfín

② la ballena

③ el tiburón

④ la medusa

⑤ el pulpo

Listen again and write the words.

el d ....

la b ....

el t ....

la m ....

el p ....

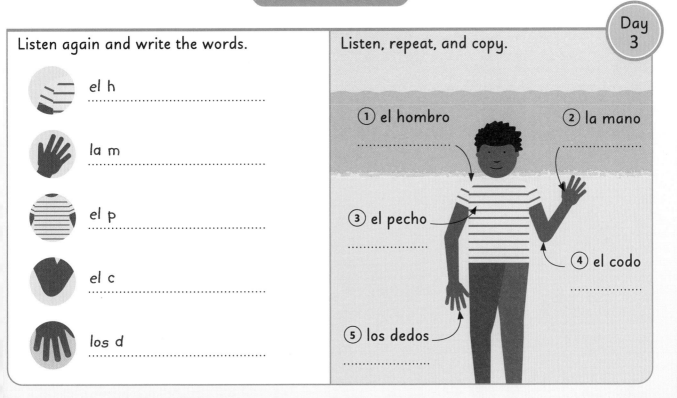

Day 3

Listen again and write the words.

el h ....

la m ....

el p ....

el c ....

los d ....

Listen, repeat, and copy.

① el hombro ....

② la mano ....

③ el pecho ....

④ el codo ....

⑤ los dedos ....

Day 4

Listen again and write the words.

el d ....

la f ....

la c ....

el l ....

la l ....

Listen, repeat, and copy.

① el durazno ....

② la fresa ....

③ la cereza ....

④ el limón ....

⑤ la lima ....

Day 5

What can you remember from this week?

1. Read the words and mark the correct pictures.

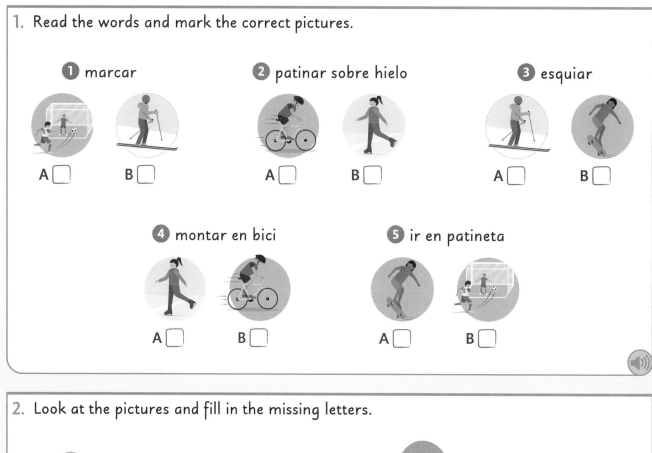

① marcar
A ☐   B ☐

② patinar sobre hielo
A ☐   B ☐

③ esquiar
A ☐   B ☐

④ montar en bici
A ☐   B ☐

⑤ ir en patineta
A ☐   B ☐

2. Look at the pictures and fill in the missing letters.

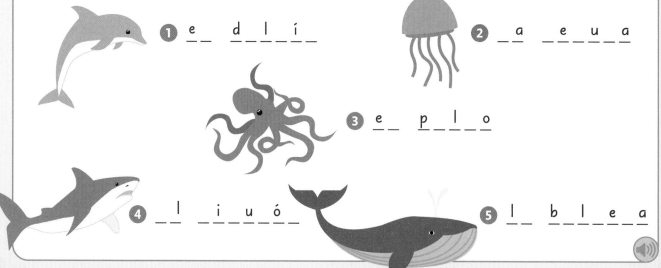

① e _ d _ l _ _ i _

② _ a _ _ e _ u _ a

③ e _ p _ l _ o

④ _ _ l _ _ i u ó _

⑤ _ l _ b _ l _ e _ a

3. Match the pictures to the correct words.

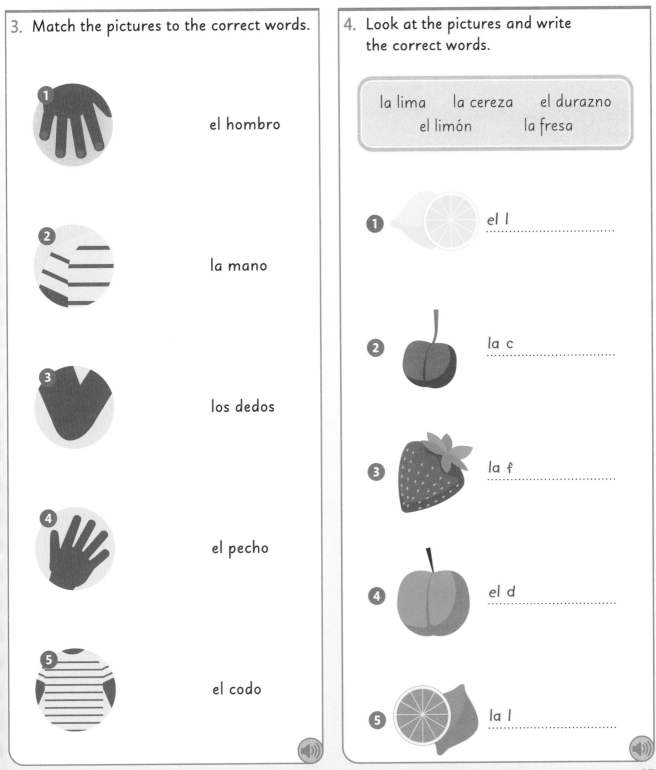

1

el hombro

2

la mano

3

los dedos

4

el pecho

5

el codo

4. Look at the pictures and write the correct words.

la lima   la cereza   el durazno
el limón   la fresa

1   el l ....

2   la c ....

3   la f ....

4   el d ....

5   la l ....

Day 1

Listen, repeat, and copy.

① el pueblo

② el café

③ la oficina de correos

④ la juguetería   ⑤ la librería

Listen again and write the words.

el p

el c

la o

la j

la l

Day 2

Listen, repeat, and copy.

② la estrella de cine

① el cine

③ la película

④ el boleto

⑤ el asiento

Listen again and write the words.

el c

la e

la p

el b

el a

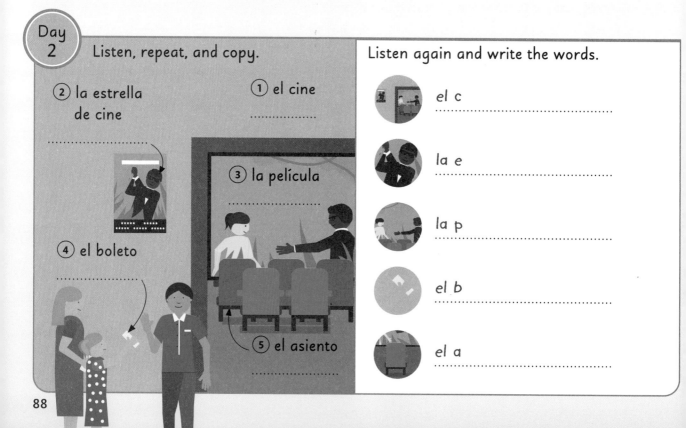

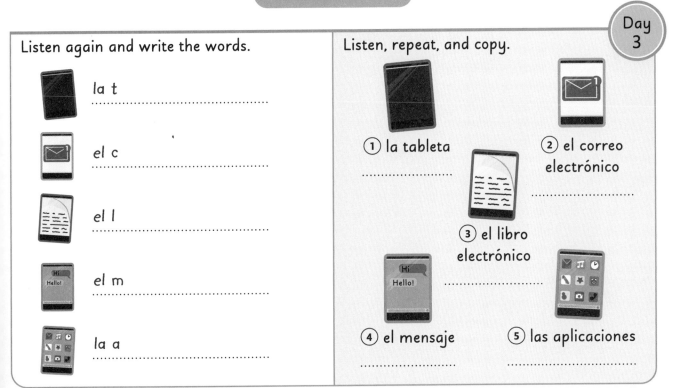

Day 3

Listen again and write the words.

la t ....

el c ....

el l ....

el m ....

la a ....

Listen, repeat, and copy.

① la tableta
....

② el correo electrónico
....

③ el libro electrónico
....

④ el mensaje
....

⑤ las aplicaciones
....

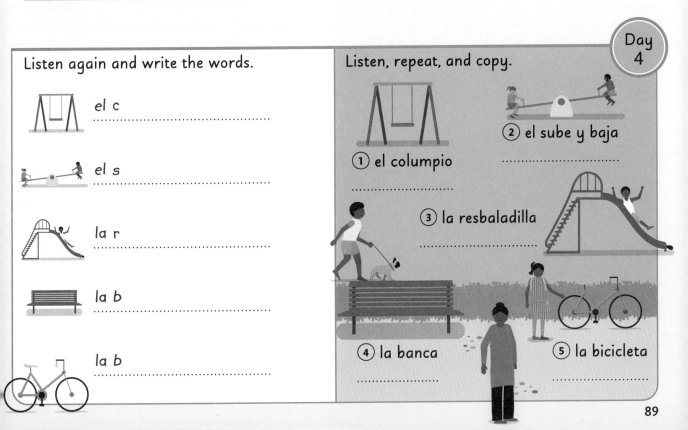

Day 4

Listen again and write the words.

el c ....

el s ....

la r ....

la b ....

la b ....

Listen, repeat, and copy.

① el columpio
....

② el sube y baja
....

③ la resbaladilla

④ la banca
....

⑤ la bicicleta
....

Day
5

What can you remember from this week?

1. Look at the pictures and write the correct words.

1 la t ....

2 el l ....

3 el m ....

4 las a ....

5 el c ....

2. Match the pictures to the correct words.

1 la oficina de correos

2 el café

3 la librería

4 el pueblo

5 la juguetería

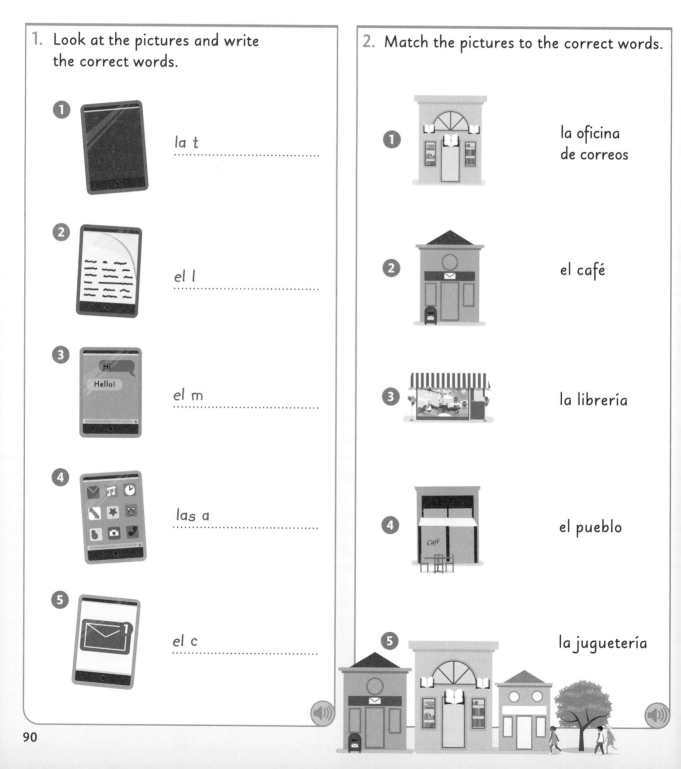

3. Look at the pictures and circle the correct words.

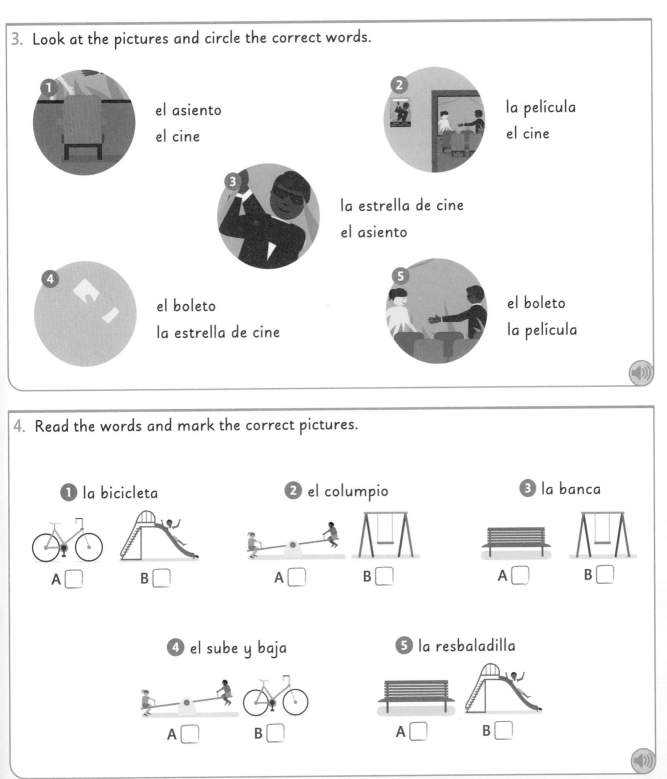

1. el asiento
   el cine

2. la película
   el cine

3. la estrella de cine
   el asiento

4. el boleto
   la estrella de cine

5. el boleto
   la película

4. Read the words and mark the correct pictures.

1 la bicicleta
   A ☐ B ☐

2 el columpio
   A ☐ B ☐

3 la banca
   A ☐ B ☐

4 el sube y baja
   A ☐ B ☐

5 la resbaladilla
   A ☐ B ☐

Day 1

Listen, repeat, and copy.

① la fecha ....

② la pregunta ....

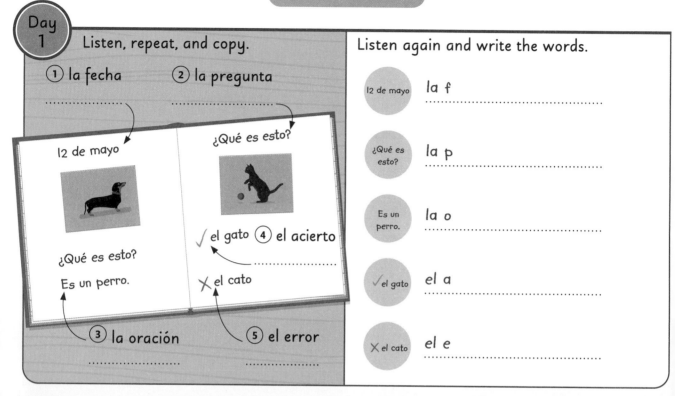

12 de mayo

¿Qué es esto?

¿Qué es esto?

Es un perro.

✓ el gato ④ el acierto ....

✗ el cato

③ la oración ....

⑤ el error ....

Listen again and write the words.

12 de mayo — la f ....

¿Qué es esto? — la p ....

Es un perro. — la o ....

✓ el gato — el a ....

✗ el cato — el e ....

Day 2

Listen, repeat, and copy.

① el pasillo ....

② piso de arriba ....

③ piso de abajo ....

④ el sótano ....

⑤ las escaleras ....

Listen again and write the words.

el p ....

p ....

p ....

el s ....

las e ....

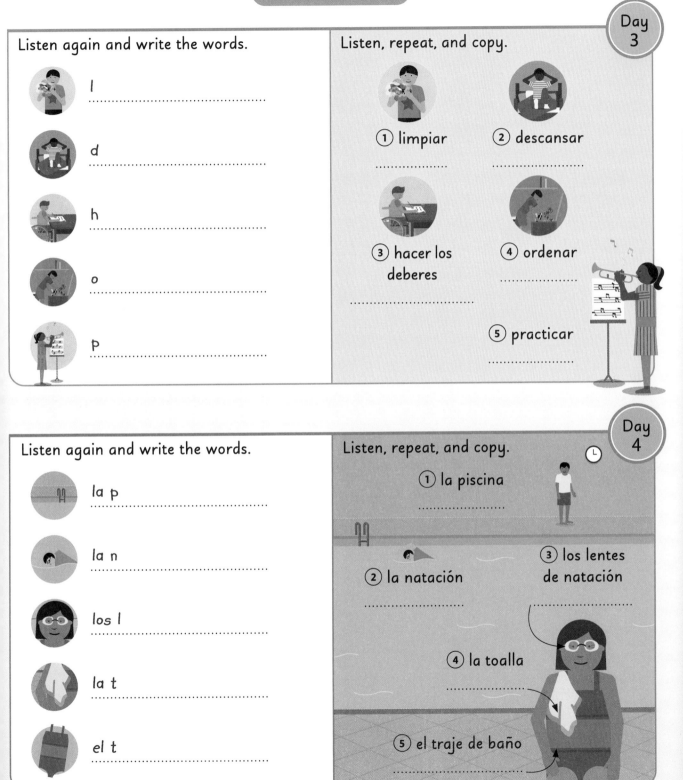

Day 3

Listen again and write the words.

l ....

d ....

h ....

o ....

p ....

Listen, repeat, and copy.

1 limpiar ....

2 descansar ....

3 hacer los deberes ....

4 ordenar ....

5 practicar ....

Day 4

Listen again and write the words.

la p ....

la n ....

los l ....

la t ....

el t ....

Listen, repeat, and copy.

1 la piscina ....

2 la natación ....

3 los lentes de natación ....

4 la toalla ....

5 el traje de baño ....

Day 5   What can you remember from this week?

1. Look at the picture and write the correct words.

piso de arriba

el sótano

el pasillo

las escaleras

piso de abajo

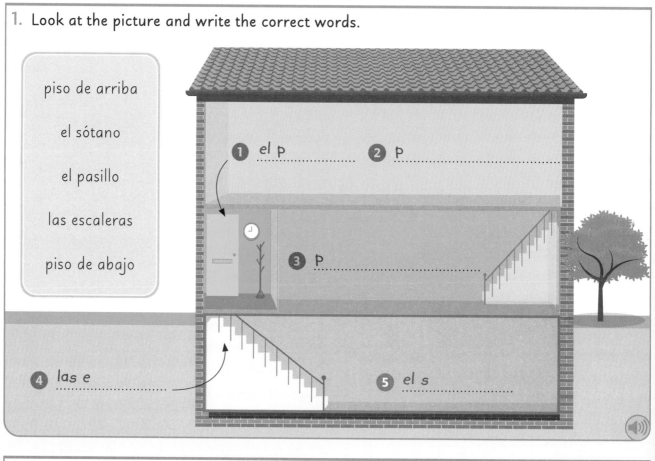

1 el p _____   2 P _____

3 P _____

4 las e _____   5 el s _____

2. Match the pictures to the correct words.

ordenar   descansar   hacer los deberes   limpiar   practicar

3. Look at the pictures and circle the correct words.

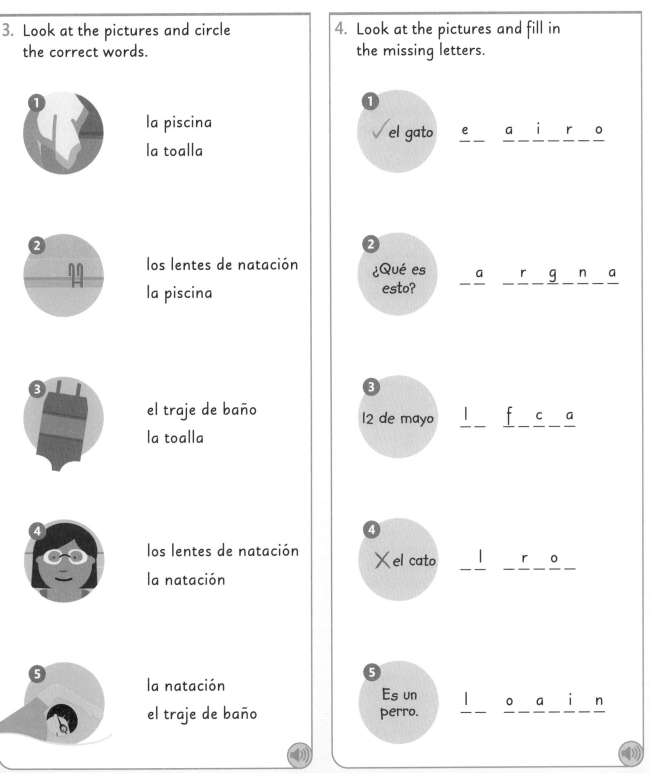

1
la piscina
la toalla

2
los lentes de natación
la piscina

3
el traje de baño
la toalla

4
los lentes de natación
la natación

5
la natación
el traje de baño

4. Look at the pictures and fill in the missing letters.

1 ✓ el gato
e _ _ a _ _ i _ r _ o

2 ¿Qué es esto?
_ _ a _ _ r _ g _ n _ _ a

3 12 de mayo
l _ _ f _ c _ _ a

4 ✗ el cato
_ _ l _ _ r _ o _

5 Es un perro.
l _ _ o _ a _ i _ n

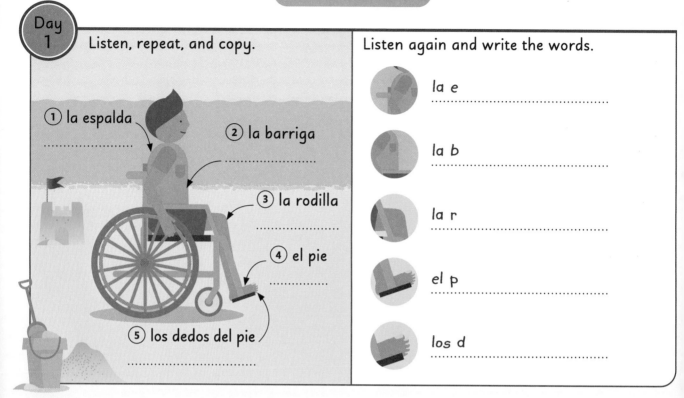

Day 1

Listen, repeat, and copy.

1. la espalda
   ....
2. la barriga
   ....
3. la rodilla
   ....
4. el pie
   ....
5. los dedos del pie
   ....

Listen again and write the words.

la e ....

la b ....

la r ....

el p ....

los d ....

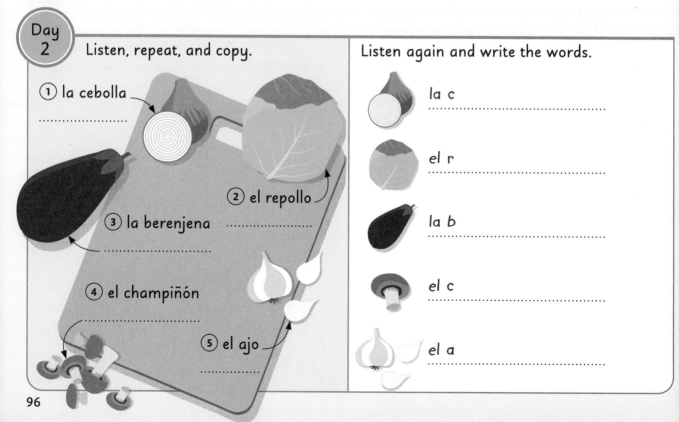

Day 2

Listen, repeat, and copy.

1. la cebolla
   ....
2. el repollo
   ....
3. la berenjena
   ....
4. el champiñón
   ....
5. el ajo
   ....

Listen again and write the words.

la c ....

el r ....

la b ....

el c ....

el a ....

Week 23

Listen again and write the words.

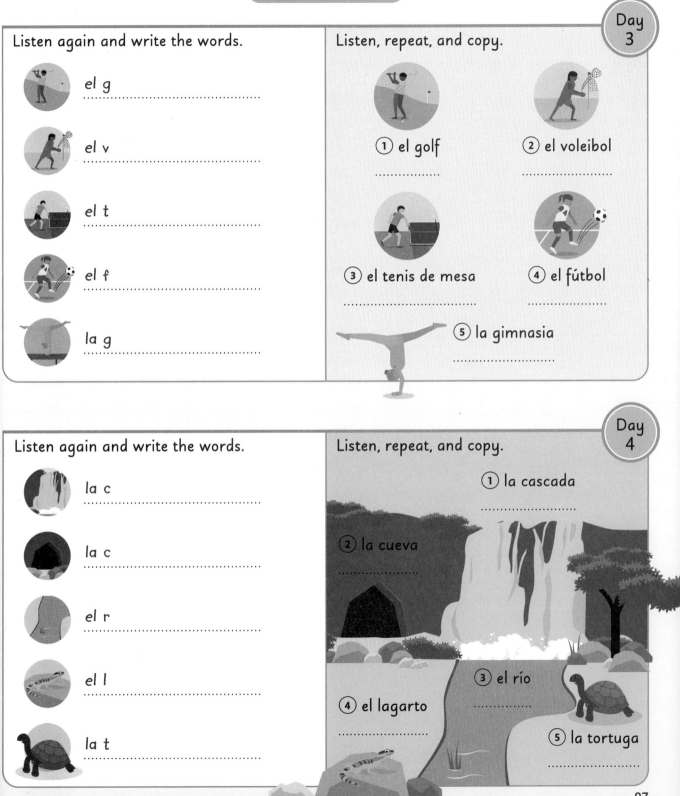

el g ....

el v ....

el t ....

el f ....

la g ....

Listen, repeat, and copy.

① el golf
....

② el voleibol
....

③ el tenis de mesa
....

④ el fútbol
....

⑤ la gimnasia
....

Listen again and write the words.

la c ....

la c ....

el r ....

el l ....

la t ....

Listen, repeat, and copy.

① la cascada
....

② la cueva
....

③ el río
....

④ el lagarto
....

⑤ la tortuga
....

Day 5

What can you remember from this week?

1. Look at the pictures and mark the correct words.

1. la cebolla ☐
   el repollo ☐

2. el champiñón ☐
   el ajo ☐

3. el repollo ☐
   la berenjena ☐

4. la cebolla ☐
   el champiñón ☐

5. el ajo ☐
   la berenjena ☐

2. Look at the pictures and write the correct words.

1. el r _____

2. la c _____

3. la c _____

4. el l _____

5. la t _____

3. Look at the pictures and circle the correct words.

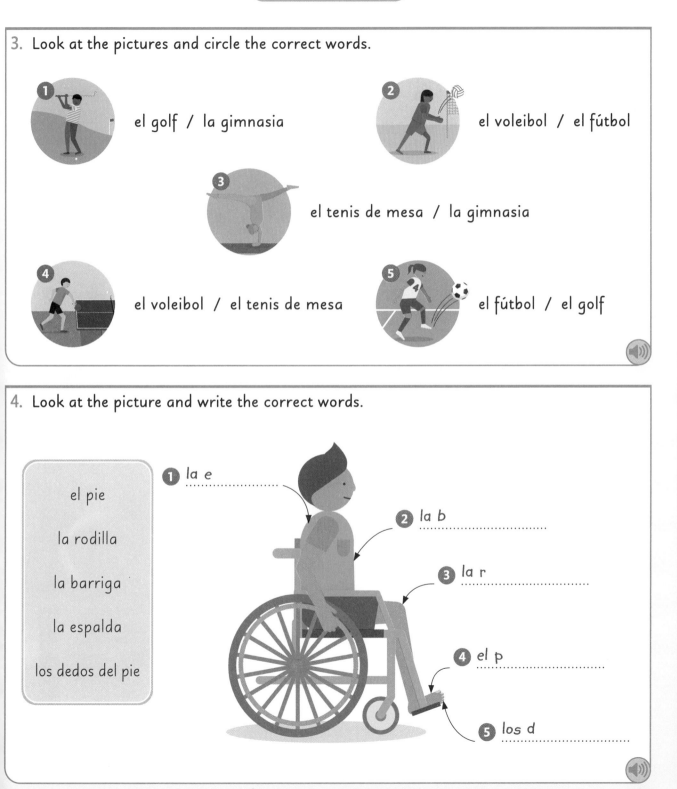

1. el golf / la gimnasia

2. el voleibol / el fútbol

3. el tenis de mesa / la gimnasia

4. el voleibol / el tenis de mesa

5. el fútbol / el golf

4. Look at the picture and write the correct words.

el pie

la rodilla

la barriga

la espalda

los dedos del pie

1. la e ....

2. la b ....

3. la r ....

4. el p ....

5. los d ....

Day 1

Listen, repeat, and copy.

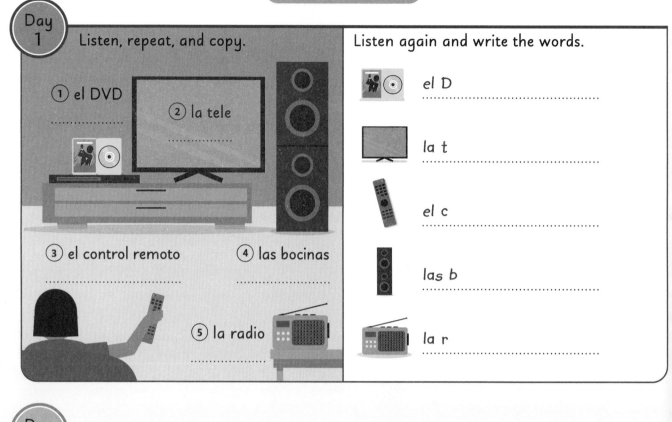

1. el DVD
2. la tele
3. el control remoto
4. las bocinas
5. la radio

Listen again and write the words.

el D ....

la t ....

el c ....

las b ....

la r ....

Day 2

Listen, repeat, and copy.

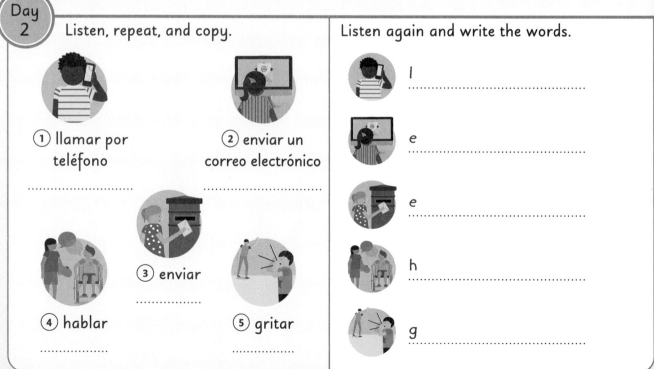

1. llamar por teléfono
2. enviar un correo electrónico
3. enviar
4. hablar
5. gritar

Listen again and write the words.

l ....

e ....

e ....

h ....

g ....

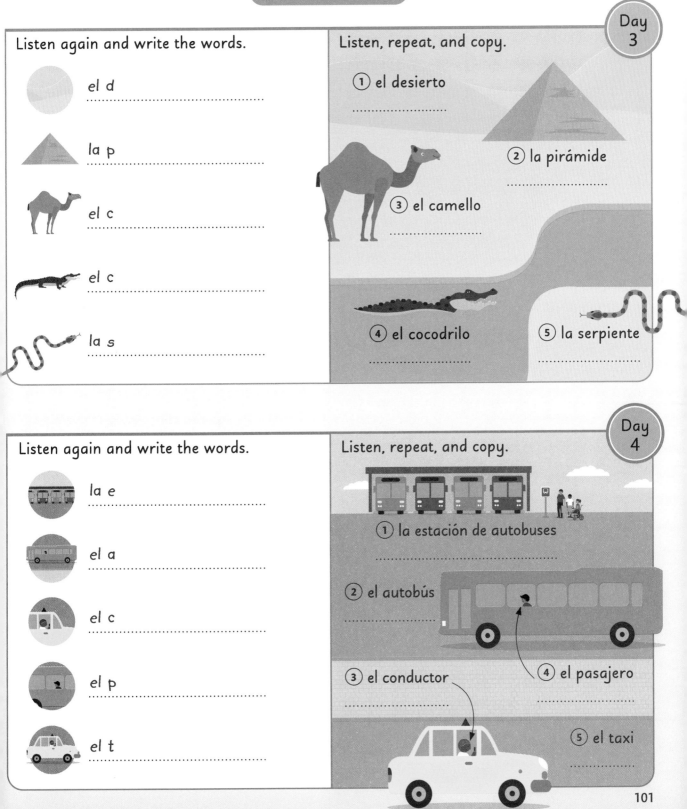

Day 3

Listen again and write the words.

el d ....

la p ....

el c ....

el c ....

la s ....

Listen, repeat, and copy.

1 el desierto
....

2 la pirámide
....

3 el camello
....

4 el cocodrilo
....

5 la serpiente
....

Day 4

Listen again and write the words.

la e ....

el a ....

el c ....

el p ....

el t ....

Listen, repeat, and copy.

1 la estación de autobuses
....

2 el autobús
....

3 el conductor
....

4 el pasajero
....

5 el taxi
....

What can you remember from this week?

1. Read the words and mark the correct pictures.

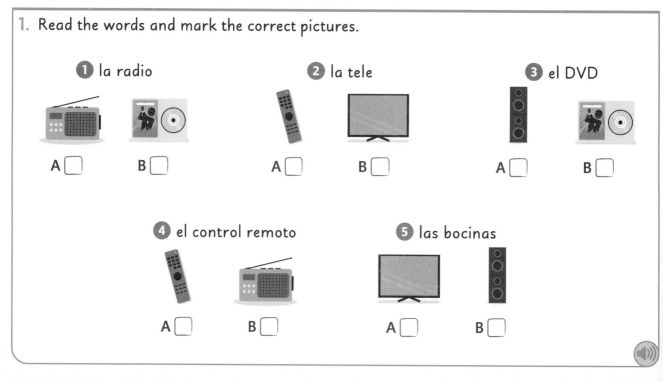

① la radio
A ☐ B ☐

② la tele
A ☐ B ☐

③ el DVD
A ☐ B ☐

④ el control remoto
A ☐ B ☐

⑤ las bocinas
A ☐ B ☐

2. Look at the pictures and write the correct words.

① el c ....

② la p ....

③ el d ....

④ la s ....

⑤ el c ....

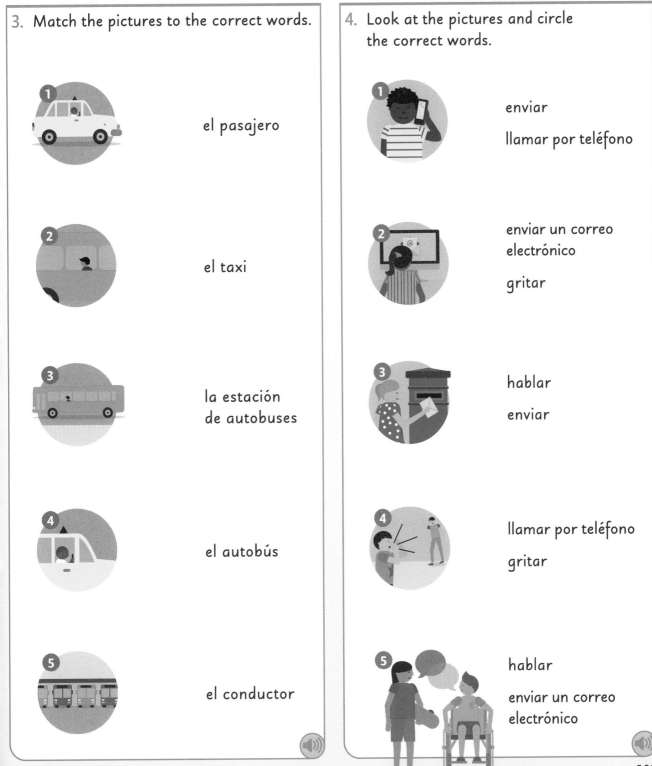

3. Match the pictures to the correct words.

el pasajero

el taxi

la estación
de autobuses

el autobús

el conductor

4. Look at the pictures and circle
the correct words.

enviar

llamar por teléfono

enviar un correo
electrónico

gritar

hablar

enviar

llamar por teléfono

gritar

hablar

enviar un correo
electrónico

Day 1

Listen, repeat, and copy.

① la escalera de mano

② el muro

③ el portón

④ el tapete

⑤ el escalón

Listen again and write the words.

la e ....

el m ....

el p ....

el t ....

el e ....

Day 2

Listen, repeat, and copy.

① nuevo ....

② viejo ....

③ iguales ....

④ diferentes ....

⑤ favorito ....

Listen again and write the words.

n ....

v ....

i ....

d ....

f ....

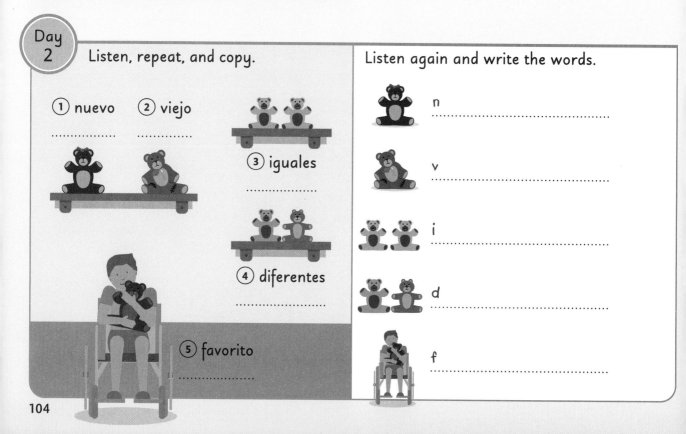

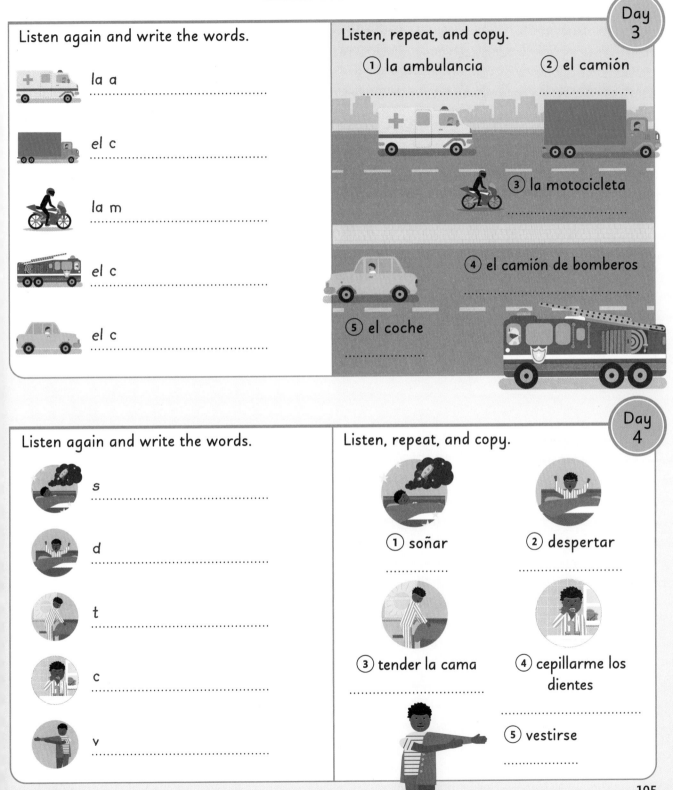

Listen again and write the words.

la a ....

el c ....

la m ....

el c ....

el c ....

Listen, repeat, and copy.

① la ambulancia ....

② el camión

③ la motocicleta ....

④ el camión de bomberos ....

⑤ el coche ....

Listen again and write the words.

s ....

d ....

t ....

c ....

v ....

Listen, repeat, and copy.

① soñar ....

② despertar ....

③ tender la cama ....

④ cepillarme los dientes ....

⑤ vestirse ....

Day 5

What can you remember from this week?

1. Look at the pictures and write the correct words.

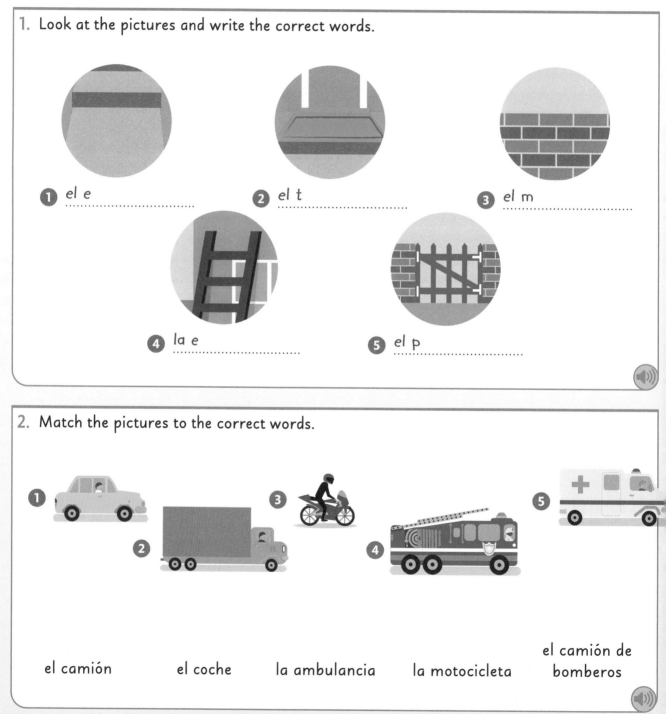

1 el e _____

2 el t _____

3 el m _____

4 la e _____

5 el p _____

2. Match the pictures to the correct words.

el camión   el coche   la ambulancia   la motocicleta   el camión de bomberos

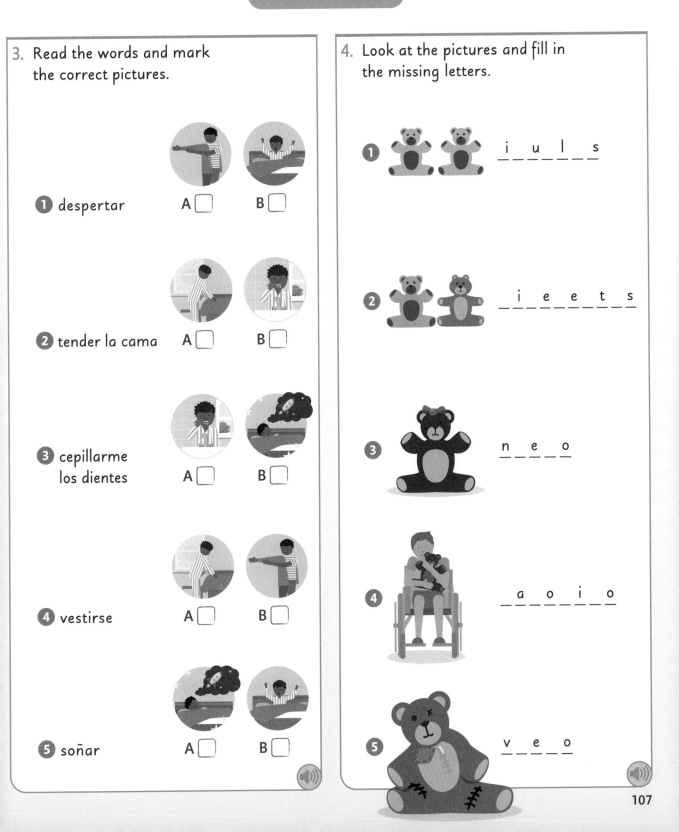

3. Read the words and mark the correct pictures.

1 despertar   A ☐   B ☐

2 tender la cama   A ☐   B ☐

3 cepillarme los dientes   A ☐   B ☐

4 vestirse   A ☐   B ☐

5 soñar   A ☐   B ☐

4. Look at the pictures and fill in the missing letters.

1 _ i u _ l _ s

2 _ i _ e _ e t _ s

3 _ n _ e _ o

4 _ a _ o _ i _ o

5 _ v _ e _ o

Day 1

Listen, repeat, and copy.

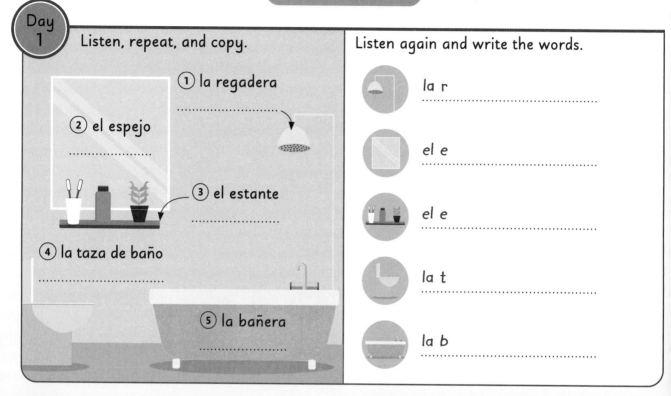

① la regadera

② el espejo

③ el estante

④ la taza de baño

⑤ la bañera

Listen again and write the words.

la r

el e

el e

la t

la b

Day 2

Listen, repeat, and copy.

① el gorila

② el panda

③ el rinoceronte

④ el loro

⑤ el canguro

Listen again and write the words.

el g

el p

el r

el l

el c

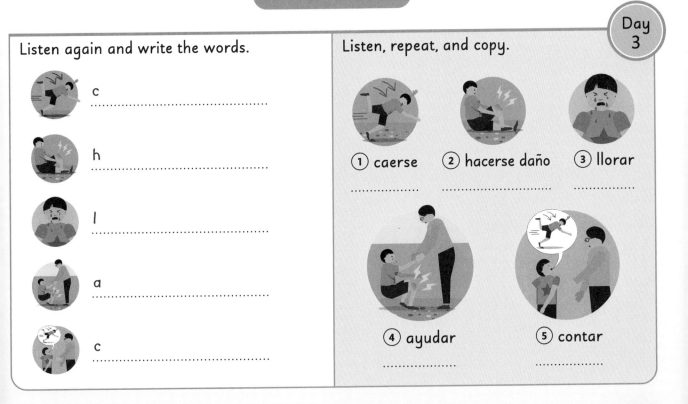

Day 3

Listen again and write the words.

c ....

h ....

l ....

a ....

c ....

Listen, repeat, and copy.

① caerse ....

② hacerse daño ....

③ llorar ....

④ ayudar ....

⑤ contar ....

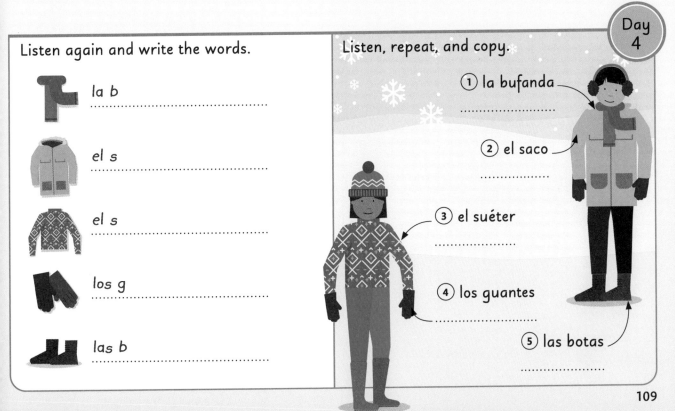

Day 4

Listen again and write the words.

la b ....

el s ....

el s ....

los g ....

las b ....

Listen, repeat, and copy.

① la bufanda ....

② el saco ....

③ el suéter ....

④ los guantes ....

⑤ las botas ....

What can you remember from this week?

1. Look at the pictures and write the correct words.

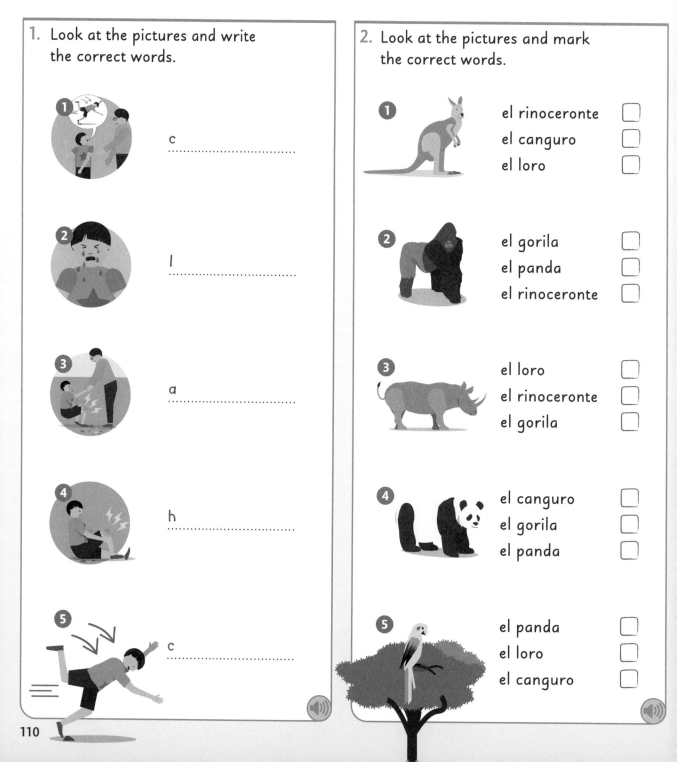

1. c ....

2. l ....

3. a ....

4. h ....

5. c ....

2. Look at the pictures and mark the correct words.

1.
el rinoceronte ☐
el canguro ☐
el loro ☐

2.
el gorila ☐
el panda ☐
el rinoceronte ☐

3.
el loro ☐
el rinoceronte ☐
el gorila ☐

4.
el canguro ☐
el gorila ☐
el panda ☐

5.
el panda ☐
el loro ☐
el canguro ☐

3. Look at the pictures and write the correct words.

el saco   las botas   los guantes   la bufanda   el suéter

1. las b ....

2. el s ....

3. la b ....

4. el s ....

5. los g ....

4. Look at the pictures and circle the correct words.

1. la regadera
   la bañera

2. la taza de baño
   el estante

3. la bañera
   el espejo

4. el espejo
   el estante

5. la regadera
   la taza de baño

Week 27

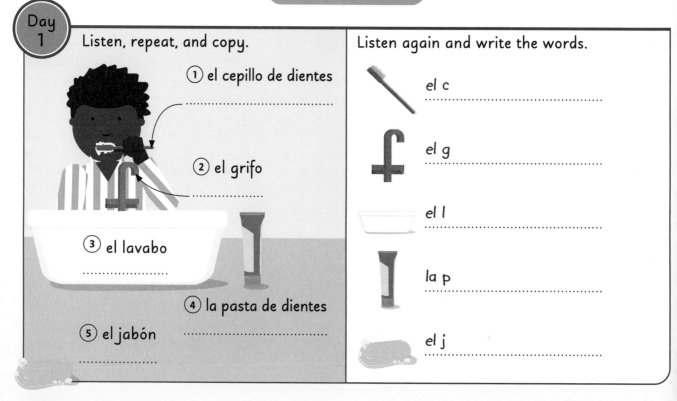

Day 1

Listen, repeat, and copy.

① el cepillo de dientes

....

② el grifo

....

③ el lavabo

....

④ la pasta de dientes

⑤ el jabón ....

....

Listen again and write the words.

el c ....

el g ....

el l ....

la p ....

el j ....

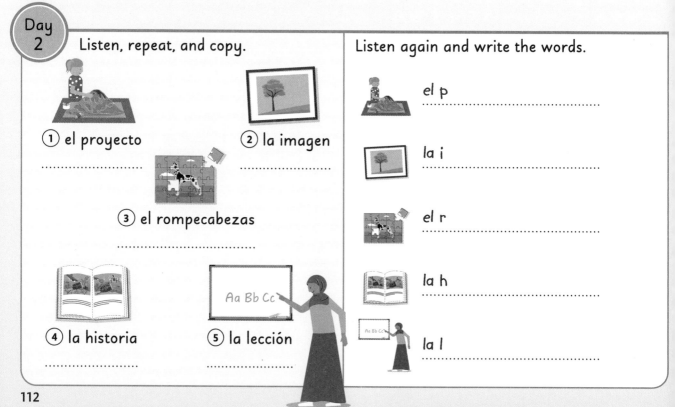

Day 2

Listen, repeat, and copy.

① el proyecto

....

② la imagen

....

③ el rompecabezas

....

④ la historia

....

⑤ la lección

....

Listen again and write the words.

el p ....

la i ....

el r ....

la h ....

la l ....

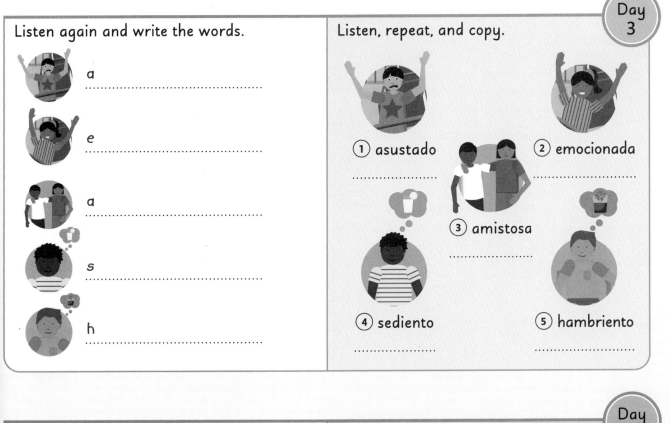

Day 3

Listen again and write the words.

a ....

e ....

a ....

s ....

h ....

Listen, repeat, and copy.

① asustado

② emocionada

③ amistosa

④ sediento

⑤ hambriento

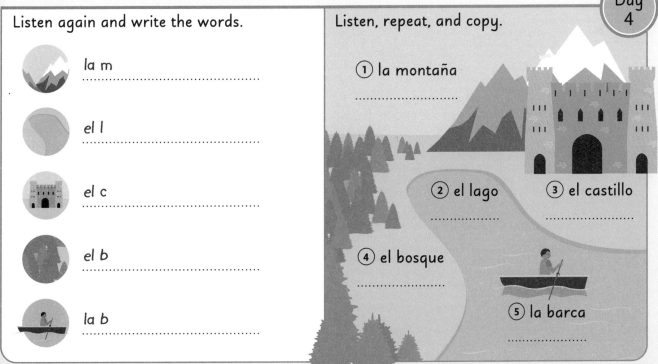

Day 4

Listen again and write the words.

la m ....

el l ....

el c ....

el b ....

la b ....

Listen, repeat, and copy.

① la montaña

② el lago

③ el castillo

④ el bosque

⑤ la barca

Day 5

What can you remember from this week?

1. Look at the pictures and write the letters in the correct order.

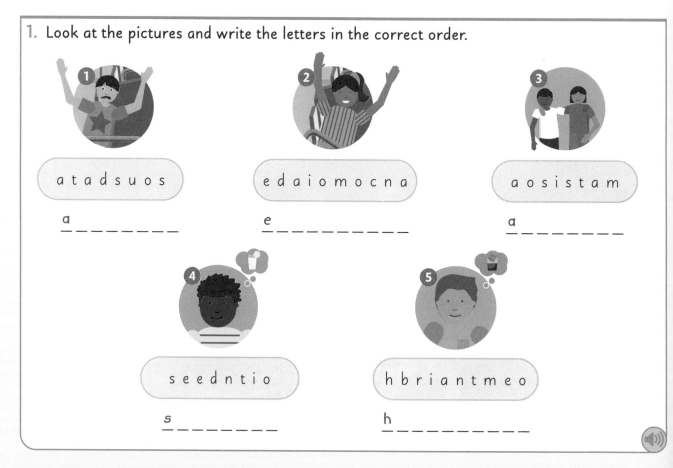

1 a t a d s u o s

a _ _ _ _ _ _ _

2 e d a i o m o c n a

e _ _ _ _ _ _ _ _ _

3 a o s i s t a m

a _ _ _ _ _ _ _

4 s e e d n t i o

s _ _ _ _ _ _ _

5 h b r i a n t m e o

h _ _ _ _ _ _ _ _ _

2. Match the pictures to the correct words.

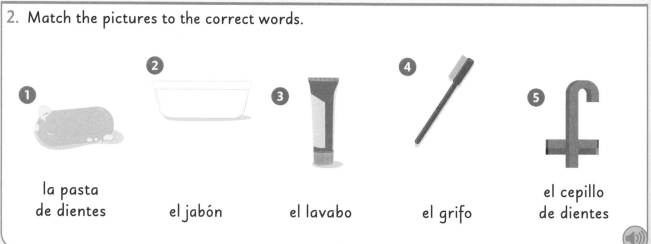

1 la pasta de dientes

2 el jabón

3 el lavabo

4 el grifo

5 el cepillo de dientes

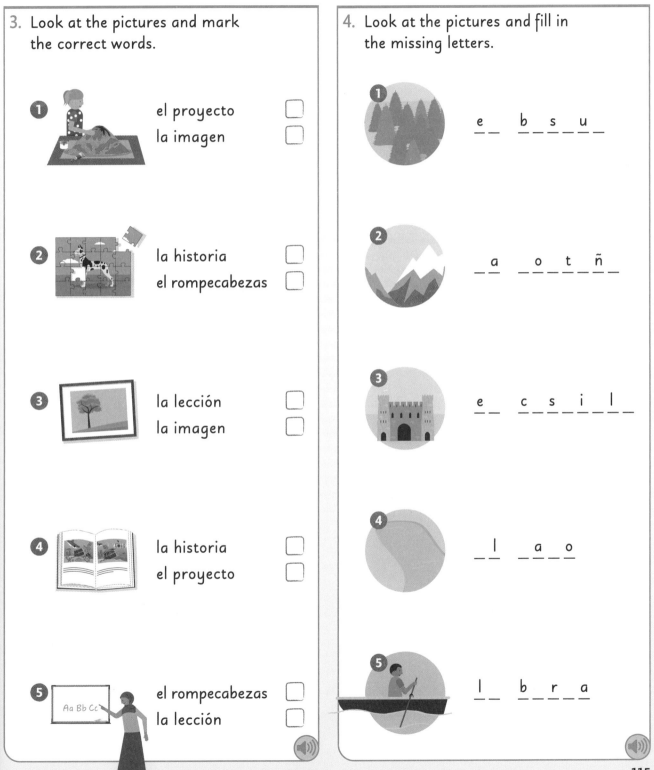

3. Look at the pictures and mark the correct words.

① el proyecto ☐
la imagen ☐

② la historia ☐
el rompecabezas ☐

③ la lección ☐
la imagen ☐

④ la historia ☐
el proyecto ☐

⑤ el rompecabezas ☐
la lección ☐

4. Look at the pictures and fill in the missing letters.

① e _ b _ s u _

② _ a _ o t ñ _

③ e _ c _ s _ i _ l _

④ _ l _ a _ o

⑤ l _ b _ r _ a

Day 1

Listen, repeat, and copy.

① la computadora

....

② la pantalla

....

③ la impresora

....

④ el teclado

....

⑤ el ratón

....

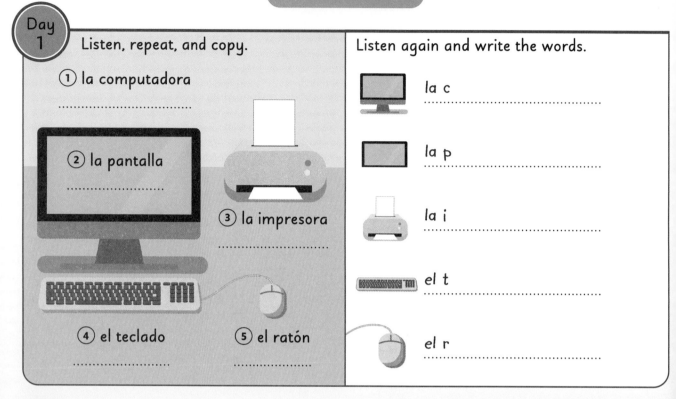

Listen again and write the words.

la c ....

la p ....

la i ....

el t ....

el r ....

Day 2

Listen, repeat, and copy.

① dentro

....

② fuera

....

③ entre

....

④ encima

....

⑤ debajo

....

Listen again and write the words.

d ....

f ....

e ....

e ....

d ....

Week 28

Listen again and write the words.

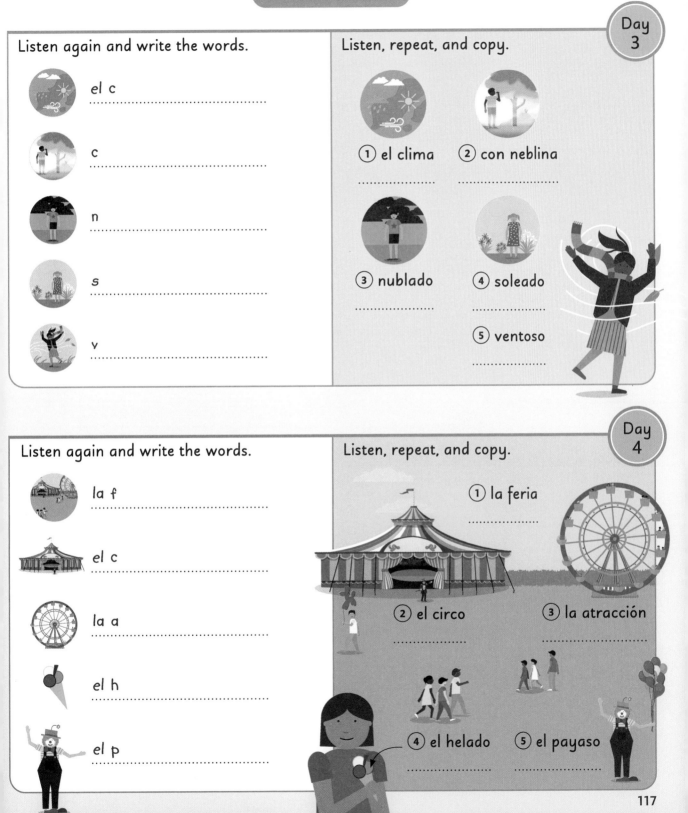

el c ....

c ....

n ....

s ....

v ....

Listen, repeat, and copy.

1 el clima   2 con neblina

....

3 nublado   4 soleado

....

5 ventoso

....

Listen again and write the words.

la f ....

el c ....

la a ....

el h ....

el p ....

Listen, repeat, and copy.

1 la feria

....

2 el circo   3 la atracción

....

4 el helado   5 el payaso

Day 5

What can you remember from this week?

1. Read the words and mark the correct pictures.

1 dentro   A ☐   B ☐

2 fuera   A ☐   B ☐

3 entre   A ☐   B ☐

4 encima   A ☐   B ☐

5 debajo   A ☐   B ☐

2. Look at the pictures and write the correct words.

1   c ....

2   s ....

3   el c ....

4   v ....

5   n ....

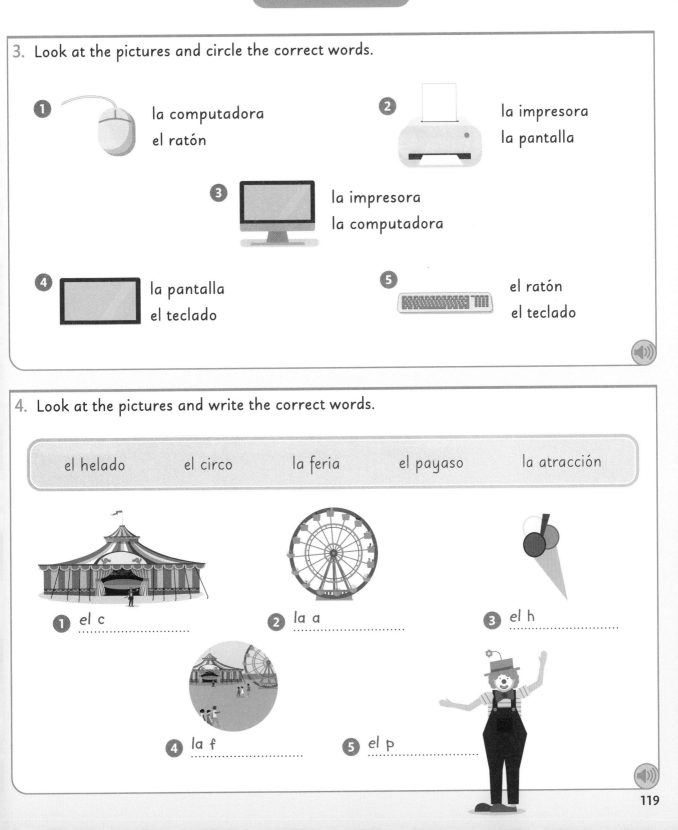

3. Look at the pictures and circle the correct words.

1 la computadora
el ratón

2 la impresora
la pantalla

3 la impresora
la computadora

4 la pantalla
el teclado

5 el ratón
el teclado

4. Look at the pictures and write the correct words.

el helado   el circo   la feria   el payaso   la atracción

1 el c ....

2 la a ....

3 el h ....

4 la f ....

5 el p ....

Week 29

Day 1

Listen, repeat, and copy.

① la sopa　② la tarta

③ el arroz
....

④ los frijoles
....

⑤ la carne
....

Listen again and write the words.

la s ....

la t ....

el a ....

los f ....

la c ....

Day 2

Listen, repeat, and copy.

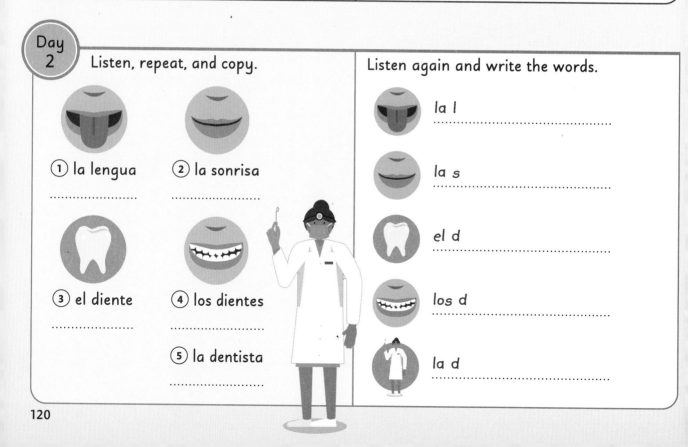

① la lengua　② la sonrisa
....　............

③ el diente　④ los dientes
....　............

⑤ la dentista
....

Listen again and write the words.

la l ....

la s ....

el d ....

los d ....

la d ....

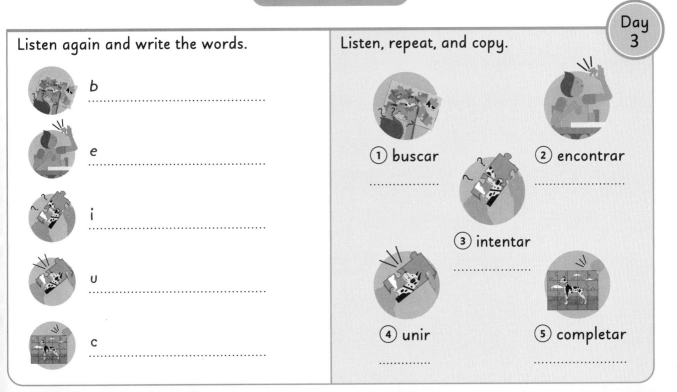

Day 3

Listen again and write the words.

b ....

e ....

i ....

u ....

c ....

Listen, repeat, and copy.

① buscar
....

② encontrar
....

③ intentar
....

④ unir
....

⑤ completar
....

Day 4

Listen again and write the words.

la p ....

el c ....

la c ....

el p ....

la r ....

Listen, repeat, and copy.

① la pesca
....

② el chaleco salvavidas
....

③ la caña de pescar
....

④ el pez
....

⑤ la red
....

Day 5

What can you remember from this week?

1. Look at the pictures and fill in the missing letters.

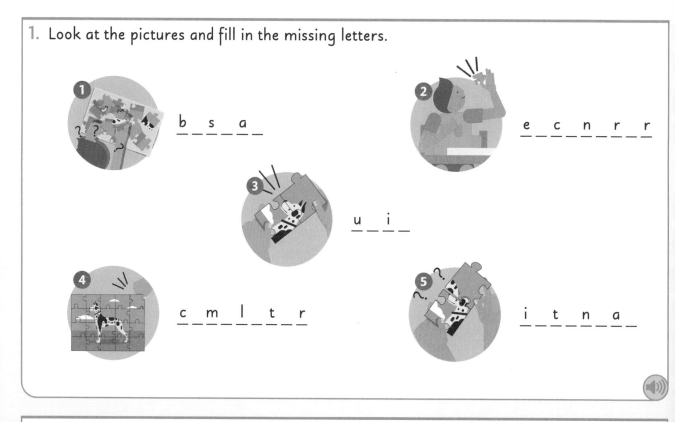

1. b _ s _ a _

2. e _ c _ n _ r _ r

3. u _ _ i _

4. c _ m _ l _ t _ r

5. i _ t _ n _ a _

2. Match the pictures to the correct words.

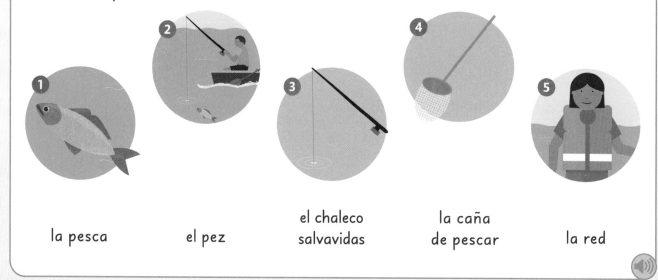

la pesca   el pez   el chaleco salvavidas   la caña de pescar   la red

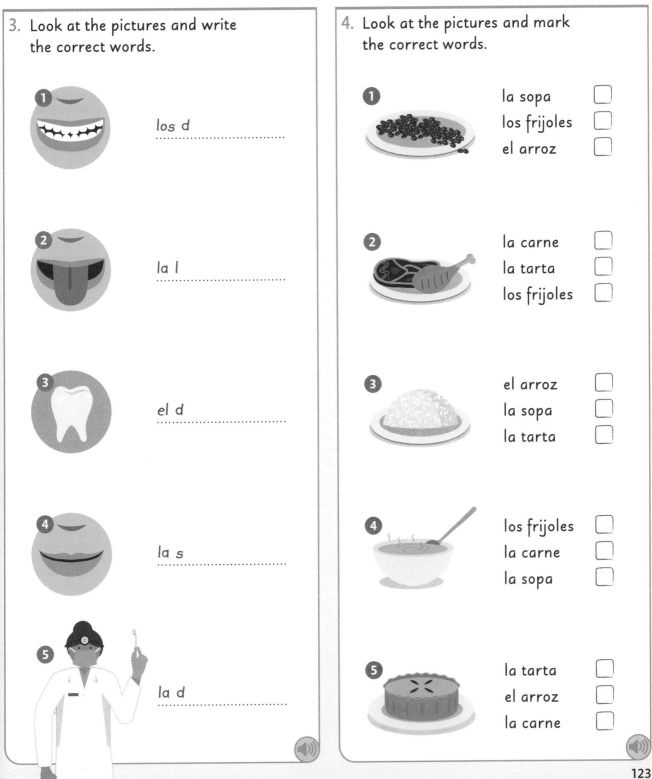

3. Look at the pictures and write the correct words.

1. los d ....

2. la l ....

3. el d ....

4. la s ....

5. la d ....

4. Look at the pictures and mark the correct words.

1. la sopa ☐
   los frijoles ☐
   el arroz ☐

2. la carne ☐
   la tarta ☐
   los frijoles ☐

3. el arroz ☐
   la sopa ☐
   la tarta ☐

4. los frijoles ☐
   la carne ☐
   la sopa ☐

5. la tarta ☐
   el arroz ☐
   la carne ☐

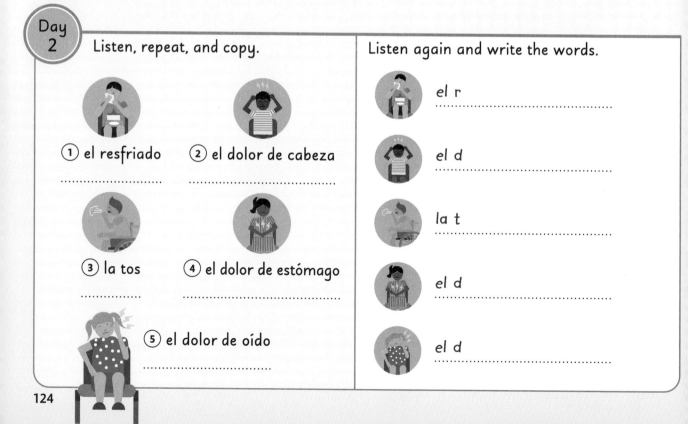

Day 1

Listen, repeat, and copy.

① el techo

....

② la puerta

....

③ la ventana

....

④ la llave

....

⑤ el piso

....

Listen again and write the words.

el t ....

la p ....

la v ....

la l ....

el p ....

Day 2

Listen, repeat, and copy.

① el resfriado

....

② el dolor de cabeza

....

③ la tos

....

④ el dolor de estómago

....

⑤ el dolor de oído

....

Listen again and write the words.

el r ....

el d ....

la t ....

el d ....

el d ....

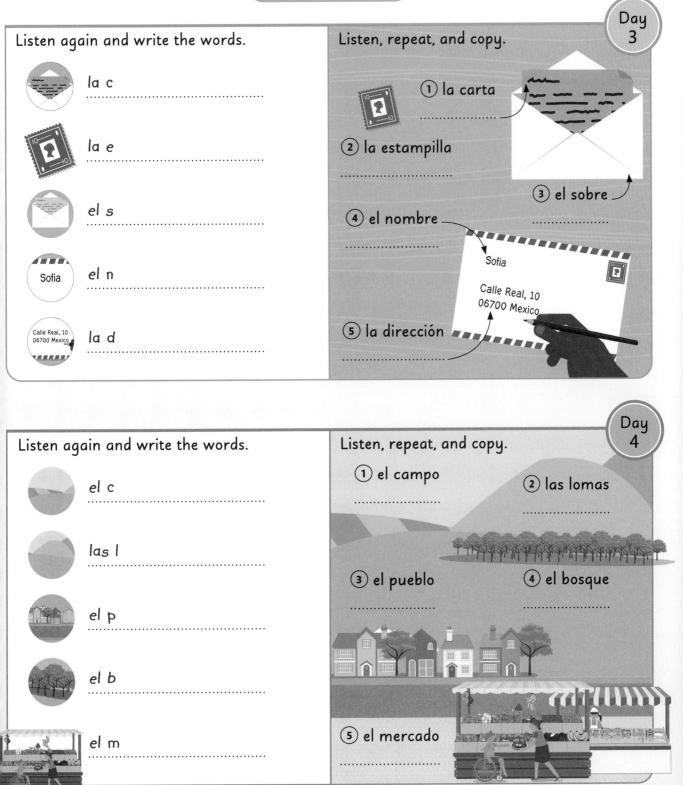

Day 3

Listen again and write the words.

la c ....

la e ....

el s ....

Sofia   el n ....

Calle Real, 10
06700 Mexico   la d ....

Listen, repeat, and copy.

① la carta ....

② la estampilla ....

③ el sobre ....

④ el nombre ....

Sofia

Calle Real, 10
06700 Mexico

⑤ la dirección ....

Day 4

Listen again and write the words.

el c ....

las l ....

el p ....

el b ....

el m ....

Listen, repeat, and copy.

① el campo ....

② las lomas ....

③ el pueblo ....

④ el bosque ....

⑤ el mercado ....

Day 5

What can you remember from this week?

1. Look at the pictures and write the correct words.

| las lomas | el pueblo | el bosque |
| el campo | el mercado | |

1. el p ....

2. las l ....

3. el c ....

4. el b ....

5. el m ....

2. Look at the pictures and mark the correct words.

1. la carta ☐
   la estampilla ☐

2. Calle Real, 10
   06700 Mexico

   el nombre ☐
   la dirección ☐

3. el sobre ☐
   la carta ☐

4. la dirección ☐
   la estampilla ☐

5. Sofia

   el sobre ☐
   el nombre ☐

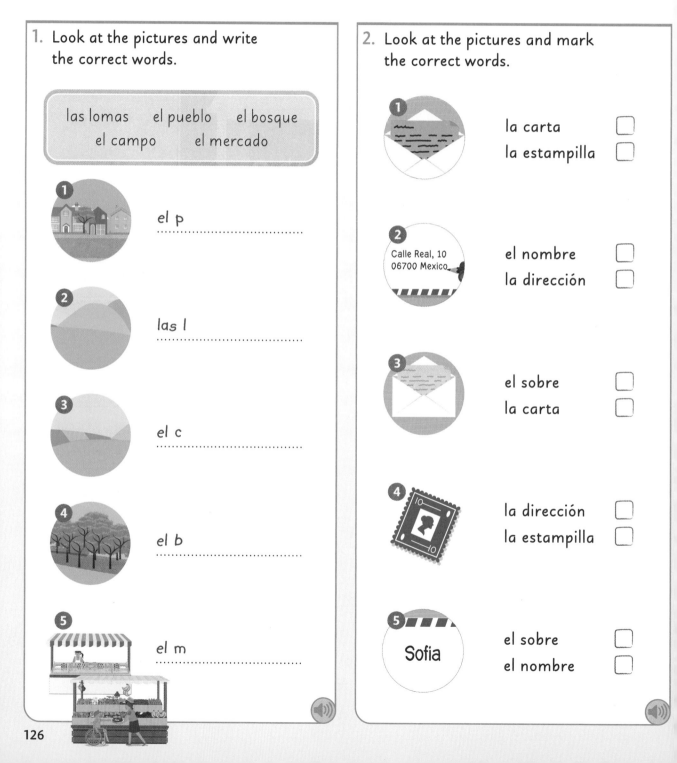

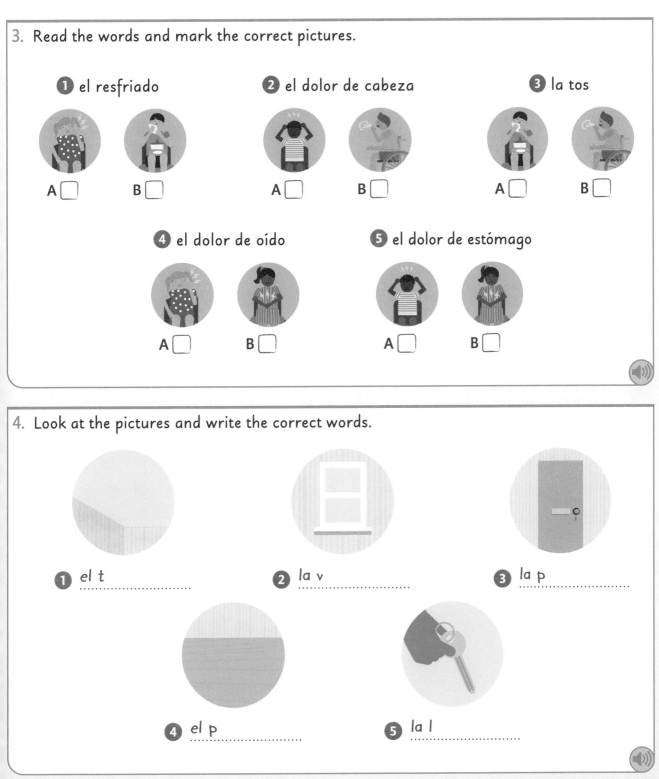

3. Read the words and mark the correct pictures.

1 el resfriado

A ☐   B ☐

2 el dolor de cabeza

A ☐   B ☐

3 la tos

A ☐   B ☐

4 el dolor de oído

A ☐   B ☐

5 el dolor de estómago

A ☐   B ☐

4. Look at the pictures and write the correct words.

1 el t _____

2 la v _____

3 la p _____

4 el p _____

5 la l _____

Day 1

Listen, repeat, and copy.

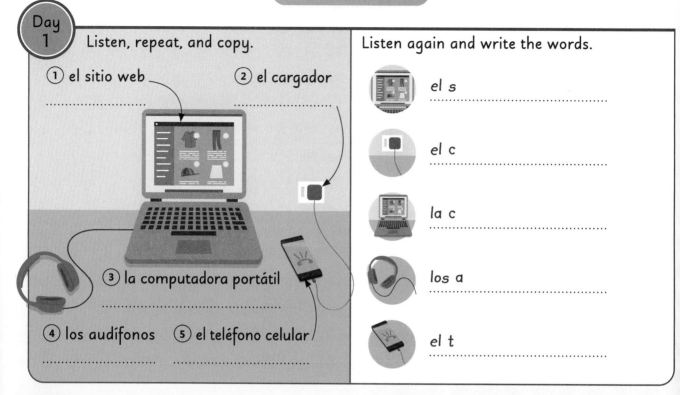

1. el sitio web
2. el cargador
3. la computadora portátil
4. los audífonos
5. el teléfono celular

Listen again and write the words.

el s ....

el c ....

la c ....

los a ....

el t ....

Day 2

Listen, repeat, and copy.

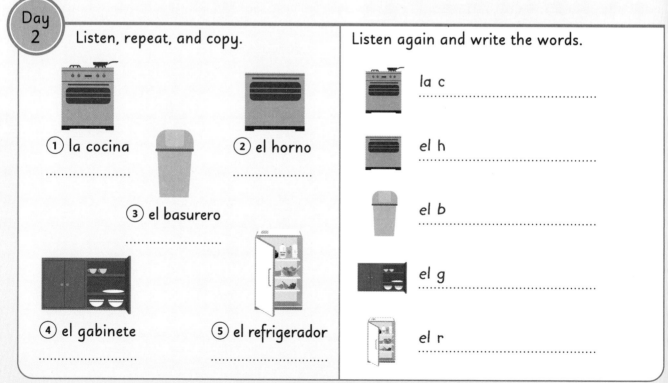

1. la cocina
2. el horno
3. el basurero
4. el gabinete
5. el refrigerador

Listen again and write the words.

la c ....

el h ....

el b ....

el g ....

el r ....

Listen again and write the words.

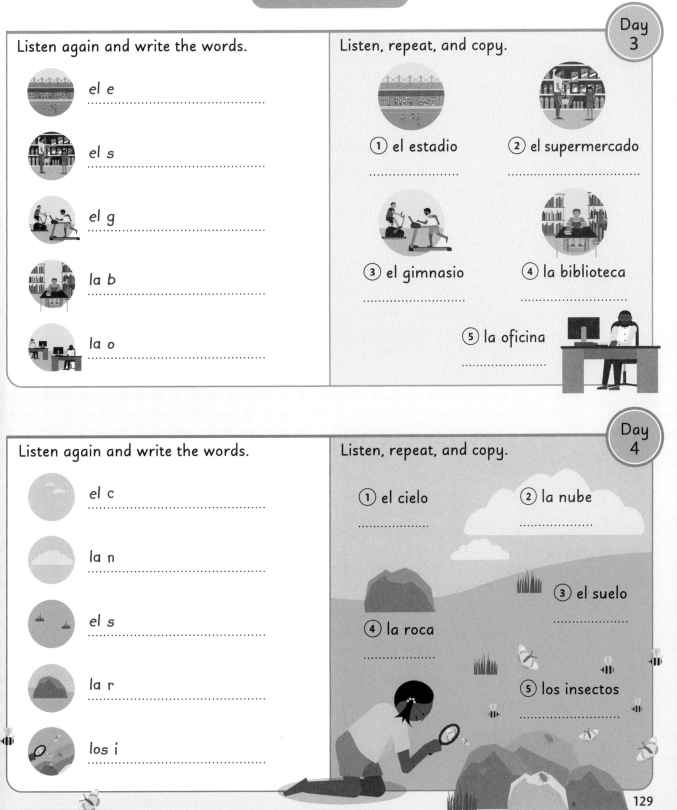

el e ....

el s ....

el g ....

la b ....

la o ....

Listen, repeat, and copy.

① el estadio
....

② el supermercado
....

③ el gimnasio
....

④ la biblioteca
....

⑤ la oficina
....

Listen again and write the words.

el c ....

la n ....

el s ....

la r ....

los i ....

Listen, repeat, and copy.

① el cielo
....

② la nube
....

③ el suelo
....

④ la roca
....

⑤ los insectos
....

Day 5

What can you remember from this week?

1. Read the words and mark the correct pictures.

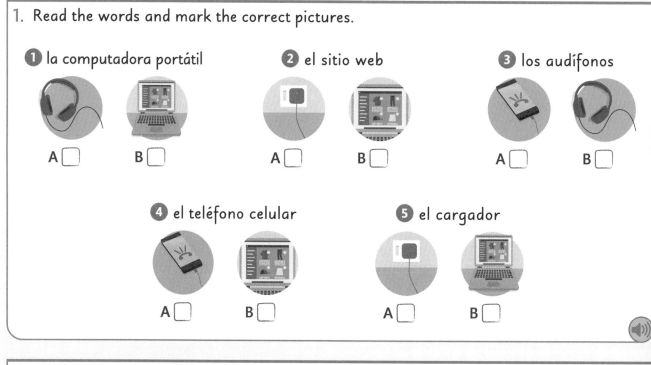

❶ la computadora portátil
A ☐   B ☐

❷ el sitio web
A ☐   B ☐

❸ los audífonos
A ☐   B ☐

❹ el teléfono celular
A ☐   B ☐

❺ el cargador
A ☐   B ☐

2. Look at the pictures and write the correct words.

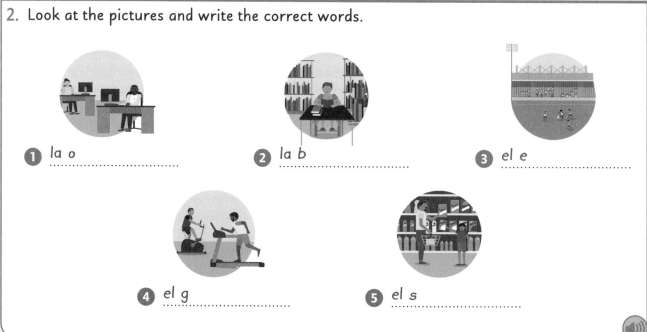

❶ la o _____

❷ la b _____

❸ el e _____

❹ el g _____

❺ el s _____

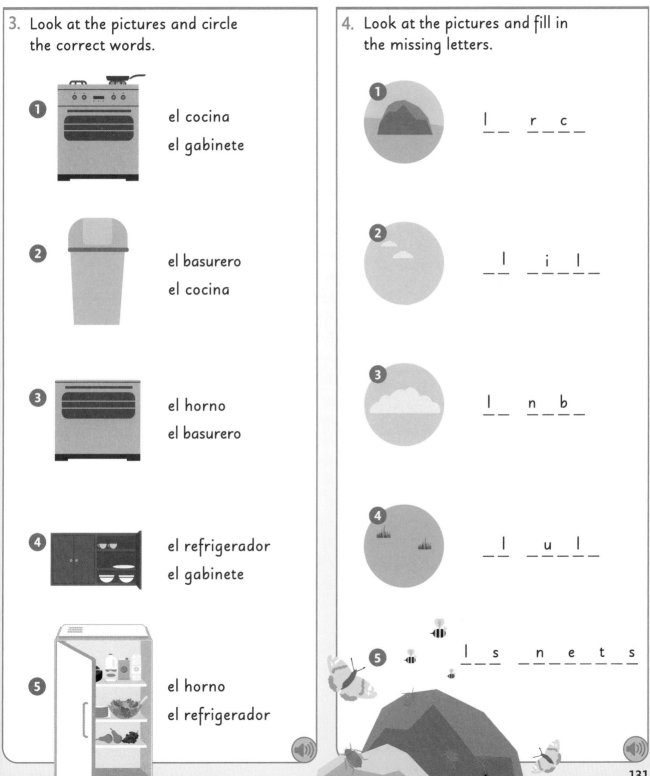

Week 31

3. Look at the pictures and circle the correct words.

1. el cocina
   el gabinete

2. el basurero
   el cocina

3. el horno
   el basurero

4. el refrigerador
   el gabinete

5. el horno
   el refrigerador

4. Look at the pictures and fill in the missing letters.

1. l _ r _ c _

2. _ l _ i _ l

3. l _ n _ b _

4. _ l _ u _ l _

5. _ _ s _ n e t s

Day 1

Listen, repeat, and copy.

① el copo de nieve

....

② el muñeco de nieve

....

③ la bola de nieve

....

④ la nieve

....

⑤ el hielo

....

Listen again and write the words.

el c

....

el m

....

la b

....

la n

....

el h

....

Day 2

Listen, repeat, and copy.

① saltar

....

② girar

....

③ columpiarse

....

④ jugar

....

⑤ silbar

....

Listen again and write the words.

s

....

g

....

c

....

j

....

s

....

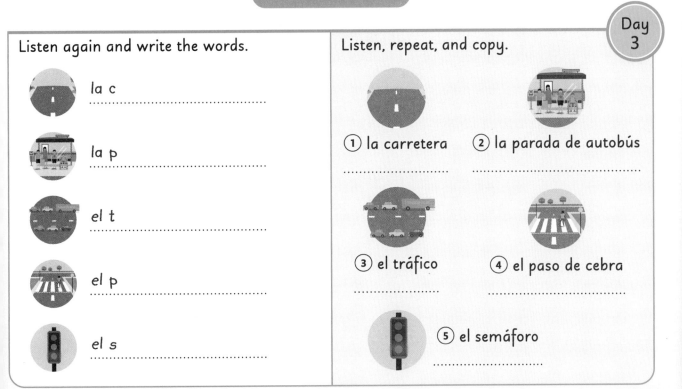

Listen again and write the words.

la c
....

la p
....

el t
....

el p
....

el s
....

Listen, repeat, and copy.

① la carretera
....

② la parada de autobús
....

③ el tráfico
....

④ el paso de cebra
....

⑤ el semáforo
....

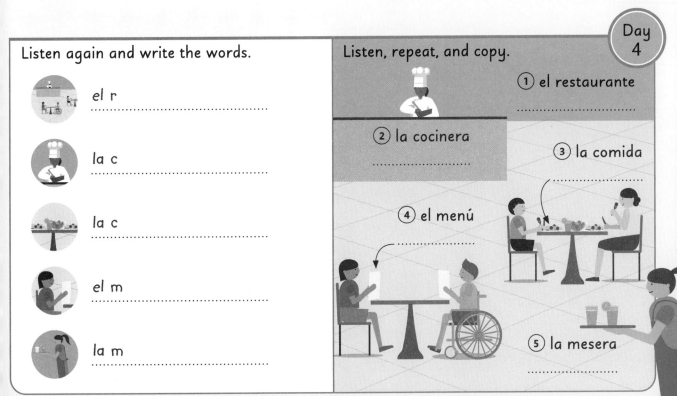

Listen again and write the words.

el r
....

la c
....

la c
....

el m
....

la m
....

Listen, repeat, and copy.

① el restaurante
....

② la cocinera
....

③ la comida
....

④ el menú
....

⑤ la mesera
....

Day 5

What can you remember from this week?

1. Read the words and mark the correct pictures.

① el muñeco de nieve   A ☐   B ☐

② la nieve   A ☐   B ☐

③ el copo de nieve   A ☐   B ☐

④ la bola de nieve   A ☐   B ☐

⑤ el hielo   A ☐   B ☐

2. Look at the pictures and write the correct words.

① el m ....

② el r ....

③ la c ....

④ la c ....

⑤ la m ....

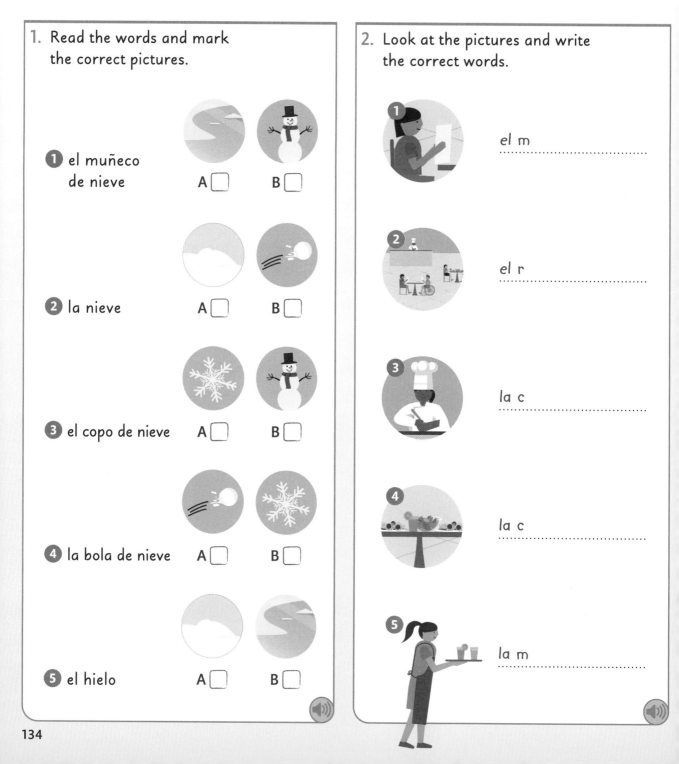

3. Look at the pictures and write the letters in the correct order.

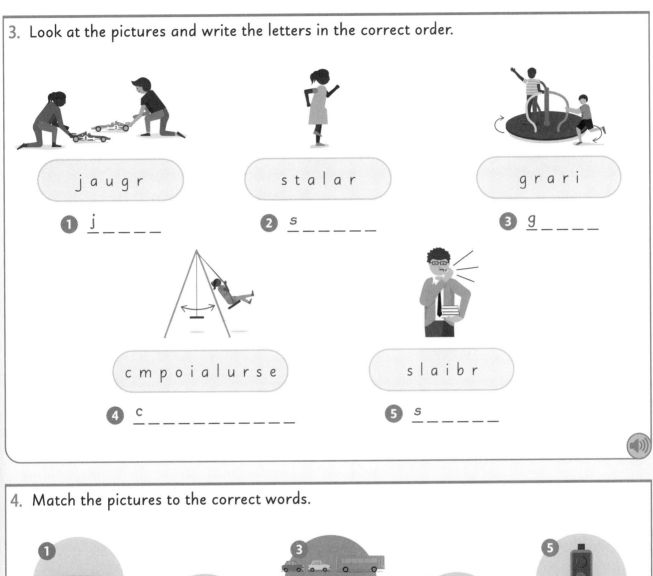

jaugr

1 j _ _ _ _

stalar

2 s _ _ _ _ _

grari

3 g _ _ _ _

cmpoialurse

4 c _ _ _ _ _ _ _ _ _ _

slaibr

5 s _ _ _ _ _

4. Match the pictures to the correct words.

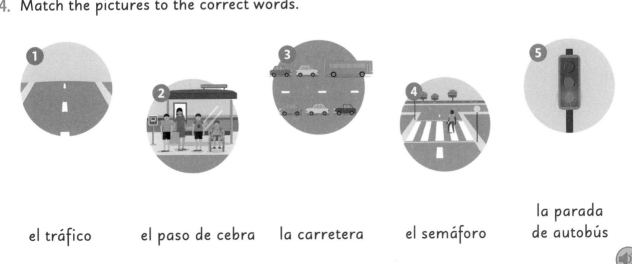

el tráfico   el paso de cebra   la carretera   el semáforo   la parada de autobús

Day 1

Listen, repeat, and copy.

① la taza

② el plato

③ el plato hondo

④ el vaso de vidrio

⑤ la botella

Listen again and write the words.

la t ....

el p ....

el p ....

el v ....

la b ....

Day 2

Listen, repeat, and copy.

① la ciudad

② el rascacielos

③ el museo

④ la universidad

⑤ el zoológico

Listen again and write the words.

la c ....

el r ....

el m ....

la u ....

el z ....

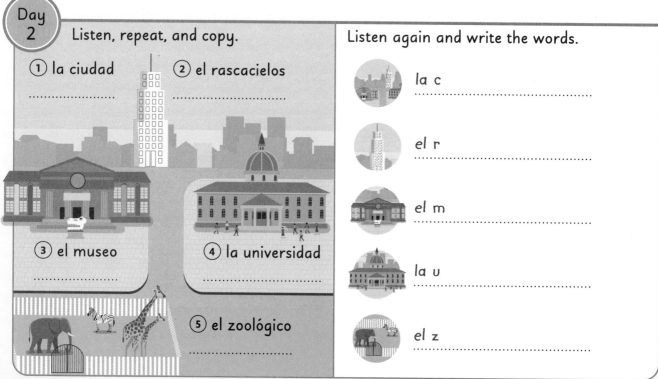

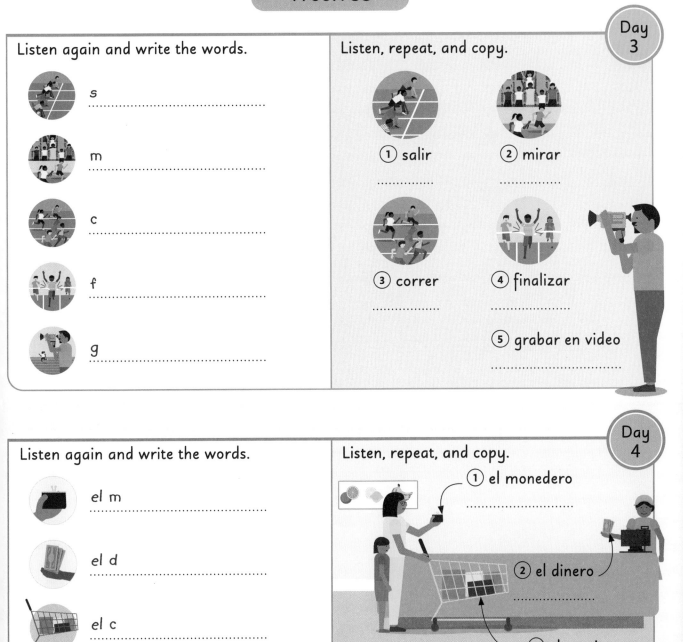

Day 3

Listen again and write the words.

s ....

m ....

c ....

f ....

g ....

Listen, repeat, and copy.

① salir
....

② mirar
....

③ correr
....

④ finalizar
....

⑤ grabar en video
....

Day 4

Listen again and write the words.

el m ....

el d ....

el c ....

la c ....

las c ....

Listen, repeat, and copy.

① el monedero
....

② el dinero
....

③ el carrito

④ la canasta
....

⑤ las compras
....

137

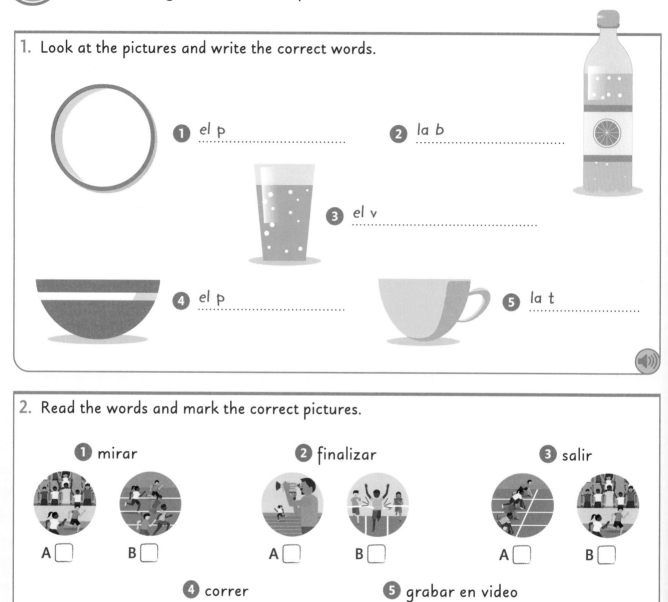

Day 5

What can you remember from this week?

1. Look at the pictures and write the correct words.

1 el p ....

2 la b ....

3 el v ....

4 el p ....

5 la t ....

2. Read the words and mark the correct pictures.

1 mirar

A ☐   B ☐

2 finalizar

A ☐   B ☐

3 salir

A ☐   B ☐

4 correr

A ☐   B ☐

5 grabar en video

A ☐   B ☐

Week 33

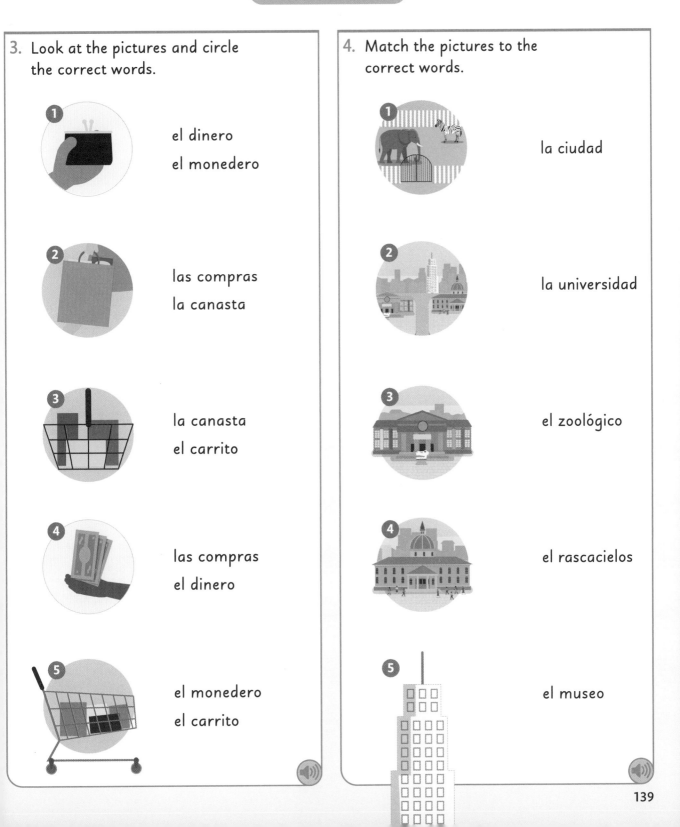

3. Look at the pictures and circle the correct words.

1. el dinero
   el monedero

2. las compras
   la canasta

3. la canasta
   el carrito

4. las compras
   el dinero

5. el monedero
   el carrito

4. Match the pictures to the correct words.

1. la ciudad

2. la universidad

3. el zoológico

4. el rascacielos

5. el museo

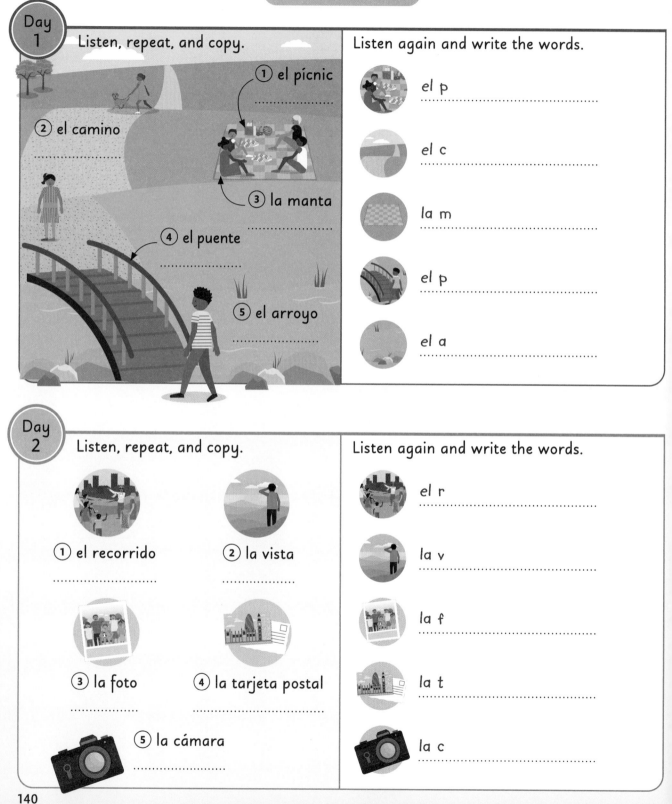

Day 1

Listen, repeat, and copy.

1. el pícnic
....
2. el camino
....
3. la manta
....
4. el puente
....
5. el arroyo
....

Listen again and write the words.

el p ....

el c ....

la m ....

el p ....

el a ....

Day 2

Listen, repeat, and copy.

1. el recorrido
....
2. la vista
....
3. la foto
....
4. la tarjeta postal
....
5. la cámara
....

Listen again and write the words.

el r ....

la v ....

la f ....

la t ....

la c ....

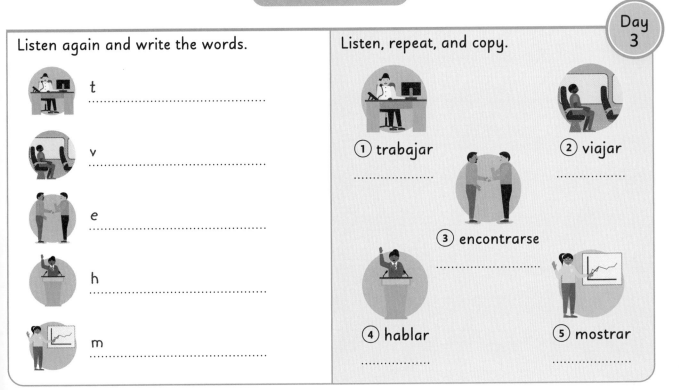

Day 3

Listen again and write the words.

t ....

v ....

e ....

h ....

m ....

Listen, repeat, and copy.

① trabajar

②viajar

....

③ encontrarse

....

④ hablar

....

⑤ mostrar

....

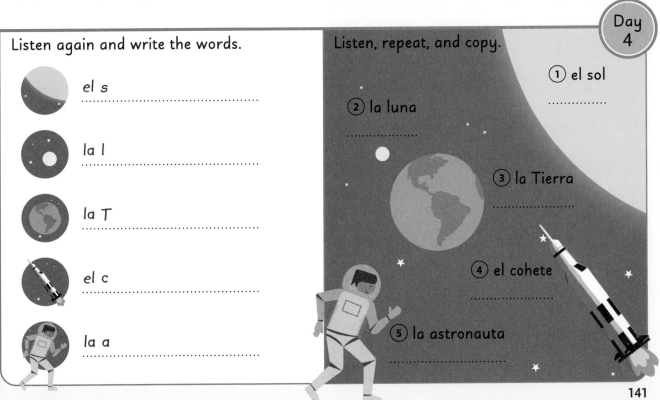

Day 4

Listen again and write the words.

el s ....

la l ....

la T ....

el c ....

la a ....

Listen, repeat, and copy.

① el sol

....

② la luna

....

③ la Tierra

....

④ el cohete

....

⑤ la astronauta

....

Day 5

What can you remember from this week?

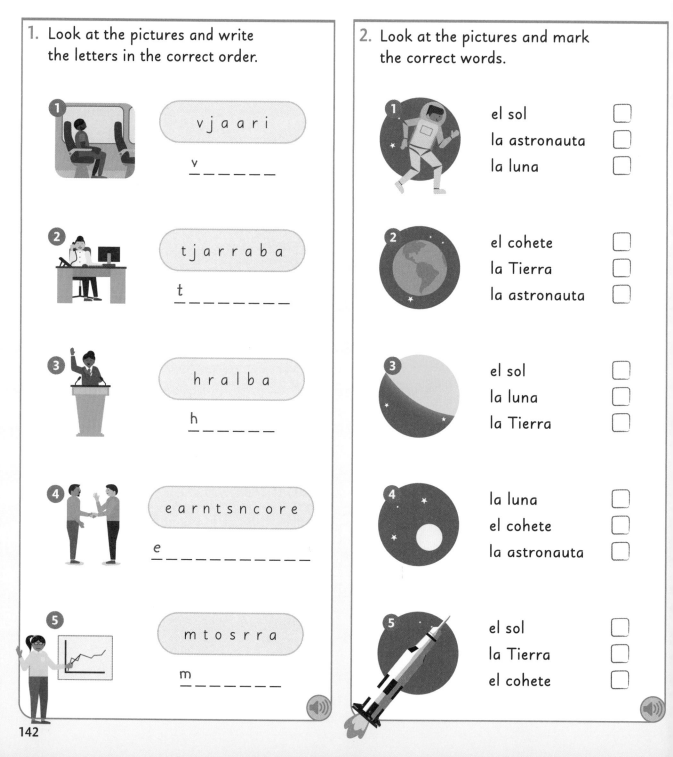

1. Look at the pictures and write the letters in the correct order.

1. v j a a r i

v _ _ _ _ _

2. t j a r r a b a

t _ _ _ _ _ _ _

3. h r a l b a

h _ _ _ _ _

4. e a r n t s n c o r e

e _ _ _ _ _ _ _ _ _ _

5. m t o s r r a

m _ _ _ _ _ _

2. Look at the pictures and mark the correct words.

1. el sol ☐
la astronauta ☐
la luna ☐

2. el cohete ☐
la Tierra ☐
la astronauta ☐

3. el sol ☐
la luna ☐
la Tierra ☐

4. la luna ☐
el cohete ☐
la astronauta ☐

5. el sol ☐
la Tierra ☐
el cohete ☐

3. Look at the pictures and write the correct words.

| el camino | el puente | el pícnic | el arroyo | la manta |

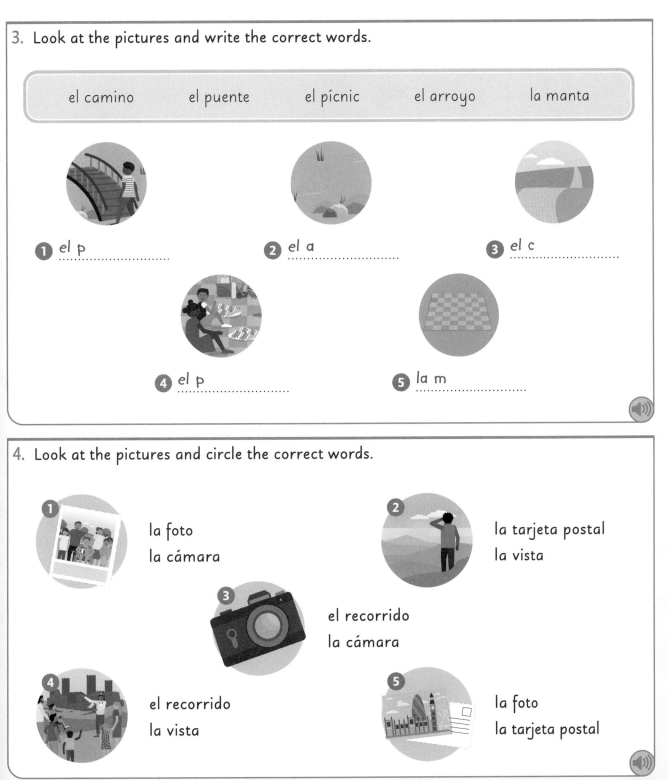

1 el p ....

2 el a ....

3 el c ....

4 el p ....

5 la m ....

4. Look at the pictures and circle the correct words.

1 la foto
la cámara

2 la tarjeta postal
la vista

3 el recorrido
la cámara

4 el recorrido
la vista

5 la foto
la tarjeta postal

Day 1

Listen, repeat, and copy.

① arriba

② en medio

③ abajo

④ pequeña

⑤ alto

Listen again and write the words.

a ....

e ....

a ....

p ....

a ....

Day 2

Listen, repeat, and copy.

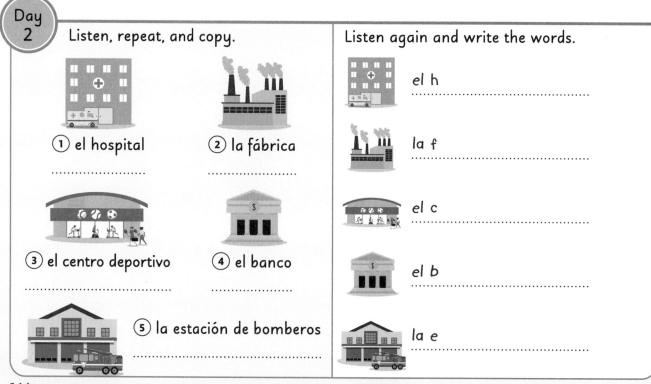

① el hospital

② la fábrica

③ el centro deportivo

④ el banco

⑤ la estación de bomberos

Listen again and write the words.

el h ....

la f ....

el c ....

el b ....

la e ....

Week 35

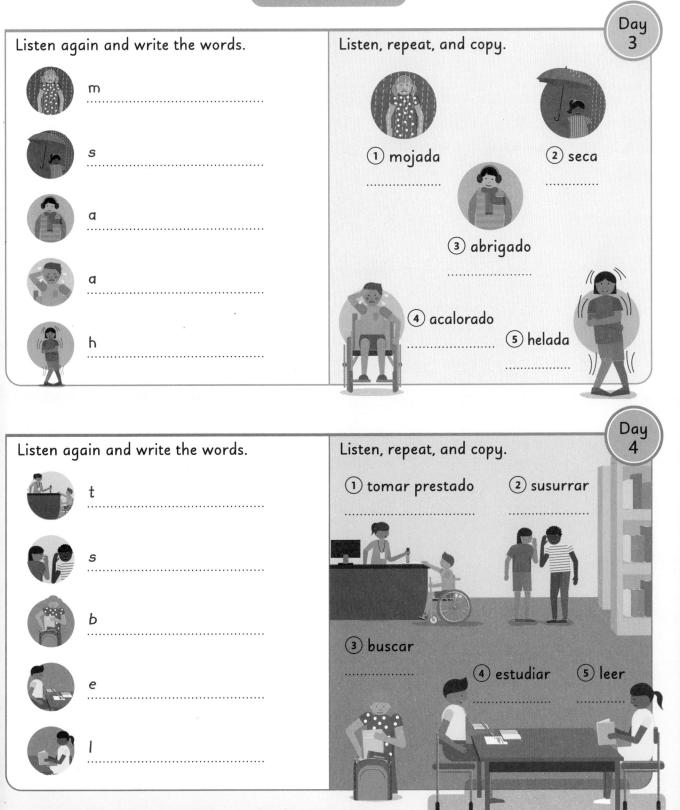

Listen again and write the words.

m ....

s ....

a ....

a ....

h ....

Listen, repeat, and copy.

① mojada

② seca ....

③ abrigado ....

④ acalorado ....

⑤ helada ....

Listen again and write the words.

t ....

s ....

b ....

e ....

l ....

Listen, repeat, and copy.

① tomar prestado ....

② susurrar ....

③ buscar ....

④ estudiar ....

⑤ leer ....

Day 5

What can you remember from this week?

1. Read the words and mark the correct pictures.

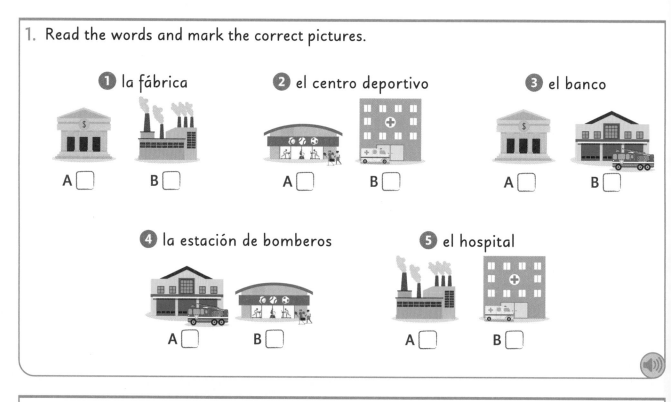

1 la fábrica

A ☐   B ☐

2 el centro deportivo

A ☐   B ☐

3 el banco

A ☐   B ☐

4 la estación de bomberos

A ☐   B ☐

5 el hospital

A ☐   B ☐

2. Look at the pictures and fill in the missing letters.

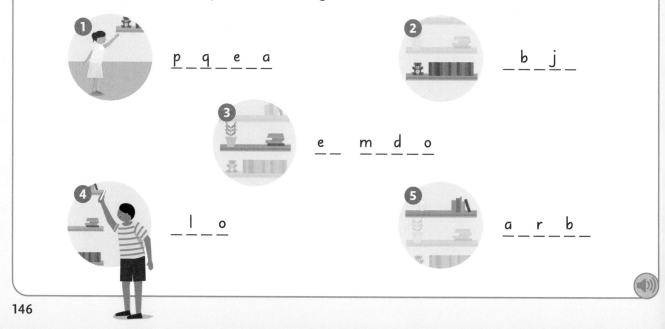

1   p _ q _ e _ a

2   _ _ _ b _ j _

3   e _   _ m _ d _ o

4   _ _ l _ o

5   a _ r _ b _

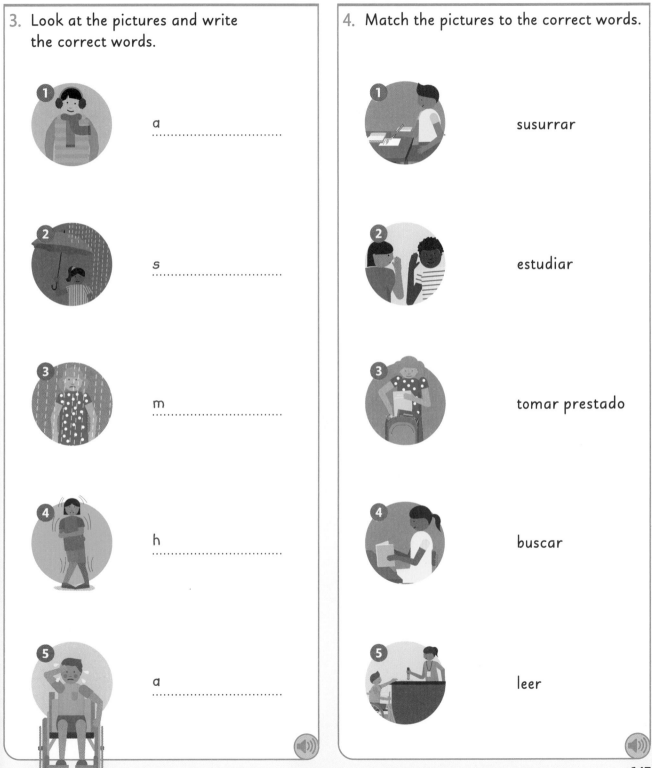

3. Look at the pictures and write the correct words.

1. a ....

2. s ....

3. m ....

4. h ....

5. a ....

4. Match the pictures to the correct words.

1.   susurrar

2.   estudiar

3.   tomar prestado

4.   buscar

5.   leer

Day 1

Listen, repeat, and copy.

① el té
....

② la leche
....

③ el azúcar
....

④ el café
....

⑤ la galleta
....

Listen again and write the words.

el t
....

la l
....

el a
....

el c
....

la g
....

Day 2

Listen, repeat, and copy.

① despegar
....

② aterrizar
....

③ bajar
....

④ subir
....

⑤ darse prisa
....

Listen again and write the words.

d
....

a
....

b
....

s
....

d
....

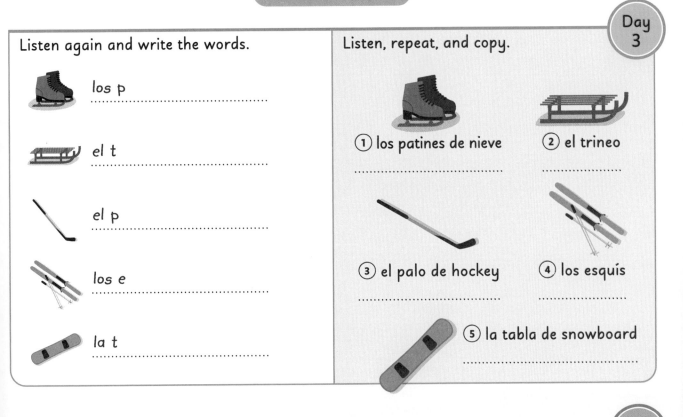

Day 3

Listen again and write the words.

los p ....

el t ....

el p ....

los e ....

la t ....

Listen, repeat, and copy.

① los patines de nieve ....

② el trineo ....

③ el palo de hockey ....

④ los esquís ....

⑤ la tabla de snowboard ....

Day 4

Listen again and write the words.

el o ....

la p ....

el b ....

la c ....

el g ....

Listen, repeat, and copy.

① el oro ....

② la plata ....

③ el bronce ....

④ la carrera ....

⑤ el ganador ....

Day 5

What can you remember from this week?

1. Look at the pictures and write the correct words.

la leche   el té   el café
el azúcar   la galleta

① el t ....

② la g ....

③ el c ....

④ la l ....

⑤ el a ....

2. Look at the pictures and circle the correct words.

① la carrera / el oro

② el ganador / la plata

③ la plata / el oro

④ el ganador / el bronce

⑤ el bronce / la carrera

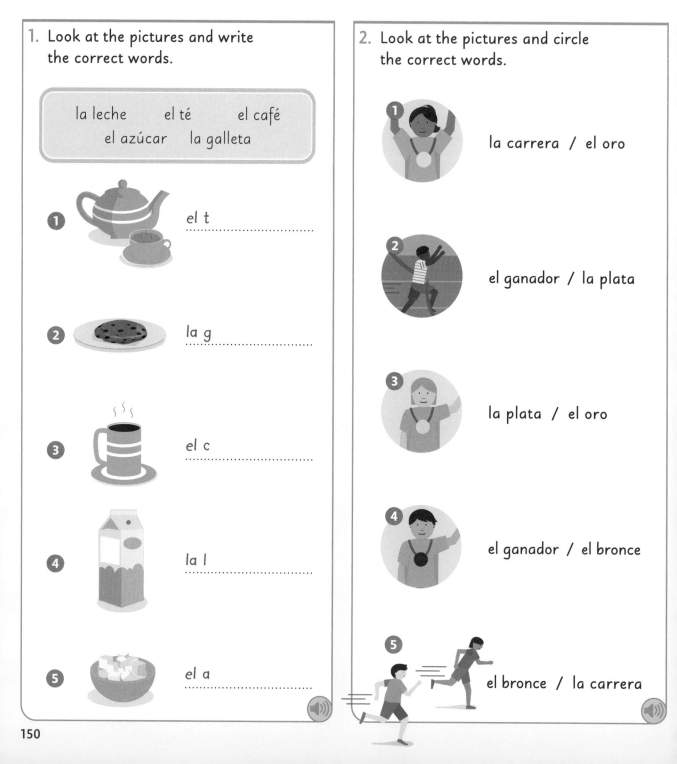

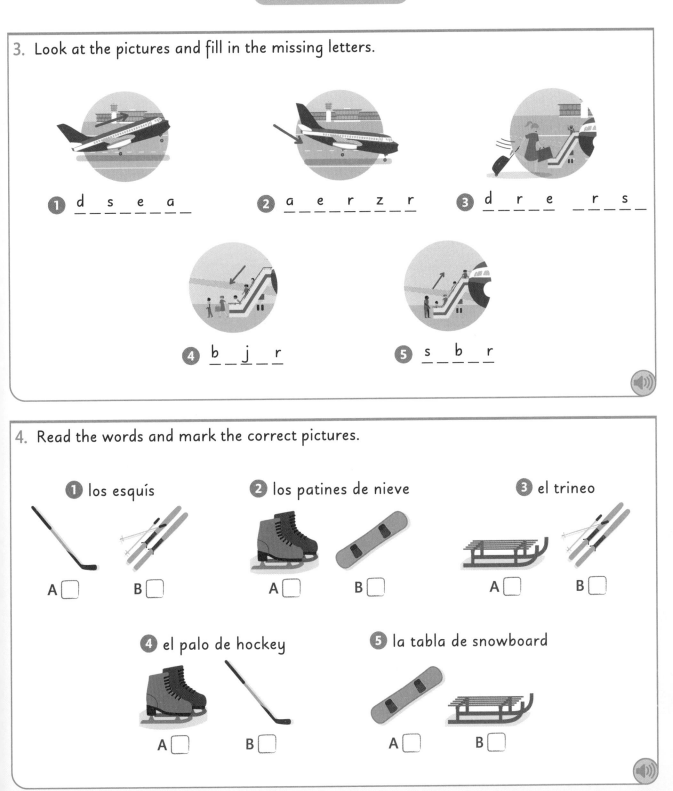

3. Look at the pictures and fill in the missing letters.

1 d _ s _ e _ a _ _ _

2 a _ e _ r _ z _ r _ _

3 d _ r _ e _ _ r _ s _

4 b _ _ j _ _ r _

5 s _ b _ _ r _

4. Read the words and mark the correct pictures.

1 los esquís

A ☐   B ☐

2 los patines de nieve

A ☐   B ☐

3 el trineo

A ☐   B ☐

4 el palo de hockey

A ☐   B ☐

5 la tabla de snowboard

A ☐   B ☐

Day 1

Listen, repeat, and copy.

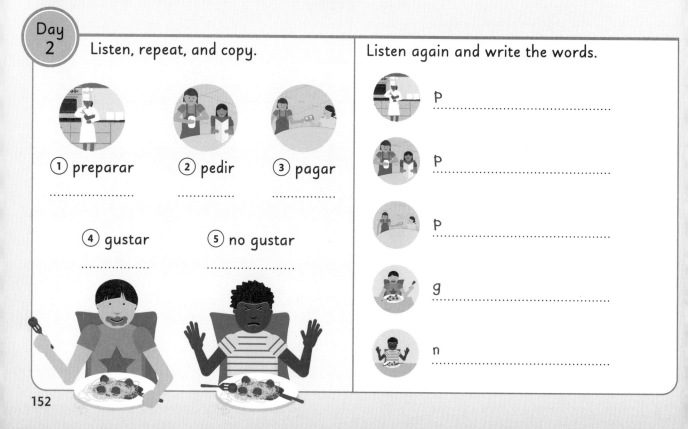

① el pasto

② el cisne

③ el pato

④ el estanque

⑤ la rana

Listen again and write the words.

el p ....

el c ....

el p ....

el e ....

la r ....

Day 2

Listen, repeat, and copy.

① preparar ....

② pedir ....

③ pagar ....

④ gustar ....

⑤ no gustar ....

Listen again and write the words.

p ....

p ....

p ....

g ....

n ....

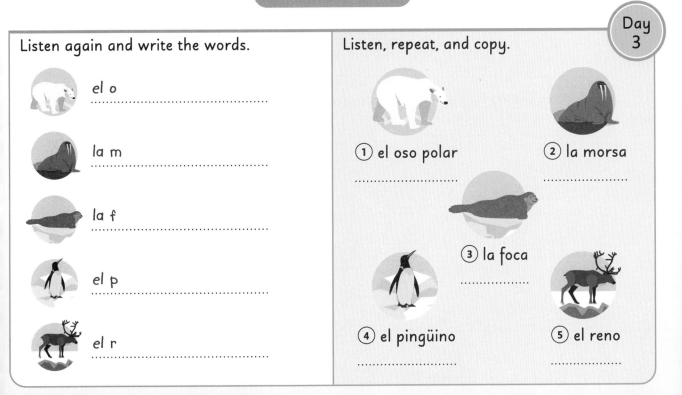

Listen again and write the words.

el o ....

la m ....

la f ....

el p ....

el r ....

Listen, repeat, and copy.

① el oso polar ....

② la morsa ....

③ la foca ....

④ el pingüino ....

⑤ el reno ....

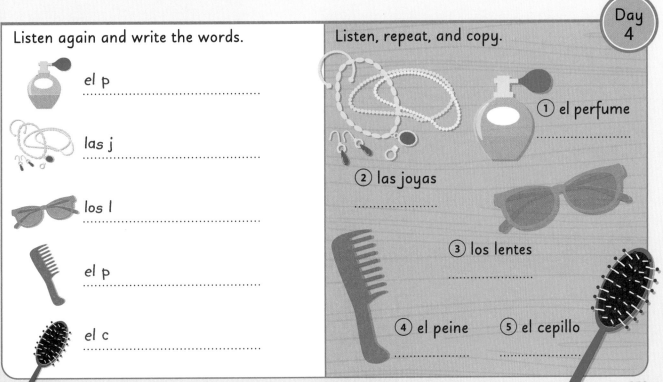

Listen again and write the words.

el p ....

las j ....

los l ....

el p ....

el c ....

Listen, repeat, and copy.

① el perfume ....

② las joyas ....

③ los lentes ....

④ el peine ....

⑤ el cepillo ....

Day 5

What can you remember from this week?

1. Look at the pictures and write the correct words.

| pagar | no gustar | gustar | pedir | preparar |

1 g ....

2 n ....

3 p ....

4 p ....

5 p ....

2. Match the pictures to the correct words.

1

2

3

4

5

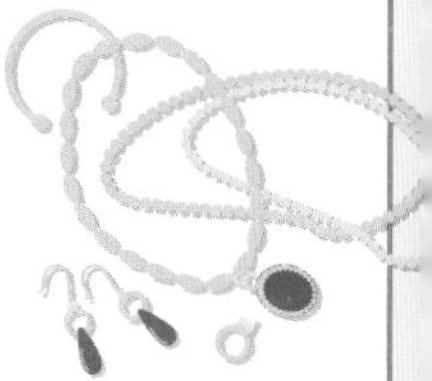

el cepillo   el peine   las joyas   los lentes   el perfume

3. Look at the pictures and mark the correct words.

1. el pingüino ☐
   la morsa ☐

2. el oso polar ☐
   el pingüino ☐

3. el reno ☐
   la foca ☐

4. el reno ☐
   el oso polar ☐

5. la foca ☐
   la morsa ☐

4. Look at the pictures and write the correct words.

1. el p...................

2. la r...................

3. el e...................

4. el c...................

5. el p...................

Day 1

Listen, repeat, and copy.

① la ensalada

....

② el tomate   ③ el queso

....

④ las aceitunas   ⑤ la lechuga

....

Listen again and write the words.

la e ....

el t ....

el q ....

las a ....

la l ....

Day 2

Listen, repeat, and copy.

① castaño
....

③ negro
....

② rubio
....

④ gris
....

⑤ pelirrojo
....

Listen again and write the words.

c ....

r ....

n ....

g ....

p ....

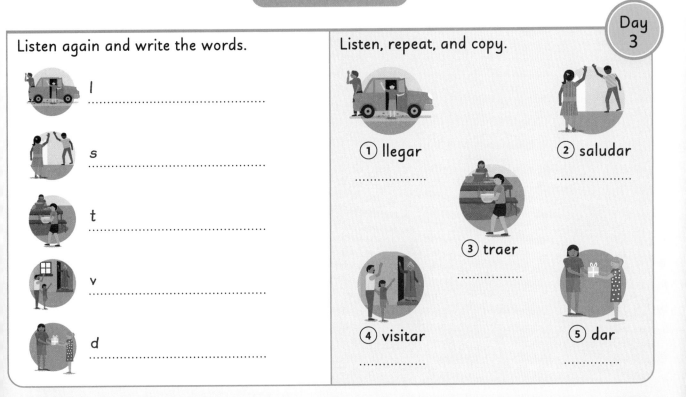

Listen again and write the words.

l ....

s ....

t ....

v ....

d ....

Listen, repeat, and copy.

① llegar ....

② saludar ....

③ traer ....

④ visitar ....

⑤ dar ....

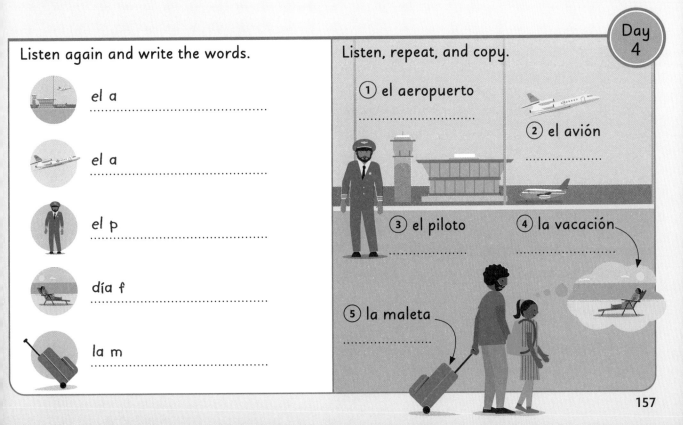

Listen again and write the words.

el a ....

el a ....

el p ....

día f ....

la m ....

Listen, repeat, and copy.

① el aeropuerto ....

② el avión ....

③ el piloto ....

④ la vacación ....

⑤ la maleta ....

Day 5

What can you remember from this week?

1. Look at the pictures and mark the correct words.

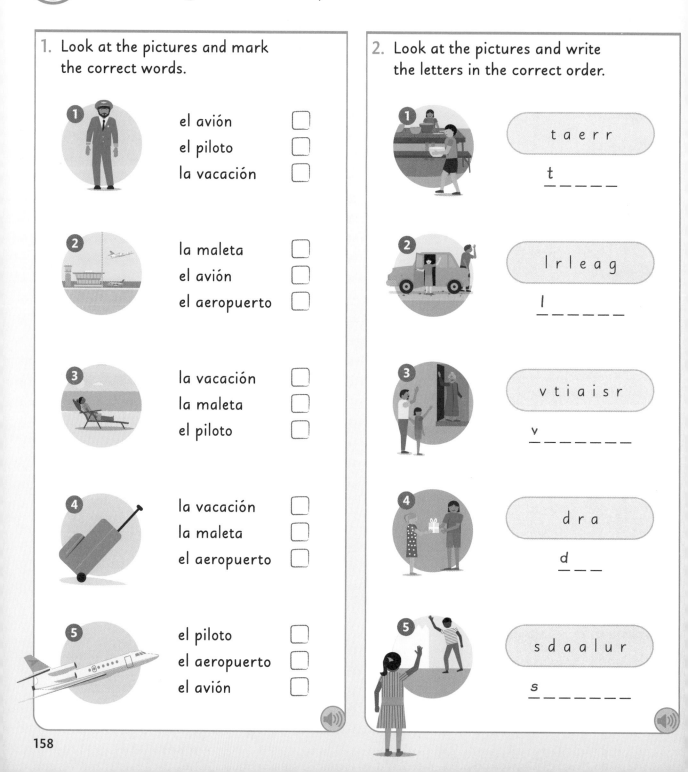

1.
- el avión ☐
- el piloto ☐
- la vacación ☐

2.
- la maleta ☐
- el avión ☐
- el aeropuerto ☐

3.
- la vacación ☐
- la maleta ☐
- el piloto ☐

4.
- la vacación ☐
- la maleta ☐
- el aeropuerto ☐

5.
- el piloto ☐
- el aeropuerto ☐
- el avión ☐

2. Look at the pictures and write the letters in the correct order.

1. t a e r r

t _ _ _ _ _

2. l r l e a g

l _ _ _ _ _

3. v t i a i s r

v _ _ _ _ _ _

4. d r a

d _ _

5. s d a a l u r

s _ _ _ _ _ _

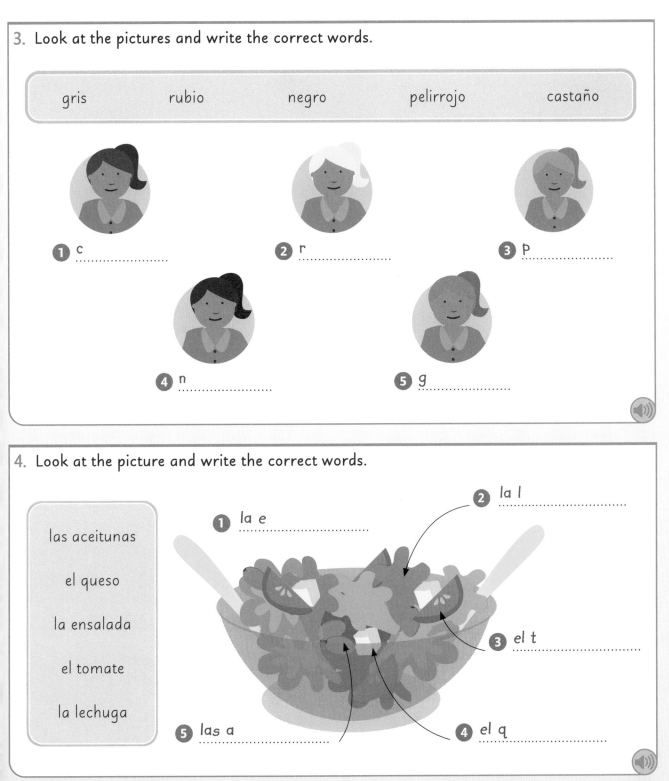

3. Look at the pictures and write the correct words.

gris   rubio   negro   pelirrojo   castaño

1 c _____

2 r _____

3 p _____

4 n _____

5 g _____

4. Look at the picture and write the correct words.

las aceitunas

el queso

la ensalada

el tomate

la lechuga

1 la e _____

2 la l _____

3 el t _____

4 el q _____

5 las a _____

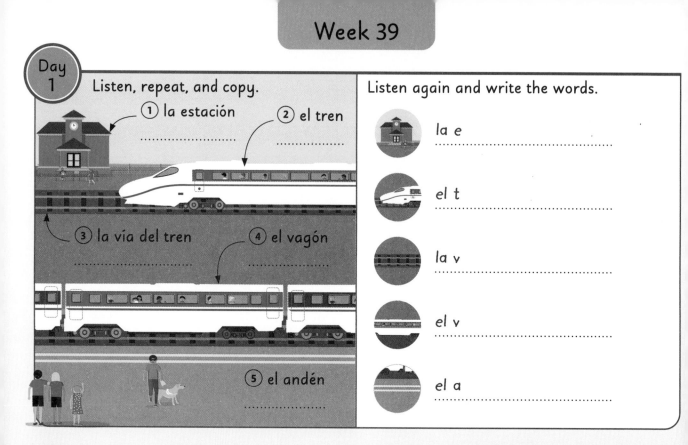

Day 1

Listen, repeat, and copy.

① la estación

② el tren

③ la vía del tren

④ el vagón

⑤ el andén

Listen again and write the words.

la e

el t

la v

el v

el a

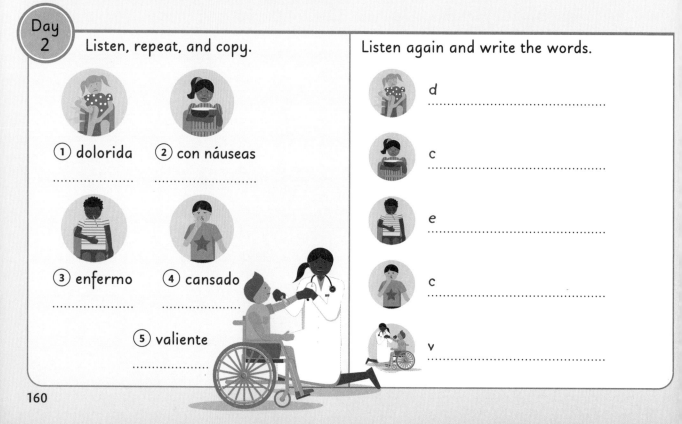

Day 2

Listen, repeat, and copy.

① dolorida

② con náuseas

③ enfermo

④ cansado

⑤ valiente

Listen again and write the words.

d

c

e

c

v

160

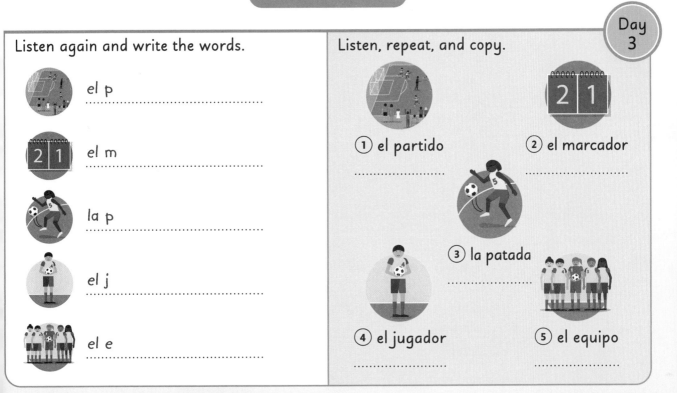

Day 3

Listen again and write the words.

el p ....

el m ....

la p ....

el j ....

el e ....

Listen, repeat, and copy.

① el partido ....

② el marcador ....

③ la patada ....

④ el jugador ....

⑤ el equipo ....

Day 4

Listen again and write the words.

la m ....

la m ....

la a ....

el e ....

el c ....

Listen, repeat, and copy.

① la mariposa ....

② la mosca ....

③ la araña ....

④ el escarabajo ....

⑤ el caracol ....

Day 5

What can you remember from this week?

1. Look at the pictures and circle the correct words.

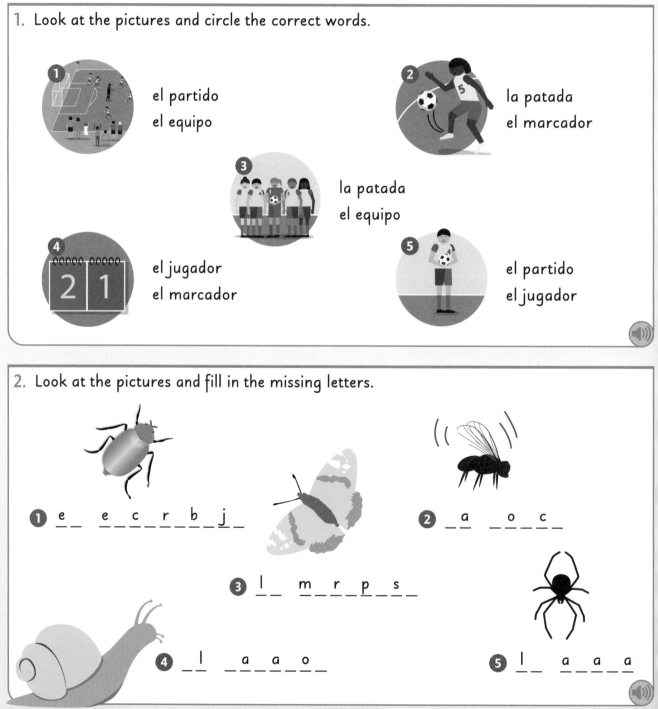

1. el partido
   el equipo

2. la patada
   el marcador

3. la patada
   el equipo

4. el jugador
   el marcador

5. el partido
   el jugador

2. Look at the pictures and fill in the missing letters.

1. e _ _ e _ _ c _ r _ b _ j _

2. _ _ a _ _ o _ c _

3. l _ _ m _ _ _ p _ s _

4. _ _ l _ a _ a _ o _

5. l _ _ a _ a _ a

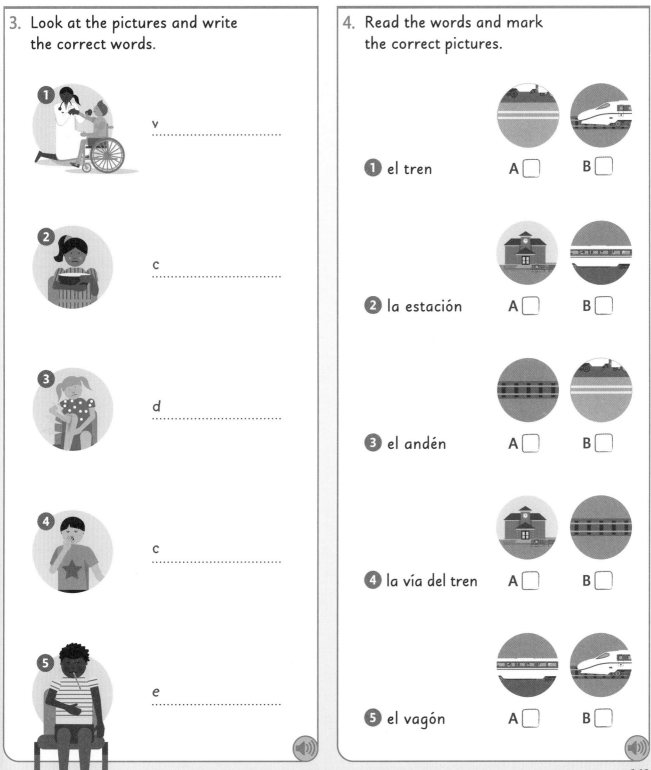

Week 39

3. Look at the pictures and write the correct words.

1. v...................................

2. c...................................

3. d...................................

4. c...................................

5. e...................................

4. Read the words and mark the correct pictures.

1. el tren   A ☐   B ☐

2. la estación   A ☐   B ☐

3. el andén   A ☐   B ☐

4. la vía del tren   A ☐   B ☐

5. el vagón   A ☐   B ☐

Week 40

Day 1

Listen, repeat, and copy.

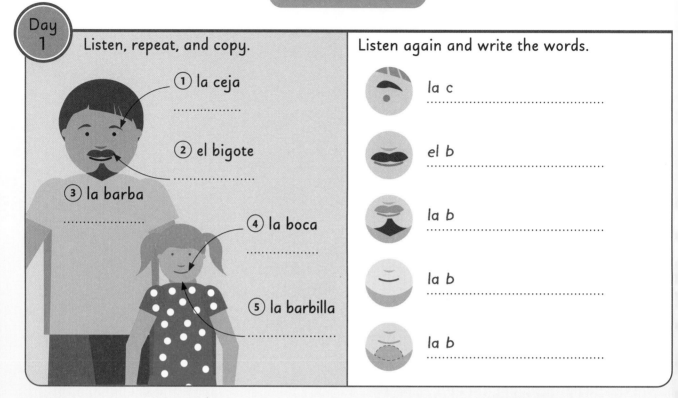

① la ceja

....

② el bigote

....

③ la barba

....

④ la boca

....

⑤ la barbilla

....

Listen again and write the words.

la c ....

el b ....

la b ....

la b ....

la b ....

Day 2

Listen, repeat, and copy.

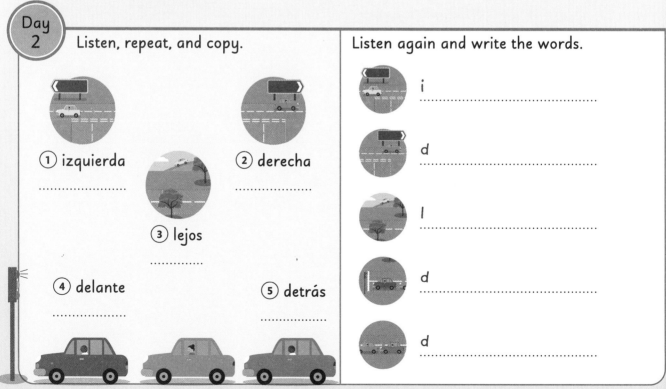

① izquierda

....

② derecha

....

③ lejos

....

④ delante

....

⑤ detrás

....

Listen again and write the words.

i ....

d ....

l ....

d ....

d ....

Week 40

Listen again and write the words.

r
....

t
....

e
....

a
....

c
....

Listen, repeat, and copy.

① romper
....

② traer
....

③ esconder
....

④ alimentar
....

⑤ cuidar
....

Listen again and write the words.

c
....

o
....

d
....

d
....

r
....

Listen, repeat, and copy.

① claro
....

② oscuro
....

③ despierto
....

④ dormido
....

⑤ ruidoso
....

165

Day 5

What can you remember from this week?

1. Look at the pictures and write the letters in the correct order.

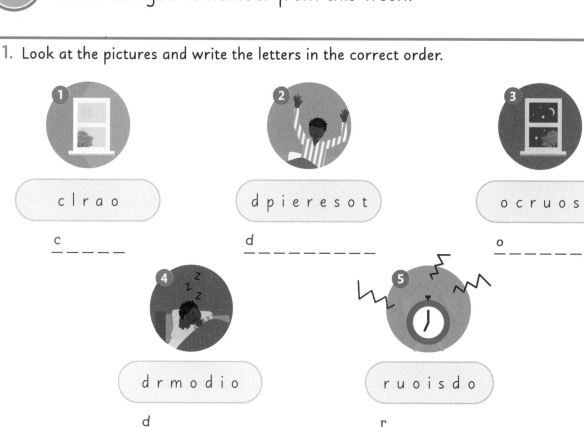

1 c l r a o

c _ _ _ _ _

2 d p i e r e s o t

d _ _ _ _ _ _ _ _ _

3 o c r u o s

o _ _ _ _ _

4 d r m o d i o

d _ _ _ _ _ _ _

5 r u o i s d o

r _ _ _ _ _ _ _

2. Match the pictures to the correct words.

traer   esconder   cuidar   alimentar   romper

3. Look at the pictures and mark the correct words.

1
lejos ☐
derecha ☐

2
detrás ☐
izquierda ☐

3
lejos ☐
detrás ☐

4
delante ☐
derecha ☐

5
delante ☐
izquierda ☐

4. Look at the pictures and write the correct words.

la ceja   la boca   la barbilla
el bigote   la barba

1 la b ....

2 la b ....

3 la c ....

4 el b ....

5 la b ....

Week 41

Day 1

Listen, repeat, and copy.

① cortar

② crecer

③ regar   ④ plantar

⑤ recoger

Listen again and write the words.

c ....

c ....

r ....

p ....

r ....

Day 2

Listen, repeat, and copy.

① la música   ② el grupo

③ el músico   ④ la estrella de pop

⑤ el festival

Listen again and write the words.

la m ....

el g ....

el m ....

la e ....

el f ....

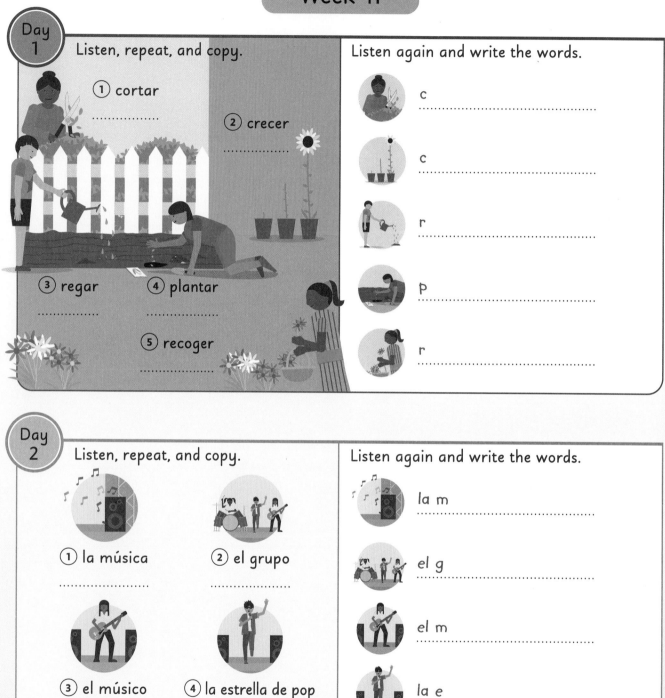

Week 41

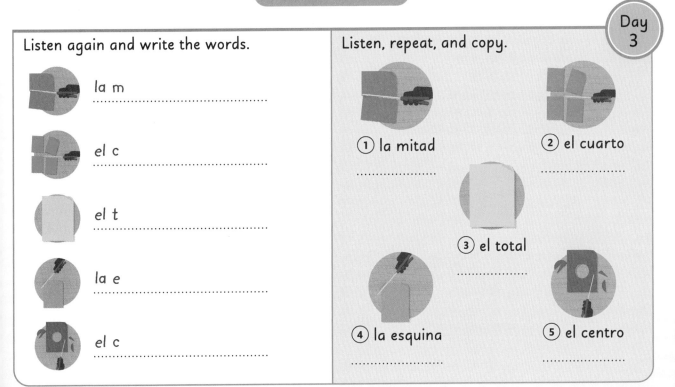

Listen again and write the words.

la m ....

el c ....

el t ....

la e ....

el c ....

Listen, repeat, and copy.

① la mitad
....

② el cuarto
....

③ el total
....

④ la esquina
....

⑤ el centro
....

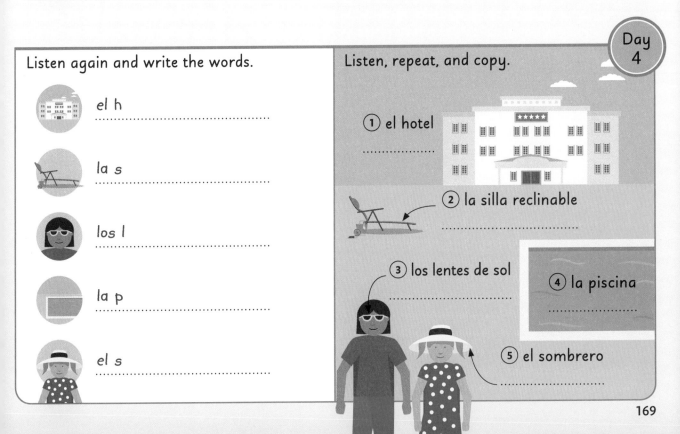

Listen again and write the words.

el h ....

la s ....

los l ....

la p ....

el s ....

Listen, repeat, and copy.

① el hotel
....

② la silla reclinable
....

③ los lentes de sol
....

④ la piscina
....

⑤ el sombrero
....

What can you remember from this week?

1. Look at the pictures and write the correct words.

| el centro | el total | la mitad |
| la esquina | | el cuarto |

1. el t ....

2. la e ....

3. la m ....

4. el c ....

5. el c ....

2. Look at the pictures and circle the correct words.

1. los lentes de sol
la piscina

2. el sombrero
la silla reclinable

3. el hotel
la piscina

4. la silla reclinable
el hotel

5. el sombrero
los lentes de sol

170

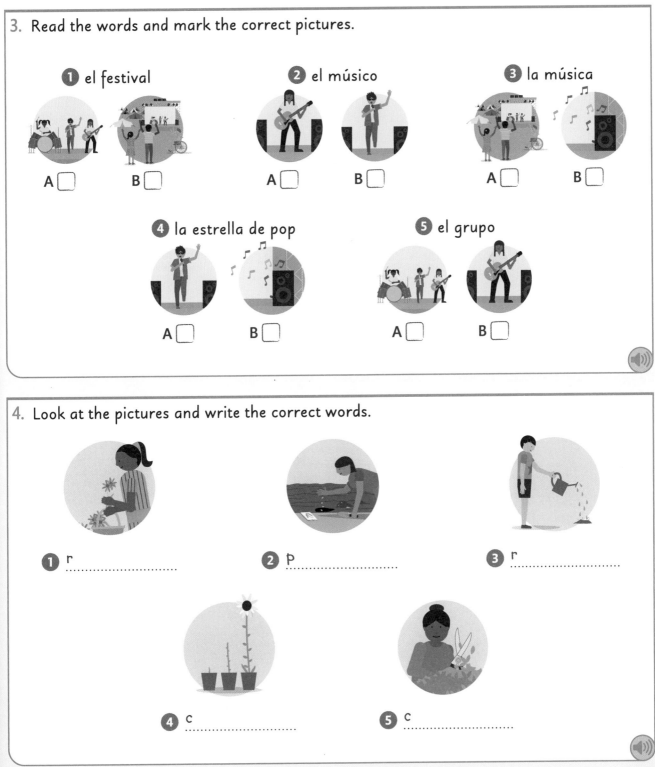

3. Read the words and mark the correct pictures.

1 el festival

A ☐   B ☐

2 el músico

A ☐   B ☐

3 la música

A ☐   B ☐

4 la estrella de pop

A ☐   B ☐

5 el grupo

A ☐   B ☐

4. Look at the pictures and write the correct words.

1 r ....

2 p ....

3 r ....

4 c ....

5 c ....

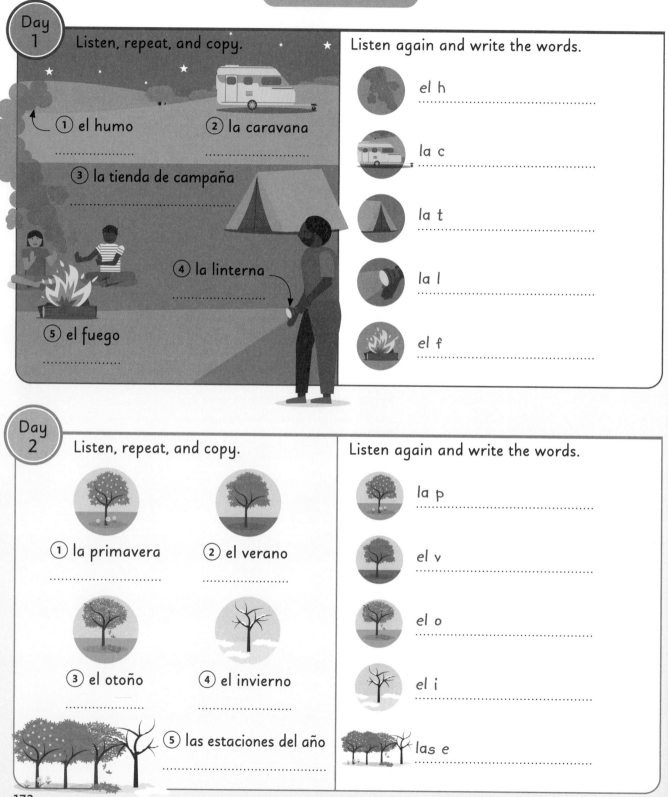

Day 1

Listen, repeat, and copy.

① el humo

② la caravana

③ la tienda de campaña

④ la linterna

⑤ el fuego

Listen again and write the words.

el h

la c

la t

la l

el f

Day 2

Listen, repeat, and copy.

① la primavera

② el verano

③ el otoño

④ el invierno

⑤ las estaciones del año

Listen again and write the words.

la p

el v

el o

el i

las e

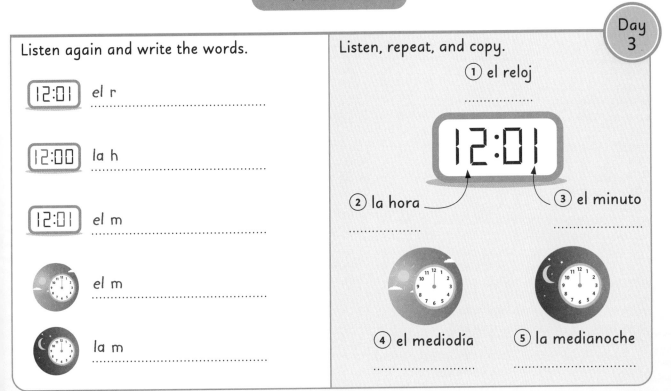

Day 3

Listen again and write the words.

`12:01` el r ....

`12:00` la h ....

`12:01` el m ....

el m ....

la m ....

Listen, repeat, and copy.

① el reloj ....

`12:01`

② la hora .... ③ el minuto ....

④ el mediodía .... ⑤ la medianoche ....

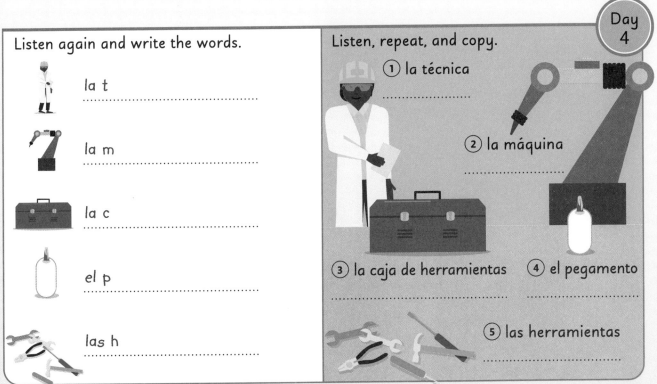

Day 4

Listen again and write the words.

la t ....

la m ....

la c ....

el p ....

las h ....

Listen, repeat, and copy.

① la técnica ....

② la máquina ....

③ la caja de herramientas ④ el pegamento
....

⑤ las herramientas
....

Day 5

What can you remember from this week?

1. Look at the pictures and fill in the missing letters.

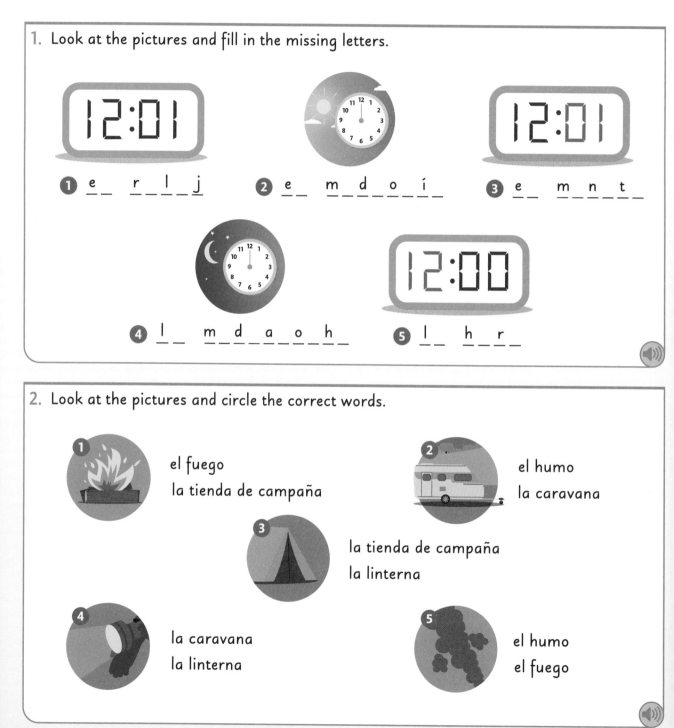

① e _ r _ l _ j

② e _ m _ _ _ d _ o _ í

③ e _ m _ n _ t

④ l _ m _ _ _ d _ a _ o _ h

⑤ l _ h _ _ r

2. Look at the pictures and circle the correct words.

① el fuego
la tienda de campaña

② el humo
la caravana

③ la tienda de campaña
la linterna

④ la caravana
la linterna

⑤ el humo
el fuego

3. Look at the pictures and write the correct words.

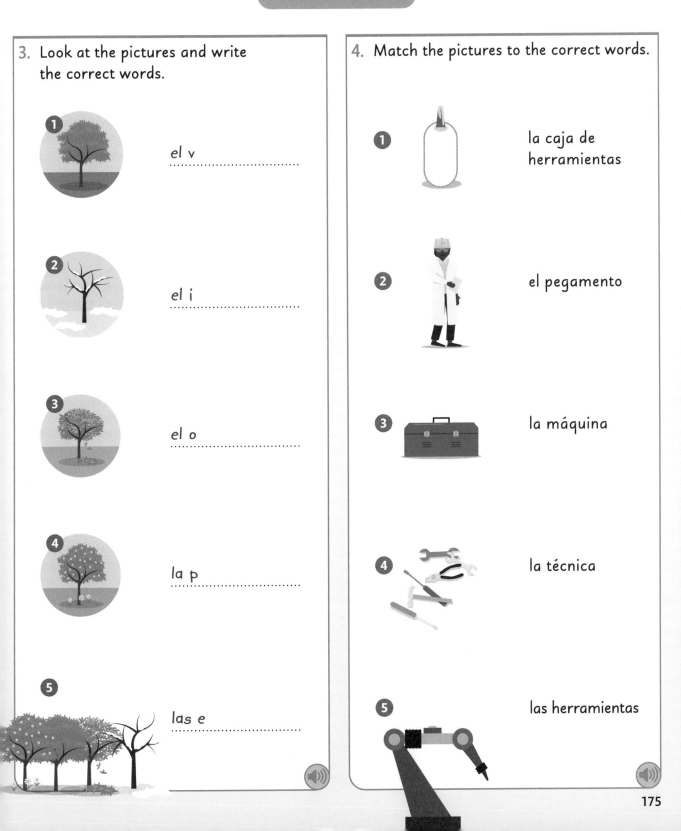

1. el v ....

2. el i ....

3. el o ....

4. la p ....

5. las e ....

4. Match the pictures to the correct words.

1.   la caja de herramientas

2.   el pegamento

3.   la máquina

4.   la técnica

5.   las herramientas

Day 1

Listen, repeat, and copy.

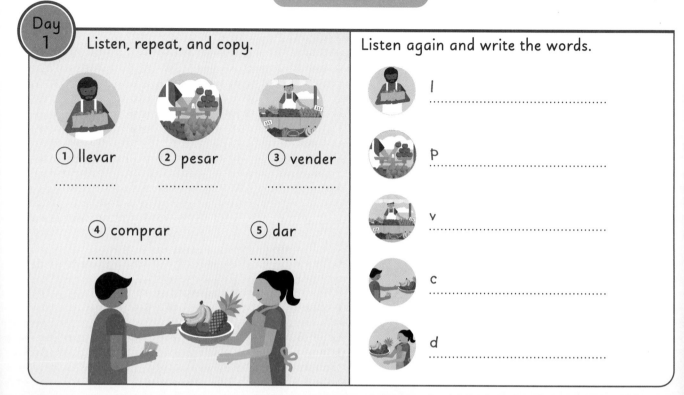

1. llevar
2. pesar
3. vender

4. comprar
5. dar

Listen again and write the words.

l

p

v

c

d

Day 2

Listen, repeat, and copy.

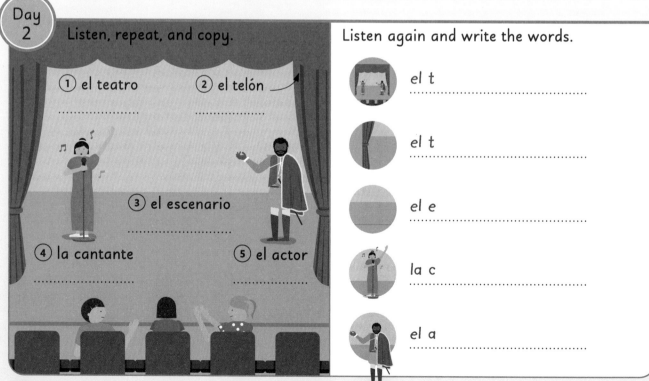

1. el teatro
2. el telón
3. el escenario
4. la cantante
5. el actor

Listen again and write the words.

el t

el t

el e

la c

el a

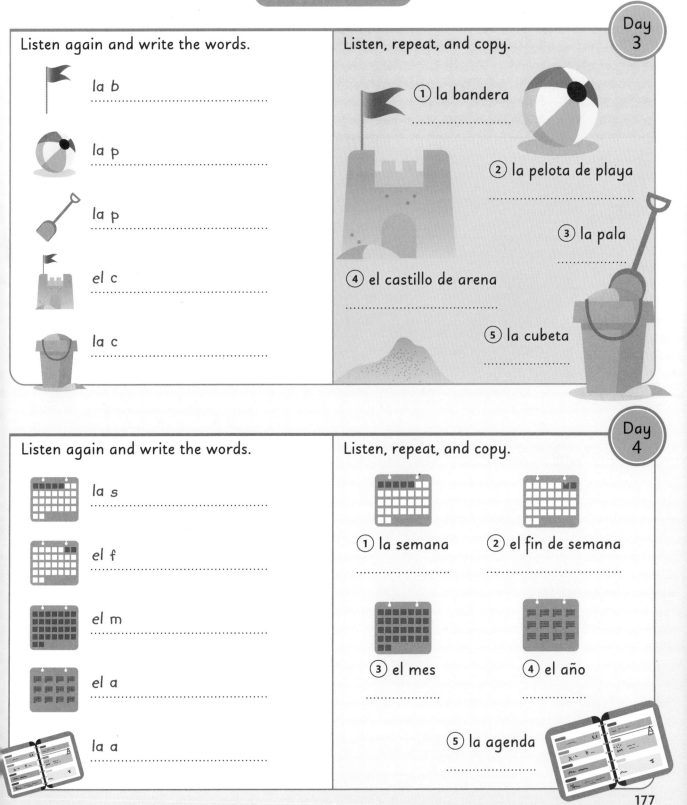

Day 3

Listen again and write the words.

la b ....

la p ....

la p ....

el c ....

la c ....

Listen, repeat, and copy.

① la bandera
....

② la pelota de playa
....

③ la pala
....

④ el castillo de arena
....

⑤ la cubeta
....

Day 4

Listen again and write the words.

la s ....

el f ....

el m ....

el a ....

la a ....

Listen, repeat, and copy.

① la semana
....

② el fin de semana
....

③ el mes
....

④ el año
....

⑤ la agenda
....

Day 5

What can you remember from this week?

1. Look at the pictures and write the letters in the correct order.

p s a r e

p _ _ _ _ _

c m o r p a r

c _ _ _ _ _ _ _

d r a

d _ _ _

v e e r n d

v _ _ _ _ _ _

l v a l e r

l _ _ _ _ _ _

2. Look at the pictures and circle the correct words.

1. el teatro
   el actor

2. el telón
   la cantante

3. el actor
   el escenario

4. la cantante
   el escenario

5. el telón
   el teatro

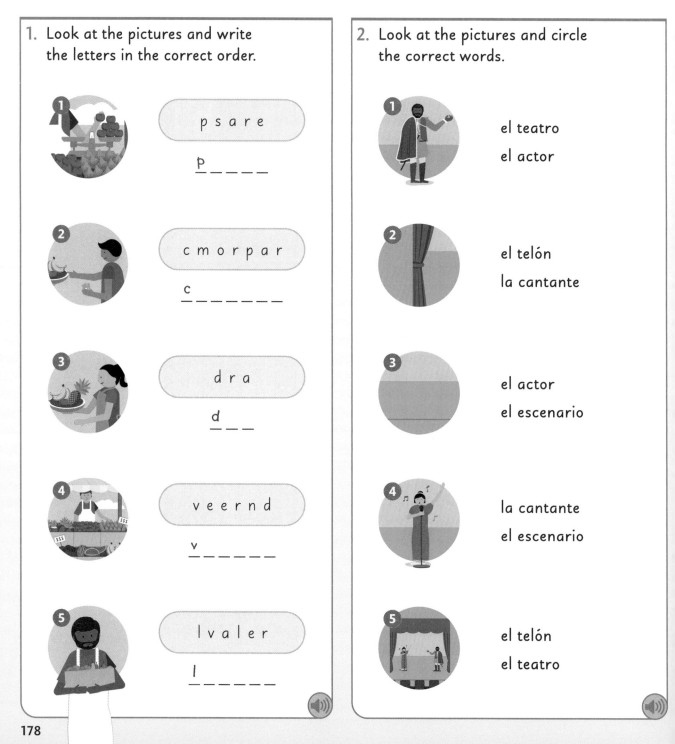

Week 43

3. Match the pictures to the correct words.

1
2
3
4
5

la cubeta   la bandera   el castillo de arena   la pelota de playa   la pala

4. Look at the pictures and write the correct words.

la semana   el mes   el fin de semana   el año   la agenda

1 el m ....

2 la s ....

3 el a ....

4 la a ....

5 el f ....

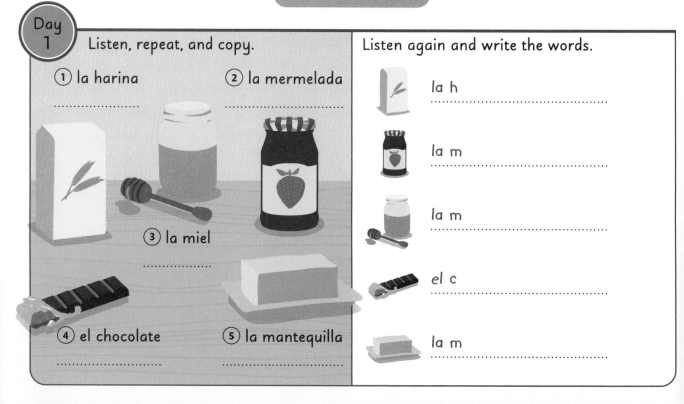

Day 1

Listen, repeat, and copy.

① la harina

② la mermelada

③ la miel

④ el chocolate

⑤ la mantequilla

Listen again and write the words.

la h ....

la m ....

la m ....

el c ....

la m ....

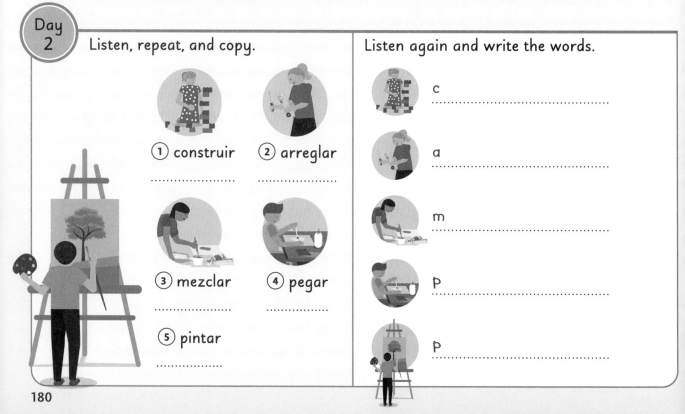

Day 2

Listen, repeat, and copy.

① construir ② arreglar

③ mezclar ④ pegar

⑤ pintar

Listen again and write the words.

c ....

a ....

m ....

p ....

p ....

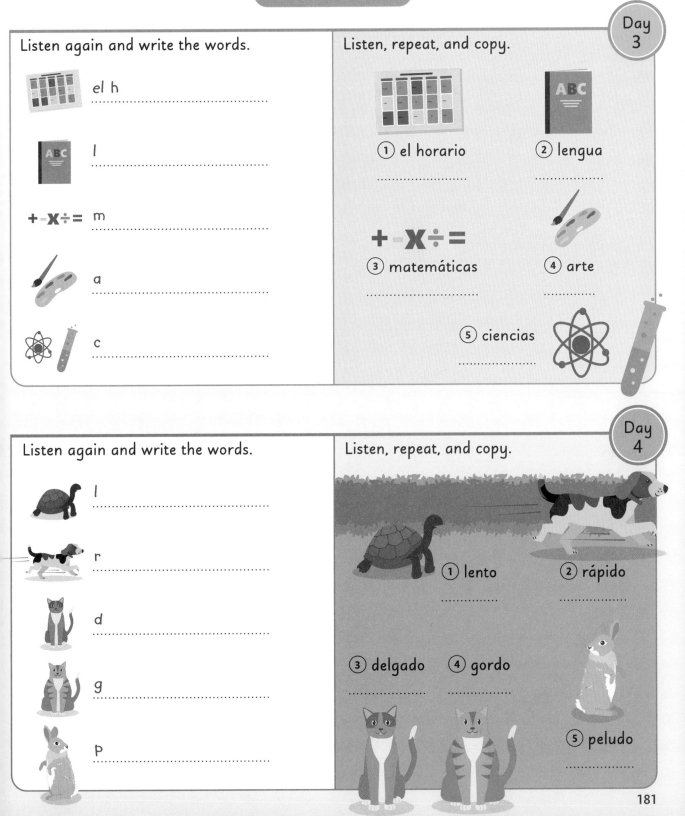

Listen again and write the words.

el h ....

l ....

m ....

a ....

c ....

Listen, repeat, and copy.

① el horario

② lengua

③ matemáticas

④ arte

⑤ ciencias

Listen again and write the words.

l ....

r ....

d ....

g ....

p ....

Listen, repeat, and copy.

① lento

② rápido

③ delgado

④ gordo

⑤ peludo

Day 5

What can you remember from this week?

1. Look at the pictures and circle the correct words.

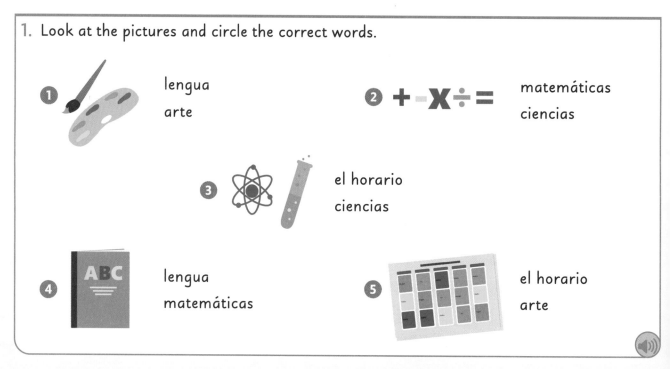

1. lengua / arte

2. matemáticas / ciencias

3. el horario / ciencias

4. lengua / matemáticas

5. el horario / arte

2. Look at the pictures and fill in the missing letters.

1. c _ n _ t _ u _ r

2. _ _ i _ t _ r

3. m _ z _ l _ r

4. _ r _ e _ l _ r

5. p _ g _ r

3. Look at the pictures and mark the correct words.

1. la mermelada ☐
   la mantequilla ☐
   el chocolate ☐

2. la harina ☐
   la miel ☐
   la mermelada ☐

3. la mantequilla ☐
   el chocolate ☐
   la miel ☐

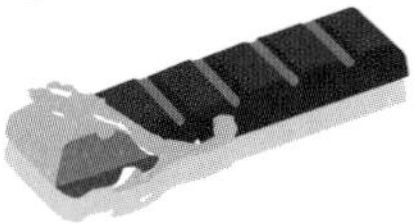

4. la harina ☐
   la mantequilla ☐
   la mermelada ☐

5. la miel ☐
   el chocolate ☐
   la harina ☐

4. Look at the pictures and write the correct words.

lento   peludo   rápido
     gordo   delgado

1. p ....

2. l ....

3. g ....

4. r ....

5. d ....

Day 1

Listen, repeat, and copy.

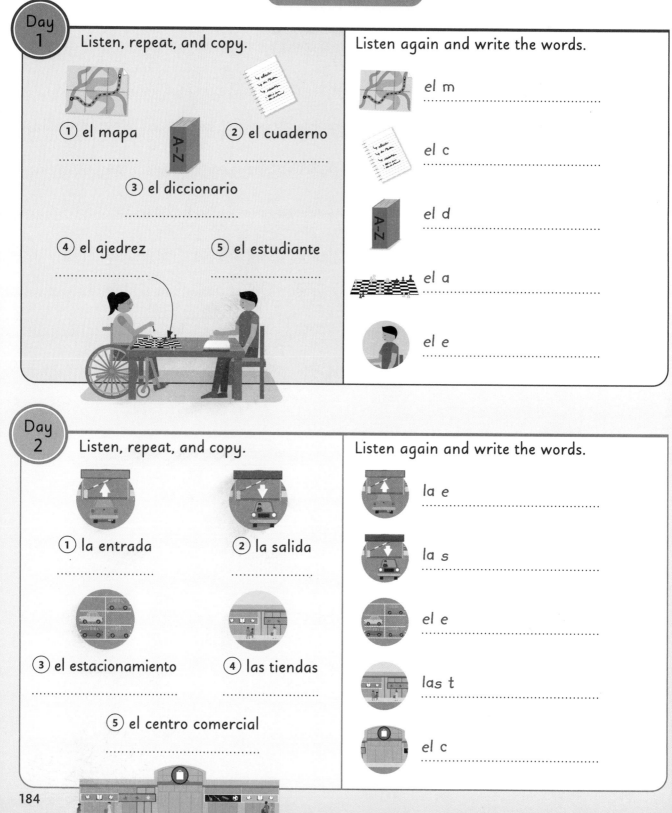

① el mapa

② el cuaderno

③ el diccionario

④ el ajedrez

⑤ el estudiante

Listen again and write the words.

el m

el c

el d

el a

el e

Day 2

Listen, repeat, and copy.

① la entrada

② la salida

③ el estacionamiento

④ las tiendas

⑤ el centro comercial

Listen again and write the words.

la e

la s

el e

las t

el c

Day 3

Listen again and write the words.

la m
....

el v
....

la r
....

la t
....

la m
....

Listen, repeat, and copy.

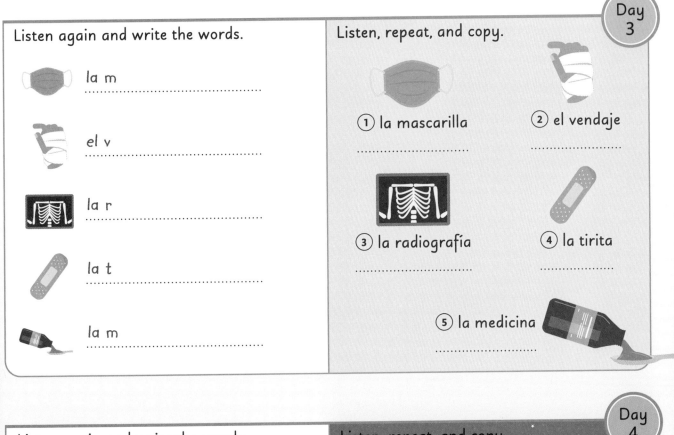

① la mascarilla
....

② el vendaje
....

③ la radiografía
....

④ la tirita
....

⑤ la medicina
....

Day 4

Listen again and write the words.

a
....

r
....

c
....

q
....

d
....

Listen, repeat, and copy.

① acampar
....

② reír
....

③ charlar
....

④ quemar
....

⑤ dormir
....

Day
5

What can you remember from this week?

1. Look at the pictures and circle the correct words.

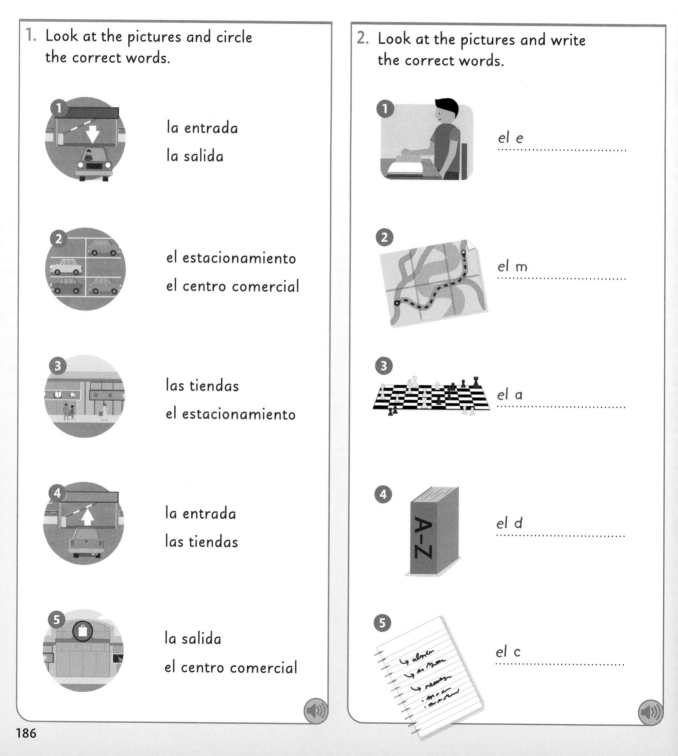

1
la entrada
la salida

2
el estacionamiento
el centro comercial

3
las tiendas
el estacionamiento

4
la entrada
las tiendas

5
la salida
el centro comercial

2. Look at the pictures and write the correct words.

1
el e ....

2
el m ....

3
el a ....

4
el d ....

5
el c ....

3. Look at the pictures and mark the correct words.

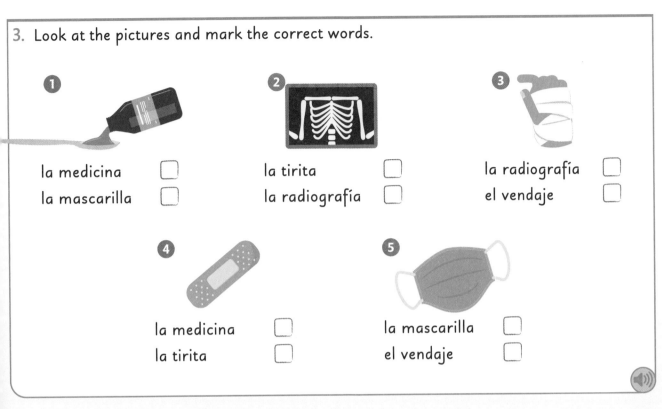

1
la medicina ☐
la mascarilla ☐

2
la tirita ☐
la radiografía ☐

3
la radiografía ☐
el vendaje ☐

4
la medicina ☐
la tirita ☐

5
la mascarilla ☐
el vendaje ☐

4. Look at the pictures and fill in the missing letters.

1 q _ e _ a _

2 _ r _ i _

3 c _ a _ l _ r

4 a _ a _ p _ r

5 d _ r _ i _

Day 1

Listen, repeat, and copy.

① el búho
....

② la ardilla
....

③ el ciervo
....

④ el lobo
....

⑤ el zorro
....

Listen again and write the words.

el b
....

la a
....

el c
....

el l
....

el z
....

Day 2

Listen, repeat, and copy.

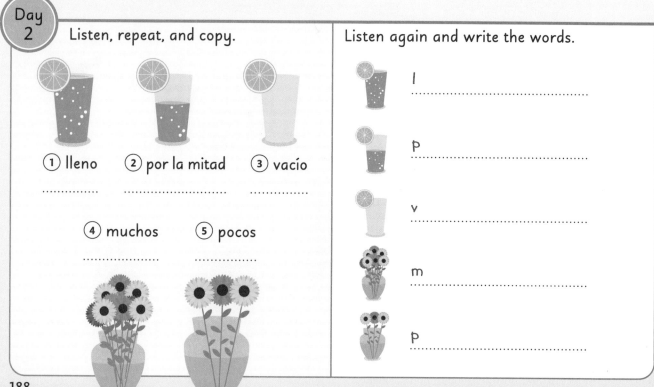

① lleno
....

② por la mitad
....

③ vacío
....

④ muchos
....

⑤ pocos
....

Listen again and write the words.

l
....

p
....

v
....

m
....

p
....

Week 46

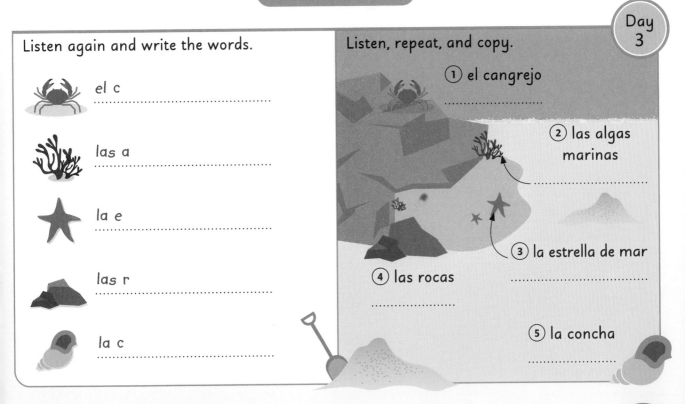

Listen again and write the words.

el c ....

las a ....

la e ....

las r ....

la c ....

Listen, repeat, and copy.

① el cangrejo ....

② las algas marinas ....

③ la estrella de mar ....

④ las rocas ....

⑤ la concha ....

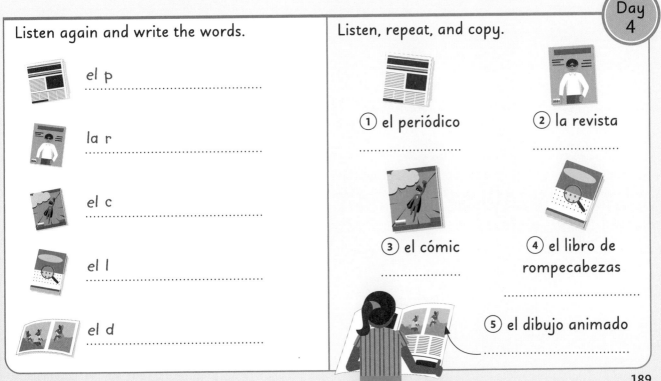

Listen again and write the words.

el p ....

la r ....

el c ....

el l ....

el d ....

Listen, repeat, and copy.

① el periódico ....

② la revista ....

③ el cómic ....

④ el libro de rompecabezas ....

⑤ el dibujo animado

Day 5

What can you remember from this week?

1. Look at the pictures and write the correct words.

el búho   el lobo   la ardilla   el ciervo   el zorro

1 el l ....

2 el b ....

3 el c ....

4 la a ....

5 el z ....

2. Match the pictures to the correct words.

1   2   3   4   5

la concha   el cangrejo   la estrella de mar   las rocas   las algas marinas

190

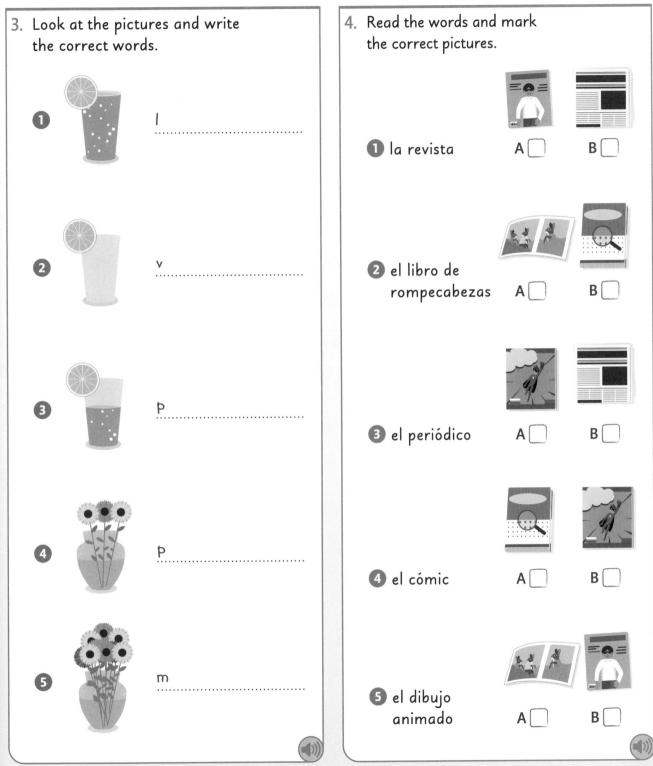

3. Look at the pictures and write the correct words.

1 l................................

2 v................................

3 p................................

4 p................................

5 m................................

4. Read the words and mark the correct pictures.

1 la revista   A ☐   B ☐

2 el libro de rompecabezas   A ☐   B ☐

3 el periódico   A ☐   B ☐

4 el cómic   A ☐   B ☐

5 el dibujo animado   A ☐   B ☐

Day 1

Listen, repeat, and copy.

① el águila   ② el ala

③ el pico

④ la garra   ⑤ el nido

Listen again and write the words.

el á ....

el a ....

el p ....

la g ....

el n ....

Day 2

Listen, repeat, and copy.

① aburrido   ② ruidoso   ③ tranquila
....

④ ordenada   ⑤ desordenada
....

Listen again and write the words.

a ....

r ....

t ....

o ....

d ....

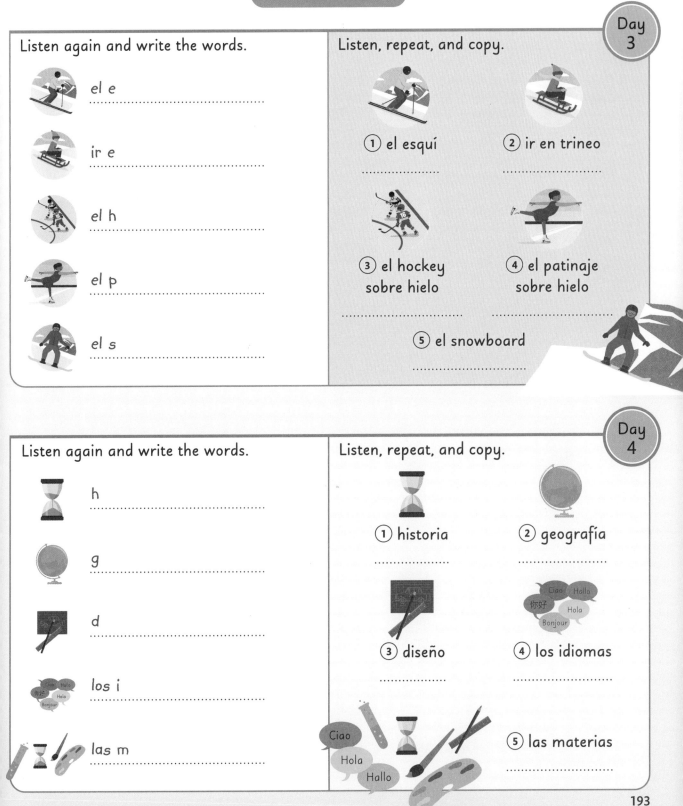

Day 3

Listen again and write the words.

el e ....

ir e ....

el h ....

el p ....

el s ....

Listen, repeat, and copy.

① el esquí ....

② ir en trineo ....

③ el hockey sobre hielo ....

④ el patinaje sobre hielo ....

⑤ el snowboard ....

Day 4

Listen again and write the words.

h ....

g ....

d ....

los i ....

las m ....

Listen, repeat, and copy.

① historia ....

② geografía ....

③ diseño ....

④ los idiomas ....

⑤ las materias ....

Day 5

What can you remember from this week?

1. Look at the pictures and mark the correct words.

1. geografía ☐
las materias ☐

2. los idiomas ☐
diseño ☐

3. historia ☐
geografía ☐

4. los idiomas ☐
historia ☐

5. diseño ☐
las materias ☐

2. Look at the pictures and fill in the missing letters.

1. e _ n _ _ d _

2. _ _ l _ _ i _ o

3. e _ _ a _ a

4. _ a _ _ _ a _ r

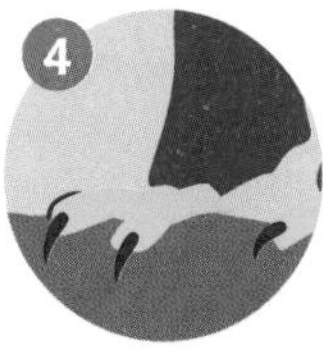

5. e _ _ á u _ l _

3. Look at the pictures and write the correct words.

1 r ....

2 t ....

3 d ....

4 o ....

5 a ....

4. Read the words and mark the correct pictures.

1 ir en trineo

A ☐   B ☐

2 el snowboard

A ☐   B ☐

3 el esquí

A ☐   B ☐

4 el patinaje sobre hielo

A ☐   B ☐

5 el hockey sobre hielo

A ☐   B ☐

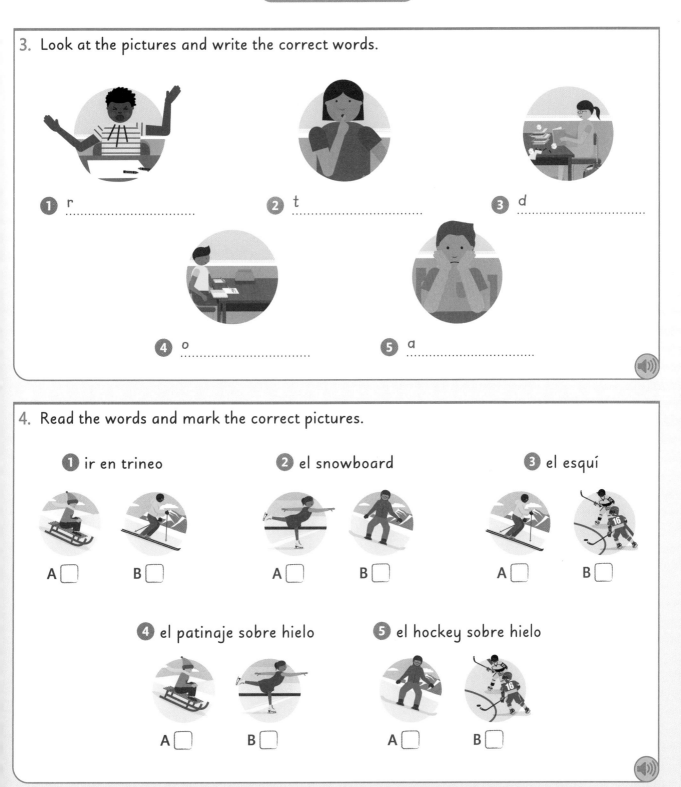

Day 1

Listen, repeat, and copy.

(1) el norte

(2) el este

(3) el sur

(4) el oeste

(5) la brújula

Listen again and write the words.

el n ....

el e ....

el s ....

el o ....

la b ....

Day 2

Listen, repeat, and copy.

(1) el espacio

(2) el cometa

(3) las estrellas

(4) el planeta

(5) el telescopio

Listen again and write the words.

el e ....

el c ....

las e ....

el p ....

el t ....

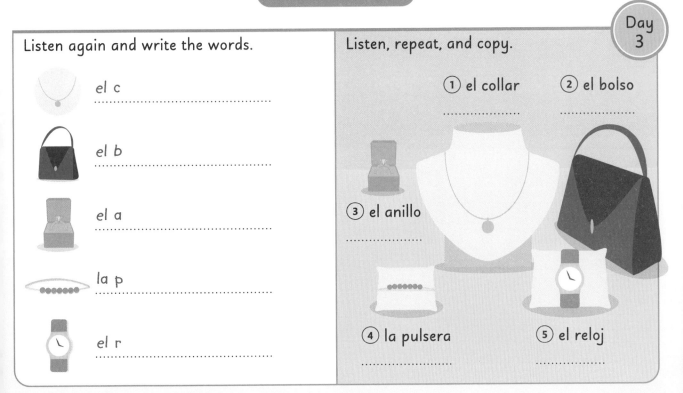

Day 3

Listen again and write the words.

el c ....

el b ....

el a ....

la p ....

el r ....

Listen, repeat, and copy.

① el collar ....

② el bolso ....

③ el anillo ....

④ la pulsera ....

⑤ el reloj ....

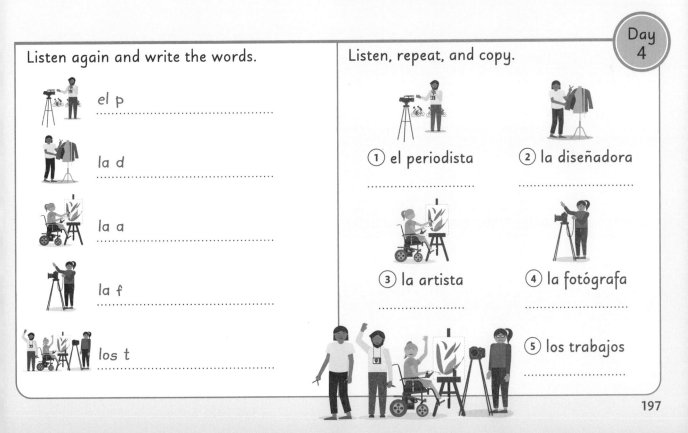

Day 4

Listen again and write the words.

el p ....

la d ....

la a ....

la f ....

los t ....

Listen, repeat, and copy.

① el periodista ....

② la diseñadora ....

③ la artista ....

④ la fotógrafa ....

⑤ los trabajos ....

Day 5

What can you remember from this week?

1. Look at the picture and write the correct words.

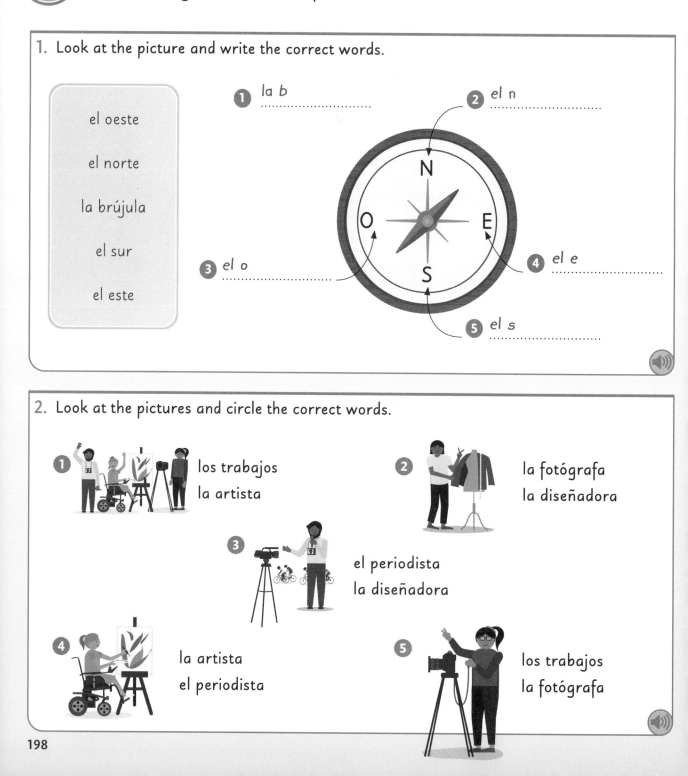

el oeste

el norte

la brújula

el sur

el este

1 la b ....

2 el n ....

3 el o ....

4 el e ....

5 el s ....

2. Look at the pictures and circle the correct words.

1 los trabajos
la artista

2 la fotógrafa
la diseñadora

3 el periodista
la diseñadora

4 la artista
el periodista

5 los trabajos
la fotógrafa

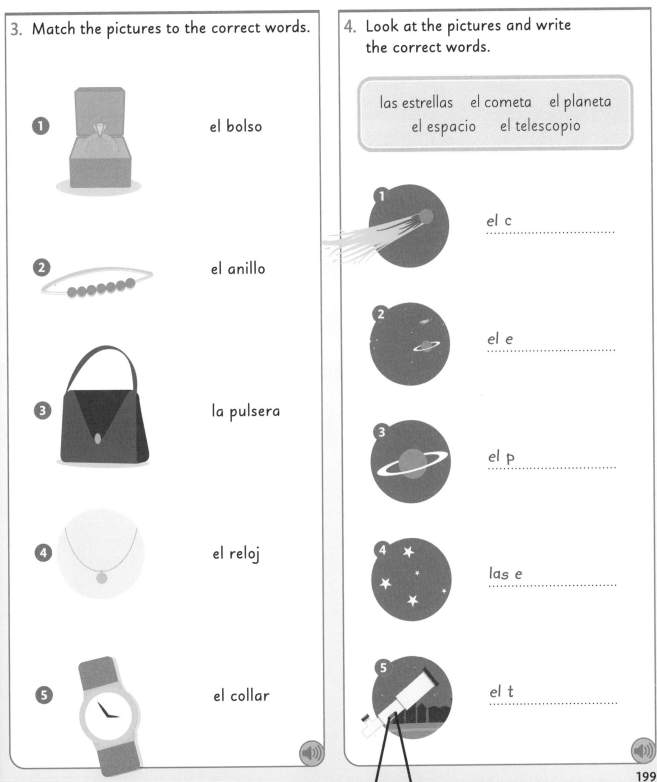

3. Match the pictures to the correct words.

① el bolso

② el anillo

③ la pulsera

④ el reloj

⑤ el collar

4. Look at the pictures and write the correct words.

las estrellas   el cometa   el planeta
el espacio   el telescopio

1 el c _____

2 el e _____

3 el p _____

4 las e _____

5 el t _____

Day 1

Listen, repeat, and copy.

① los bigotes

② el collar

③ el pelaje

④ la pata

⑤ la cola

Listen again and write the words.

los b ....

el c ....

el p ....

la p ....

la c ....

Day 2

Listen, repeat, and copy.

① inventar

② diseñar

③ pensar

④ actuar

⑤ explorar

Listen again and write the words.

i ....

d ....

p ....

a ....

e ....

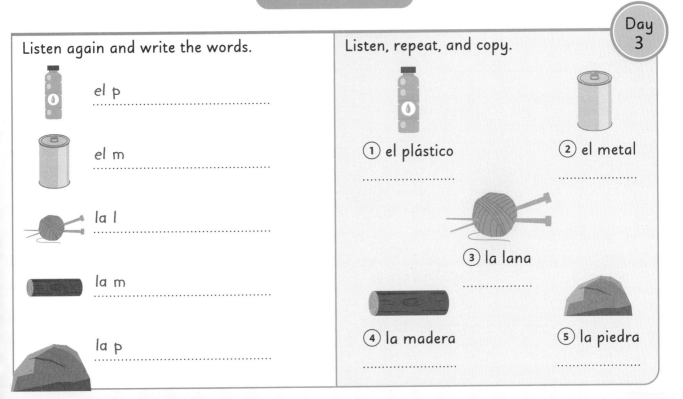

Listen again and write the words.

el p
....

el m
....

la l
....

la m
....

la p
....

Listen, repeat, and copy.

① el plástico
....

② el metal
....

③ la lana
....

④ la madera
....

⑤ la piedra
....

Listen again and write the words.

los p
....

la c
....

el c
....

el t
....

la c
....

Listen, repeat, and copy.

① los palillos
....

② la comida

③ el cuchillo
....

④ el tenedor
....

⑤ la cuchara
....

Day
5

What can you remember from this week?

1. Read the words and mark the correct pictures.

1 el tenedor

A ☐   B ☐

2 la comida

A ☐   B ☐

3 el cuchillo

A ☐   B ☐

4 los palillos

A ☐   B ☐

5 la cuchara

A ☐   B ☐

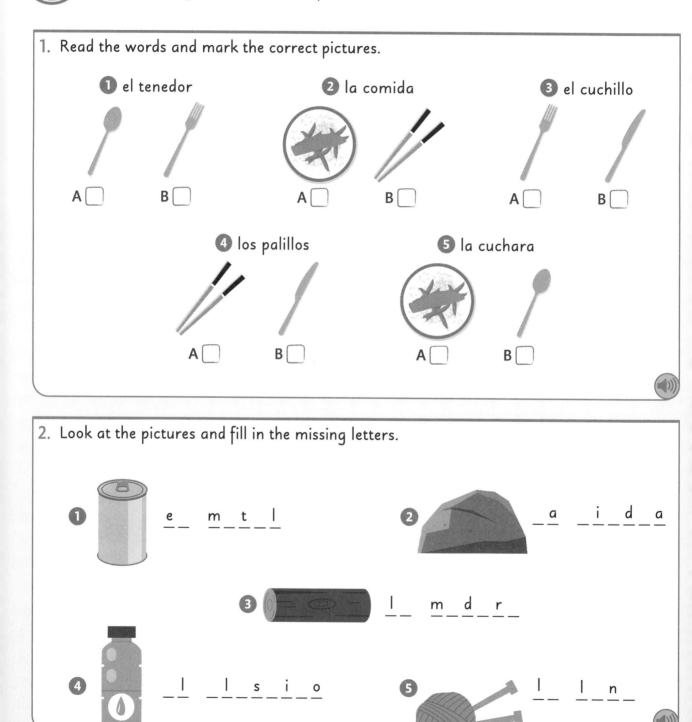

2. Look at the pictures and fill in the missing letters.

1   e _ _ m _ t _ _ l

2   _ a _ _ i _ d _ a

3   l _ _ m _ d _ r _

4   _ _ l _ _ l _ s _ i _ o

5   l _ _ l _ n _

3. Look at the pictures and mark the correct words.

1. 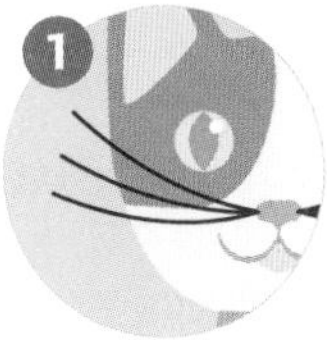 el collar ☐
   los bigotes ☐
   el pelaje ☐

2. 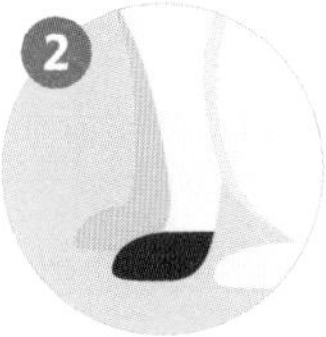 el collar ☐
   la cola ☐
   la pata ☐

3. 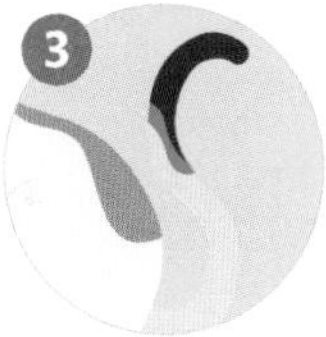 la cola ☐
   el pelaje ☐
   los bigotes ☐

4.  los bigotes ☐
   el collar ☐
   la pata ☐

5.  el pelaje ☐
   la pata ☐
   la cola ☐

4. Look at the pictures and write the letters in the correct order.

1.  i v e t r n n a

   i _ _ _ _ _ _ _

2.  p s a e n r

   p _ _ _ _ _

3.  e p r l x o a r

   e _ _ _ _ _ _ _

4.  a r a c t u

   a _ _ _ _ _

5.  d ñ i s e r a

   d _ _ _ _ _ _

Day 1

Listen, repeat, and copy.

Listen again and write the words.

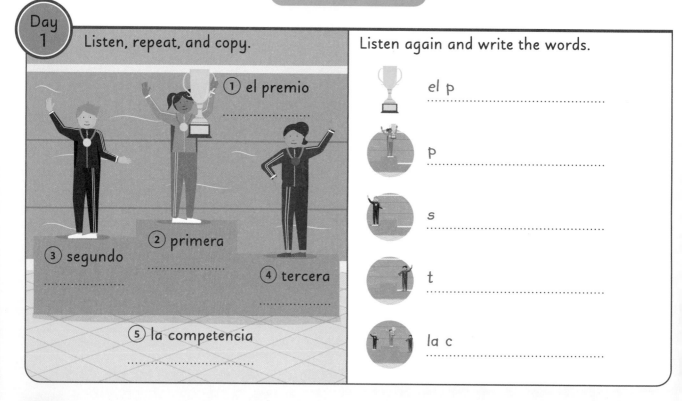

① el premio

② primera

③ segundo

④ tercera

⑤ la competencia

el p ....

p ....

s ....

t ....

la c ....

Day 2

Listen, repeat, and copy.

Listen again and write the words.

① jalar

② empujar

③ soltar

④ levantar

⑤ sujetar

j ....

e ....

s ....

l ....

s ....

Week 50

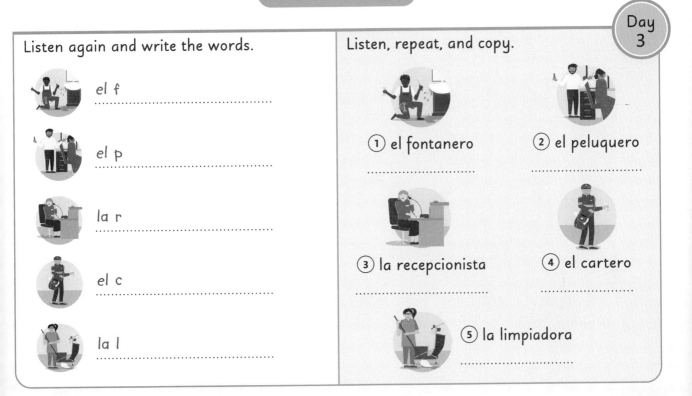

Listen again and write the words.

el f ....

el p ....

la r ....

el c ....

la l ....

Listen, repeat, and copy.

① el fontanero

② el peluquero

③ la recepcionista

④ el cartero

⑤ la limpiadora

Listen again and write the words.

las r ....

el e ....

los l ....

b ....

c ....

Listen, repeat, and copy.

① las rayas

② el estampado

③ los lunares

④ barato

⑤ caro

1. Look at the pictures and circle the correct words.

2. Look at the pictures and write the correct words.

1 empujar / jalar

2 sujetar / soltar

3 levantar / empujar

4 soltar / jalar

5 sujetar / levantar

1 las r ....

2 c ....

3 los l ....

4 el e ....

5 b ....

3. Look at the pictures and write the correct words.

> el premio　　primera　　la competencia　　segundo　　tercera

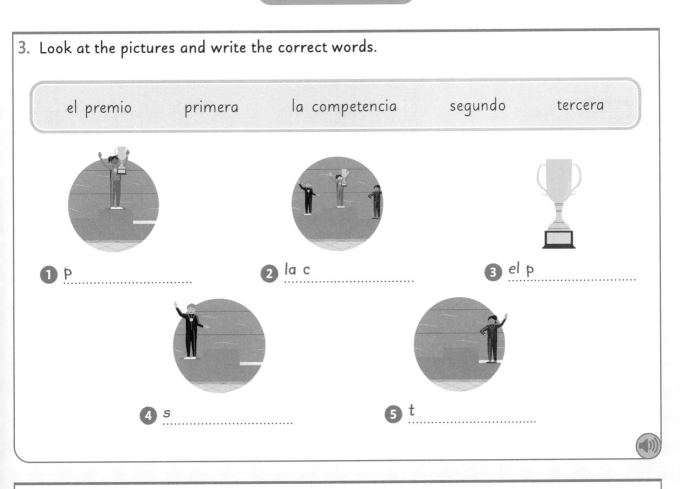

1 p ....

2 la c ....

3 el p ....

4 s ....

5 t ....

4. Match the pictures to the correct words.

el peluquero　　el cartero　　la limpiadora　　la recepcionista　　el fontanero

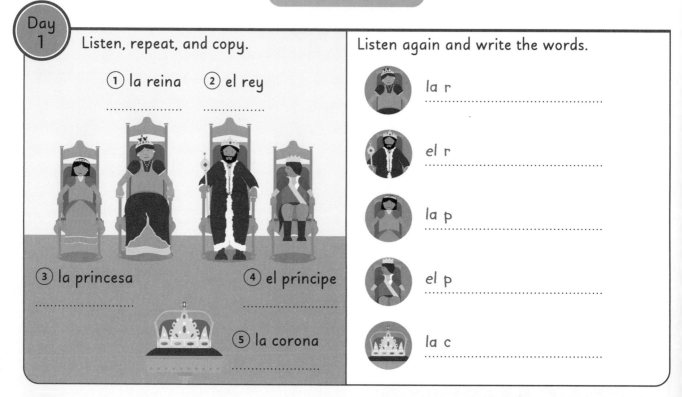

Day 1

Listen, repeat, and copy.

① la reina ② el rey

③ la princesa ④ el príncipe

⑤ la corona

Listen again and write the words.

la r ....

el r ....

la p ....

el p ....

la c ....

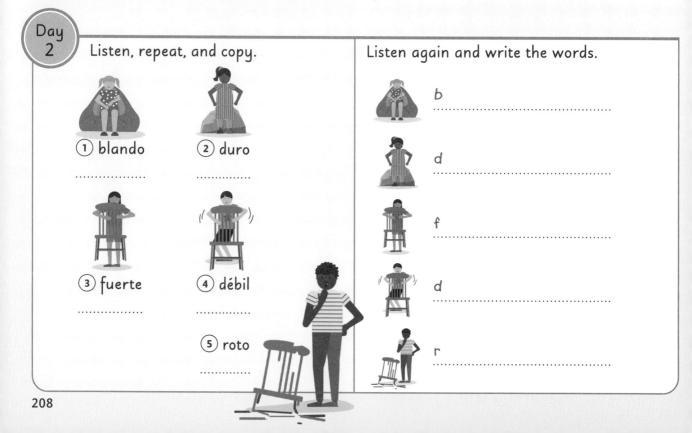

Day 2

Listen, repeat, and copy.

① blando ② duro

③ fuerte ④ débil

⑤ roto

Listen again and write the words.

b ....

d ....

f ....

d ....

r ....

Week 51

Listen again and write the words.

b ....

r ....

e ....

a ....

c ....

Listen, repeat, and copy.

① buscar

....

② reparar

....

③ encender

....

④ apagar

....

⑤ cambiar

....

Listen again and write the words.

la c ....

el c ....

el b ....

el b ....

el c ....

Listen, repeat, and copy.

① la corbata

....

② el cierre

....

③ el botón

....

④ el bolsillo

....

⑤ el cinturón

....

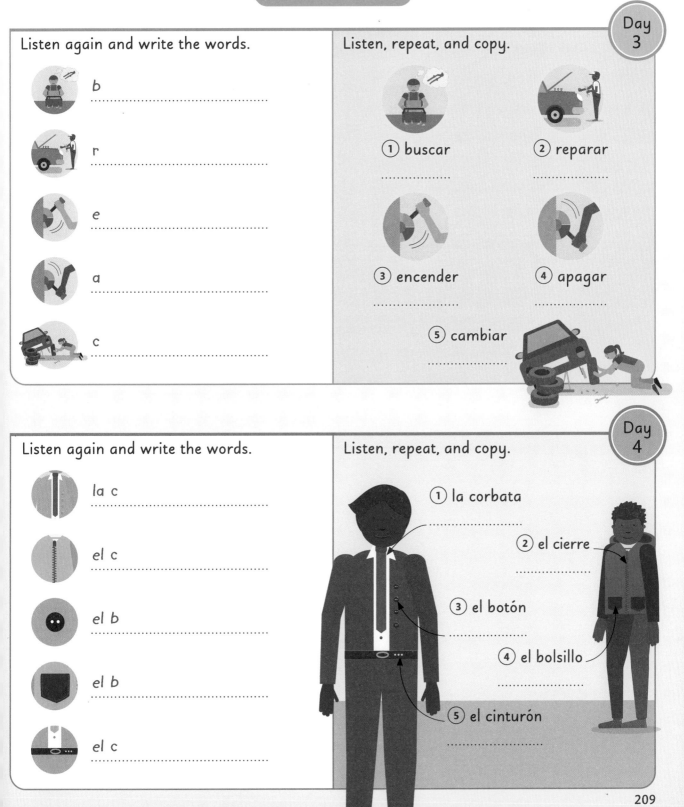

Day
5

What can you remember from this week?

1. Look at the pictures and fill in the missing letters.

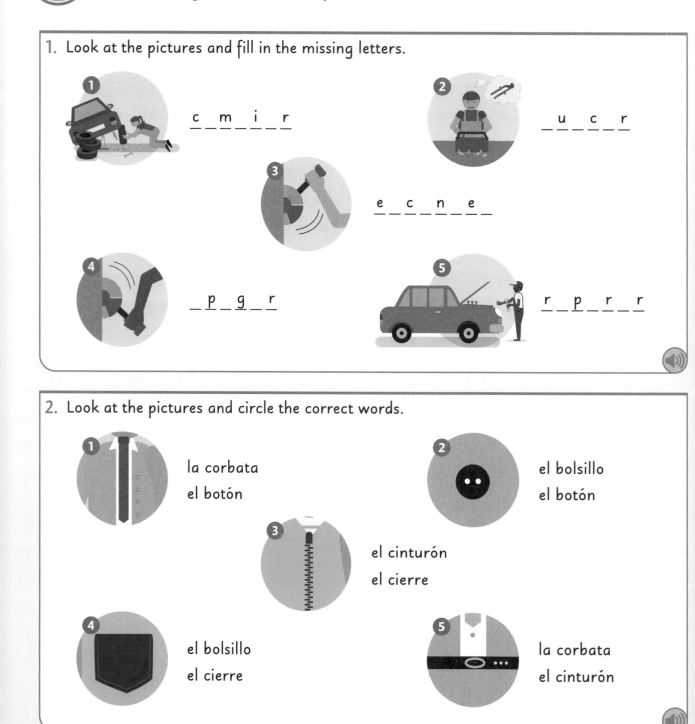

① c _ m _ i _ r

② _ u _ c _ r

③ e _ c _ n _ e _

④ _ p _ g _ r

⑤ r _ p _ r _ r

2. Look at the pictures and circle the correct words.

① la corbata
el botón

② el bolsillo
el botón

③ el cinturón
el cierre

④ el bolsillo
el cierre

⑤ la corbata
el cinturón

3. Look at the pictures and write the letters in the correct order.

① f t e u e r

f _ _ _ _ _ _

② b d l n o a

b _ _ _ _ _ _

③ d r u o

d _ _ _ _

④ r t o o

r _ _ _ _

⑤ d l é i b

d _ _ _ _ _

4. Look at the pictures and mark the correct words.

① la princesa ☐
la corona ☐

② la reina ☐
el rey ☐

③ la princesa ☐
el príncipe ☐

④ la corona ☐
el rey ☐

⑤ la reina ☐
el príncipe ☐

Day 1

Listen, repeat, and copy.

① el motor

② la llanta

③ la rueda

④ el mecánico

⑤ la caja de cartón

Listen again and write the words.

el m ....

la l ....

la r ....

el m ....

la c ....

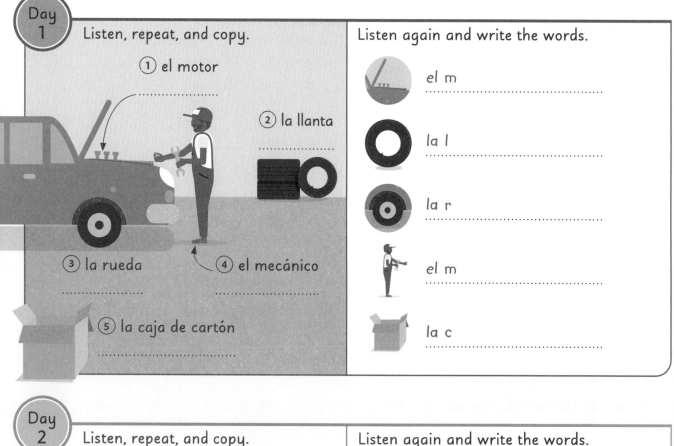

Day 2

Listen, repeat, and copy.

① sentir

② oír

③ ver

④ saborear

⑤ oler

Listen again and write the words.

s ....

o ....

v ....

s ....

o ....

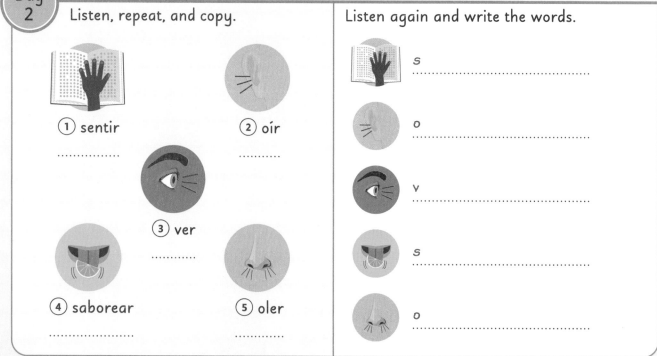

212

Week 52

Listen again and write the words.

el v ....

el t ....

los i ....

el c ....

la m ....

Listen, repeat, and copy.

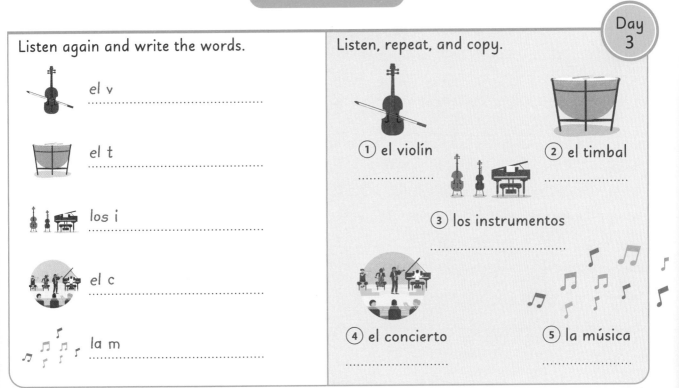

1 el violín

2 el timbal

3 los instrumentos

4 el concierto

5 la música

Listen again and write the words.

la c ....

el s ....

el m ....

la p ....

la s ....

Listen, repeat, and copy.

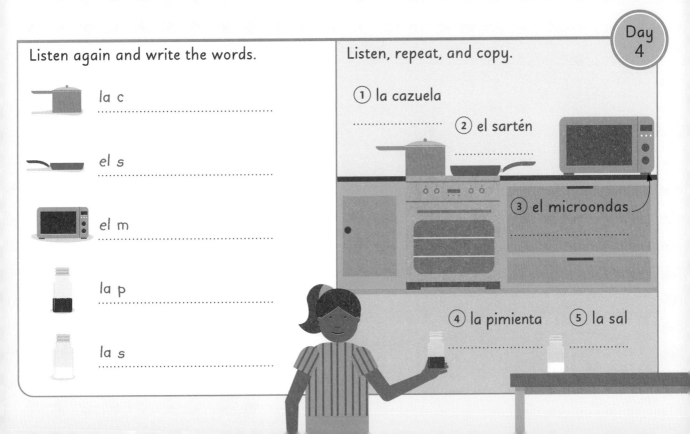

1 la cazuela

2 el sartén

3 el microondas

4 la pimienta

5 la sal

Day 5

What can you remember from this week?

1. Look at the pictures and write the correct words.

1 la p ....

2 la s ....

3 el m ....

4 la c ....

5 el s ....

2. Match the pictures to the correct words.

1 la música

2 el timbal

3 el violín

4 el concierto

5 los instrumentos

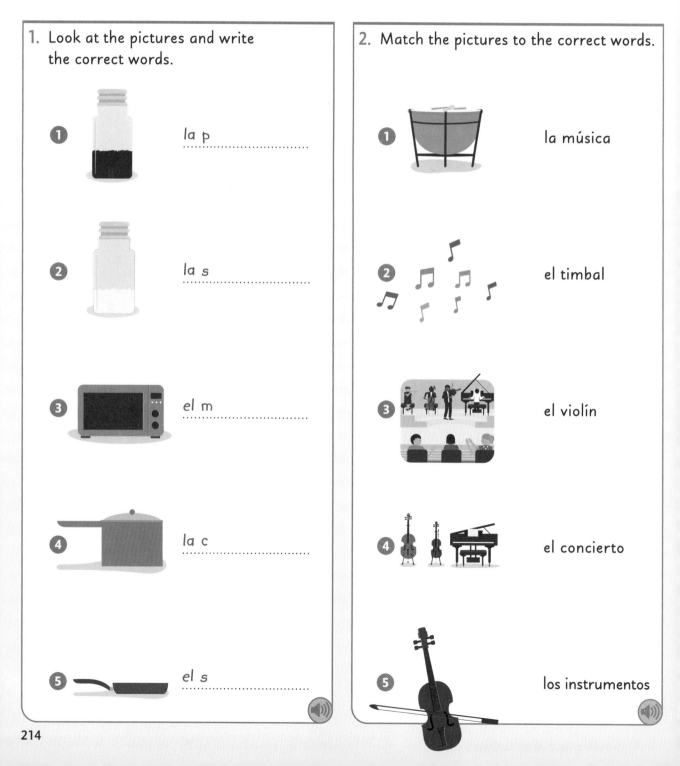

3. Look at the pictures and write the correct words.

sentir	saborear	oír	oler	ver

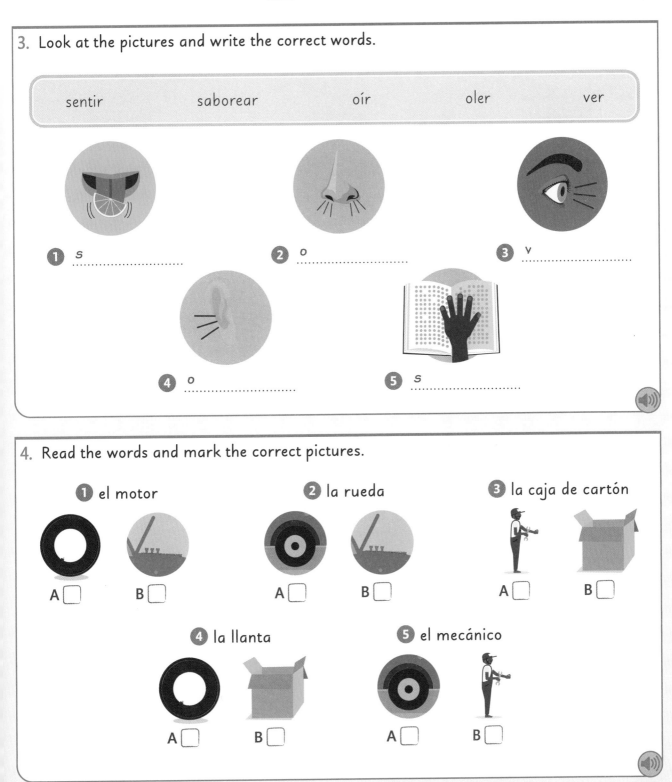

1 s ....

2 o ....

3 v ....

4 o ....

5 s ....

4. Read the words and mark the correct pictures.

1 el motor

A ☐   B ☐

2 la rueda

A ☐   B ☐

3 la caja de cartón

A ☐   B ☐

4 la llanta

A ☐   B ☐

5 el mecánico

A ☐   B ☐

Numbers

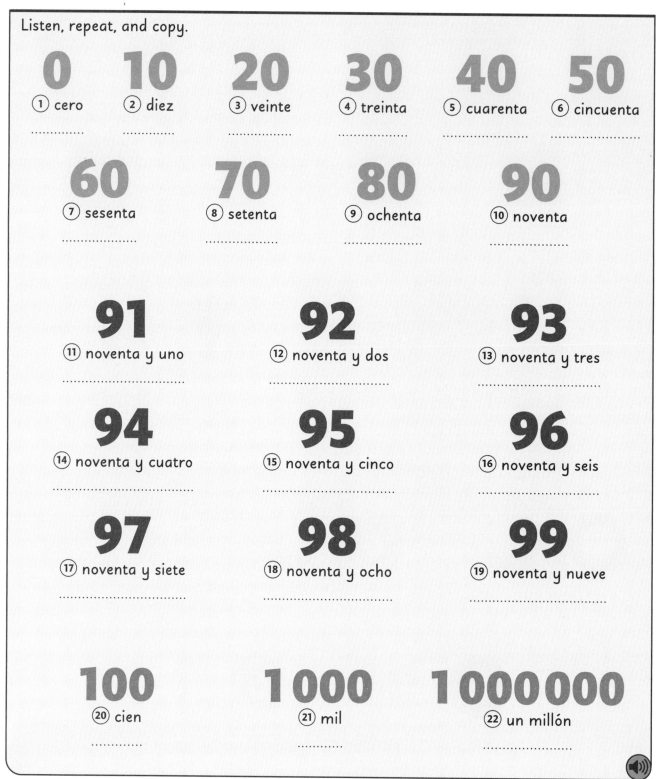

Listen, repeat, and copy.

0 ① cero

10 ② diez

20 ③ veinte

30 ④ treinta

40 ⑤ cuarenta

50 ⑥ cincuenta

60 ⑦ sesenta

70 ⑧ setenta

80 ⑨ ochenta

90 ⑩ noventa

91 ⑪ noventa y uno

92 ⑫ noventa y dos

93 ⑬ noventa y tres

94 ⑭ noventa y cuatro

95 ⑮ noventa y cinco

96 ⑯ noventa y seis

97 ⑰ noventa y siete

98 ⑱ noventa y ocho

99 ⑲ noventa y nueve

100 ⑳ cien

1 000 ㉑ mil

1 000 000 ㉒ un millón

Days

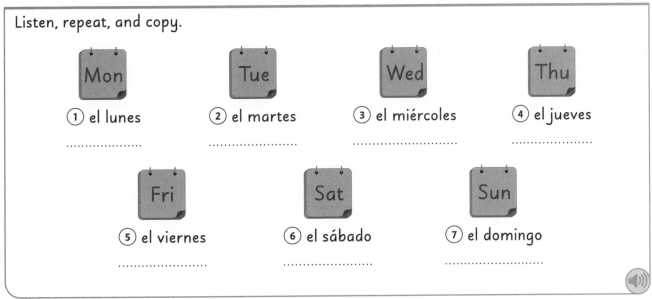

1. el lunes

2. el martes

3. el miércoles

4. el jueves

5. el viernes

6. el sábado

7. el domingo

Months

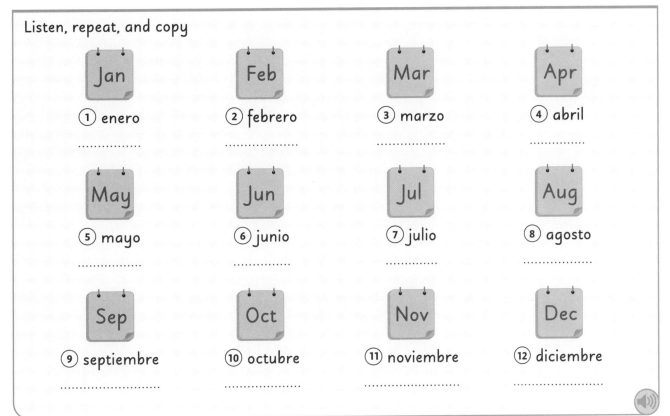

1. enero

2. febrero

3. marzo

4. abril

5. mayo

6. junio

7. julio

8. agosto

9. septiembre

10. octubre

11. noviembre

12. diciembre

English word list

Each word is followed by the number of the week it appears in. For words that are not in a weekly unit, a page number is given (for example, **p216**).

KEY

adj	adjective
n	noun
num	number
prep	preposition
v	verb

A

act *v* 49
action figure *n* 2
actor *n* 43
add *v* 10
address *n* 30
afraid *adj* 12
afternoon *n* 8
airplane *n* 38
airport *n* 38
alphabet *n* 2
ambulance *n* 25
angry *adj* 12
animals *n* 10
answer *v* 5
ant *n* 17
apartment *n* 12
apartment building *n* 12
apple *n* 1
apps *n* 21
April *n* **p217**
arm *n* 6
armchair *n* 7
arrive *v* 38
art *n* 44
artist *n* 48
ask *v* 17
asleep *adj* 40

astronaut *n* 34
August *n* **p217**
aunt *n* 14
awake *adj* 40

B

baby *n* 7
back *adj* 40
back *n* 23
backpack *n* 5
badminton *n* 6
balcony *n* 12
ball *n* 6
balloon *n* 16
banana *n* 1
band *n* 41
bandage *n* 45
band-aid *n* 45
bank *n* 35
barn *n* 10
baseball *n* 6
baseball cap *n* 11
basement *n* 22
basket *n* 33
basketball *n* 6
bat *n* 15
bathroom *n* 4
bathtub *n* 26
beach *n* 15
beach ball *n* 43
beak *n* 47
beans *n* 29
bear *n* 8
beard *n* 40
beautiful *adj* 11
bed *n* 8
bedroom *n* 4
bee *n* 17
beetle *n* 39
behind *prep* 12
belt *n* 51
bench *n* 21
between *prep* 28

bicycle *n* 21
big *adj* 11
bird *n* 19
birthday party *n* 19
black *adj* 38
black *n* 4
blanket *n* 34
blonde *adj* 38
blue *n* 1
board *n* 1
board game *n* 2
boat *n* 27
body *n* 6
book *n* 5
bookcase *n* 7
bookstore *n* 21
boots *n* 26
bored *adj* 47
borrow *v* 35
bottle *n* 33
bottom *adj* 35
bounce *v* 9
bowl *n* 33
box *n* 52
boy *n* 7
bracelet *n* 48
branch *n* 13
brave *adj* 39
bread *n* 14
break *v* 40
breakfast *n* 12
bridge *n* 34
bring *v* 38
broken *adj* 51
bronze *n* 36
brother *n* 14
brown *adj* 38
brown *n* 4
brush *n* 37
brush my teeth *v* 25
bucket *n* 43
build *v* 44
burger *n* 7
burn *v* 45
bus *n* 24
bus station *n* 24
bus stop *n* 32
butter *n* 44

butterfly *n* 39
button *n* 51
buy *v* 43

C

cabbage *n* 23
cabinet *n* 31
café *n* 21
cake *n* 19
calendar *n* 8
camel *n* 24
camera *n* 34
camp *v* 45
candle *n* 19
candy *n* 16
car *n* 25
card *n* 19
carnival *n* 28
carpet *n* 19
carrot *n* 15
carry *v* 43
cart *n* 33
cartoon *n* 46
castle *n* 27
cat *n* 6, 16
catch *v* 9
catch a bus *v* 13
caterpillar *n* 17
cave *n* 23
ceiling *n* 30
cell phone *n* 31
center *n* 41
cereal *n* 12
chair *n* 16, 19
change *v* 51
charger *n* 31
chat *v* 45
cheap *adj* 50
check *v* 10
cheese *n* 38
chef *n* 32
cherry *n* 20
chess *n* 45
chest *n* 20
chicken *n* 4
chicken *n* 7
child *n* 18
children *n* 10

subjects *n* **47**
sugar *n* **36**
suitcase *n* **38**
summer *n* **42**
sun *n* **34**
Sunday *n* **p217**
sunglasses *n* **41**
sunny *adj* **28**
supermarket *n* **31**
surf *v* **18**
surprised *adj* **12**
swan *n* **37**
sweater *n* **26**
swim *v* **18**
swimming *n* **22**
swimming pool *n* **22**
swimsuit *n* **22**
swing *n* **21**
swing *v* **32**

T

table *n* **19**
table tennis *n* **23**
tablet *n* **21**
tail *n* **49**
take a photo *v* **11**
take off *v* **36**
talk *v* **24**
tall *adj* **35**
taste *v* **52**
taxi *n* **24**
tea *n* **36**
teach *v* **5**
teacher *n* **1**
team *n* **39**
teddy bear *n* **2**
teeth *n* **29**
telephone *n* **16**
telescope *n* **48**
television *n* **7**
tell *v* **26**
ten *num* **2, p216**
tennis *n* **6**
tennis racket *n* **15**
tent *n* **42**
theater *n* **21, 43**
thin *adj* **44**
think *v* **49**

third *adj* **50**
thirsty *adj* **27**
thirteen *num* **3**
thirty *num* **p216**
three *num* **1**
throw *v* **9**
Thursday *n* **p217**
ticket *n* **21**
tidy *adj* **47**
tidy *v* **22**
tie *n* **51**
tiger *n* **8**
timetable *n* **44**
tire *n* **52**
tired *adj* **39**
toes *n* **23**
toilet *n* **26**
tomato *n* **38**
tongue *n* **29**
toolbox *n* **42**
tools *n* **42**
tooth *n* **29**
toothbrush *n* **27**
toothpaste *n* **27**
top *adj* **35**
tortoise *n* **23**
touch *v* **19**
tour *n* **34**
towel *n* **22**
town *n* **21**
toy box *n* **8**
toy store *n* **21**
toys *n* **8**
tractor *n* **10**
traffic *n* **32**
traffic lights *n* **32**
trailer *n* **42**
train *n* **39**
trash can *n* **31**
travel *v* **34**
tree *n* **13**
triangle *n* **17**
truck *n* **25**
try *v* **29**
T-shirt *n* **9**
Tuesday *n* **p217**
turn *v* **32**
turn off *v* **51**
turn on *v* **51**

TV *n* **24**
twelve *num* **3**
twenty *num* **4, p216**
two *num* **1**

U

uncle *n* **14**
under *prep* **28**
underwear *n* **7**
untidy *adj* **47**
upstairs *n* **22**

V

vacation *n* **38**
vegetables *n* **15**
vet *n* **18**
video *v* **33**
video game *n* **10**
view *n* **34**
village *n* **30**
violin *n* **52**
visit *v* **38**
volleyball *n* **23**

W

wait *v* **17**
waiter *n* **32**
wake up *v* **25**
walk *v* **13, 19**
wall *n* **25**
walrus *n* **37**
warm *adj* **35**
wash *v* **16**
watch *n* **48**
watch *v* **33**
water *n* **17**
water *v* **41**
waterfall *n* **23**
watermelon *n* **5**
wave *n* **15**
wave *v* **19**
weak *adj* **51**
weather *n* **28**
website *n* **31**
Wednesday *n* **p217**
week *n* **43**

weekend *n* **43**
weigh *v* **43**
west *n* **48**
wet *adj* **35**
whale *n* **20**
wheel *n* **52**
whiskers *n* **49**
whisper *v* **35**
whistle *v* **32**
white *n* **4**
whole *n* **41**
wind *n* **13**
window *n* **30**
windy *adj* **28**
wing *n* **47**
winner *n* **36**
winter *n* **42**
wolf *n* **46**
woman *n* **7**
women *n* **10**
wood *n* **49**
woods *n* **30**
wool *n* **49**
words *n* **1**
work *v* **34**
write *v* **3**

X

X-ray *n* **45**

Y

yard *n* **14**
year *n* **43**
yellow *n* **1**
yogurt *n* **13**
young *adj* **9**

Z

zebra *n* **5**
zero *num* **p216**
zipper *n* **51**
zoo *n* **33**

Spanish word list

Each word is followed by the number of the week it appears in. For words that are not in a weekly unit, a page number is given (for example, **p216**).

In Spanish, all nouns (things or people) are either masculine or feminine (see p6). Adjectives (describing words) also change depending on whether the noun they are describing is masculine or feminine. When two options for nouns or adjectives are given in the following list (for example, aburrido / aburrida), the masculine is given first.

KEY

adj	adjective
adv	adverb
n	noun
num	number
prep	preposition
v	verb

A

abajo adv 35
el abecedario n 2
la abeja n 17
abrigado / abrigada adj 35
abril n p217
abrir v 8
el abuelo / la abuela / los abuelos n 9
aburrido / aburrida adj 47
acalorado / acalorada adj 35
acampar v 45
las aceitunas n 38
el acierto n 22
el actor / la actriz n 43
actuar v 49
el adulto / la adulta n 18
el aeropuerto n 38
la agenda n 43
agosto n p217
agradable adj 9
el agricultor / la agricultora n 19
el agua n 17
el águila n 47
el ajedrez n 45
el ajo n 23
al lado de prep 12
el ala n 47
las albóndigas n 14
la alfombra n 7, 19
las algas marinas n 46
alimentar v 40
el almuerzo n 13
alto / alta adj 35
amarillo adj 1
la ambulancia n 25
los amigos / las amigas n 18
amistosa adj 27

el andén n 39
el anillo n 48
los animales n 10
el año n 43
apagar v 51
aplaudir v 19
las aplicaciones n 21
aprender v 5
la araña n 39
el árbol n 13
el arco iris n 13
la ardilla n 46
la arena n 15
arreglar v 44
arriba adv 35
el arroyo n 34
el arroz n 29
arte n 44
el artista / la artista n 48
el asiento n 21
el astronauta / la astronauta n 34
asustado / asustada adj 12, 27
aterrizar v 36
la atracción n 28
atrapar v 9
los audífonos n 31
el autobús n 24
el avión n 38
ayudar v 26
el azúcar n 36
azul adj 1

B

el bádminton n 6
bailar v 11
el baile n 14
bajar v 36
el balcón n 12
la ballena n 20
el baloncesto n 6
la banca n 21
el banco n 35
la bandera n 43
la bañera n 26

el baño n 4
barato / barata adj 50
la barba n 40
la barbilla n 40
la barca n 27
el barco n 6
la barriga n 23
el bate n 15
el basurero n 31
el bebé / la bebé n 7
beber v 16
las bebidas n 17
el béisbol n 6
la berenjena n 23
la biblioteca n 31
la bicicleta n 21
el bigote n 40
los bigotes n 49
blanco adj 4
blando / blanda adj 51
el bloque de apartamentos n 12
la boca n 40
las bocinas n 24
la bola de nieve n 32
el boleto n 21
el bolígrafo n 2
el bolsillo n 51
el bolso n 48
el bombero / la bombera n 18
bonito / bonita adj 9
el borrador n 5
el bosque n 27, 30
botar v 9
las botas n 26
la botella n 33
el botón n 51
el brazo n 6
el bronce n 36
la brújula n 48
la bufanda n 26

Common subjects

This is an index of common topics found in the book. Each subject is followed by the weeks it is taught in or the page number it appears on (for example, **p216**).

Answers

Week 1

1
1. el maestro
2. el pizarrón
3. los colores
4. las palabras
5. la clase

2
1. morado
2. rojo
3. amarillo
4. azul
5. verde

3
1. dos
2. cinco
3. cuatro
4. uno
5. tres

4
1. la piña
2. las uvas
3. la manzana
4. el plátano
5. la naranja

Week 2

1
1. los números
2. el abecedario
3. las letras
4. la compañera de clase
5. el salón de clases

2
1. la muñeca
2. la figura de acción
3. el osito
4. el juego de mesa
5. la marioneta

3
1. B 2. A 3. B 4. A
5. A

4
1. ocho
2. seis
3. nueve
4. siete
5. diez

Week 3

1
1. dibujar
2. colorear
3. contar
4. deletrear
5. escribir

2
1. la escuela
2. el parque infantil
3. el parque
4. la calle
5. la casa

3
1. once
2. trece
3. quince
4. catorce
5. doce

4
1. la familia
2. el padre
3. la madre
4. el hijo
5. la hija

Week 4

1
1. marrón
2. rosa
3. naranja
4. blanco
5. negro

2
1. B 2. A 3. B 4. A
5. A

3
1. la gallina
2. la cabra
3. la oveja
4. la vaca
5. el caballo

4
1. diecisiete
2. veinte
3. dieciocho
4. dieciséis
5. diecinueve

Week 5

1
1. la cebra
2. el hipopótamo
3. el león
4. la jirafa
5. el elefante

2
1. las tijeras
2. el libro
3. la regla
4. el borrador
5. la mochila

3
1. escuchar
2. enseñar
3. aprender
4. señalar
5. contestar

4
1. el kiwi
2. la pera
3. la sandía
4. el coco
5. el mango

Week 6

1
1. B 2. A 3. B 4. A
5. B

2
1. la cabeza
2. la pierna
3. el cuerpo
4. el brazo
5. el cuello

3
1. el hockey
2. el tenis
3. el béisbol
4. el baloncesto
5. el bádminton

4
1. el mar
2. la gaviota
3. la cometa
4. el barco
5. la pelota

Week 7

1
1. la niña
2. el hombre
3. el niño
4. el bebé
5. la mujer

2
1. B 2. A 3. A 4. B
5. A

3
1. el sofá
2. la alfombra
3. el sillón
4. el librero
5. la televisión

4
1. la pizza
2. los fideos
3. la hamburguesa
4. las papas fritas
5. el pollo

Week 8

1
1. el tigre
2. la rana
3. el mono
4. la selva
5. el oso

2
1. A 2. B 3. A 4. A
5. B

3
1. sentarse
2. abrir
3. cerrar
4. recoger
5. levantarse

4
1. la tarde
2. la noche
3. la mañana
4. la tarde-noche
5. el día

Week 9

1
1. los abuelos
2. la abuela
3. el abuelo
4. el nieto
5. la nieta

2
1. la camiseta
2. el vestido
3. las sandalias
4. los zapatos
5. los pantalones cortos

3
1. bonito
2. viejo
3. gruñón
4. joven
5. agradable

4
1. atrapar
2. golpear
3. patear
4. lanzar
5. botar

Week 10

1
1. la persona
2. las mujeres
3. los niños
4. las personas
5. los hombres

2
1. B 2. A 3. B 4. A
5. A

3
1. el tractor
2. el campo
3. la granja
4. los animales
5. el granero

4
1. el dinosaurio
2. el monopatín
3. el videojuego
4. el robot
5. el monstruo

Week 11

1
1. el ojo
2. los labios
3. la nariz
4. la oreja
5. la cara

2
1. A 2. B 3. A 4. A
5. B

3
1. hermoso
2. limpio
3. pequeño
4. sucio
5. grande

4
1. la camisa
2. la gorra
3. la falda
4. los pantalones
5. la chaqueta

Week 12

1
1. dentro de
2. delante de
3. detrás de
4. al lado de
5. encima de

2
1. el cereal
2. el desayuno
3. el huevo
4. el pastelito
5. la salchicha

3
1. el balcón
2. el elevador
3. el bloque de apartamentos
4. la planta baja
5. el piso

4
1. sorprendida
2. triste
3. asustado
4. feliz
5. enojada

Week 13

1
1. A 2. A 3. B 4. A
5. B

2
1. la hoja
2. la rama
3. el árbol
4. la planta
5. la flor

3

1 la tormenta
2 el viento
3 la niebla
4 la lluvia
5 el arco iris

4

1 el refrigerio
2 el yogurt
3 la fruta
4 el emparedado
5 el almuerzo

Week 14

1

1 el techo
2 la cerca
3 el jardín
4 el cobertizo
5 el hogar

2

1 el dibujo
2 el baile
3 la pintura
4 los deportes
5 los pasatiempos

3

1 el tío
2 la tía
3 la prima
4 el hermano
5 la hermana

4

1 la pasta
2 la salsa
3 la cena
4 el pan
5 las albóndigas

Week 15

1

1 la zanahoria
2 los guisantes
3 las verduras
4 la papa
5 el pimiento

2

1 el mar
2 la ola
3 la playa
4 la arena
5 la isla

3

1 el casco
2 los tenis
3 el bate
4 la raqueta de tenis
5 los patines

4

1 correr
2 saltar a la soga
3 jugar
4 trepar
5 saltar

Week 16

1

1 los dulces
2 la fiesta
3 el juego
4 la invitación
5 el globo

2

1 cocinar
2 comer
3 lavar
4 secar
5 beber

3

1 el gato
2 el ratón
3 el perro
4 el cachorro
5 el gatito

4

1 la lámpara
2 el reloj
3 el teléfono
4 el escritorio
5 la silla

Week 17

1

1 preguntar
2 elegir
3 esperar
4 ponerse
5 comprar

2

1 la mariquita
2 la abeja
3 la hormiga
4 la libélula
5 la oruga

3

1 el jugo
2 las bebidas
3 el agua
4 la limonada
5 el licuado

4

1 el triángulo
2 el círculo
3 el rectángulo
4 el cuadrado
5 las formas

Week 18

1

1 A 2 B 3 B 4 A
5 B

2

1 el pelo
2 corto
3 largo
4 liso
5 rizado

3

1 surfear
2 pescar
3 volar
4 nadar
5 navegar

4

1 el niño
2 la adulta
3 el padre
4 el grupo
5 los amigos

Week 19

1

1 moverse
2 caminar
3 tocar
4 aplaudir
5 saludar con la mano

2

1 el pájaro
2 el burro
3 el establo
4 el cerdo
5 el agricultor

3

1. el regalo
2. la tarjeta
3. la fiesta de cumpleaños
4. la vela
5. el pastel

4

1. la alfombra
2. el cojín
3. las luces
4. la silla
5. la mesa

Week 20

1

1. A 2. B 3. A 4. B
5. A

2

1. el delfín
2. la medusa
3. el pulpo
4. el tiburón
5. la ballena

3

1. los dedos
2. el hombro
3. el codo
4. la mano
5. el pecho

4

1. el limón
2. la cereza
3. la fresa
4. el durazno
5. la lima

Week 21

1

1. la tableta
2. el libro electrónico
3. el mensaje
4. las aplicaciones
5. el correo electrónico

2

1. la librería
2. la oficina de correos
3. la juguetería
4. el café
5. el pueblo

3

1. el asiento
2. el cine
3. la estrella de cine
4. el boleto
5. la película

4

1. A 2. B 3. A 4. A
5. B

Week 22

1

1. el pasillo
2. piso de arriba
3. piso de abajo
4. las escaleras
5. el sótano

2

1. hacer los deberes
2. ordenar
3. practicar
4. descansar
5. limpiar

3

1. la toalla
2. la piscina
3. el traje de baño
4. los lentes de natación
5. la natación

4

1. el acierto
2. la pregunta
3. la fecha
4. el error
5. la oración

Week 23

1

1. la cebolla
2. el ajo
3. el repollo
4. el champiñón
5. la berenjena

2

1. el río
2. la cascada
3. la cueva
4. el lagarto
5. la tortuga

3

1. el golf
2. el voleibol
3. la gimnasia
4. el tenis de mesa
5. el fútbol

4

1. la espalda
2. la barriga
3. la rodilla
4. el pie
5. los dedos del pie

Week 24

1

1. A 2. B 3. B 4. A
5. B

2

1. el camello
2. la pirámide
3. el desierto
4. la serpiente
5. el cocodrilo

3

1. el taxi
2. el pasajero
3. el autobús
4. el conductor
5. la estación de autobuses

4

1. llamar por teléfono
2. enviar un correo
   electrónico
3. enviar
4. gritar
5. hablar

Week 25

1

1. el escalón
2. el tapete
3. el muro
4. la escalera de mano
5. el portón

2

1. el coche
2. el camión
3. la motocicleta
4. el camión de bomberos
5. la ambulancia

3

1. B 2. A 3. A 4. B
5. A

4
1 iguales
2 diferentes
3 nuevo
4 favorito
5 viejo

Week 26

1
1 contar
2 llorar
3 ayudar
4 hacerse daño
5 caerse

2
1 el canguro
2 el gorila
3 el rinoceronte
4 el panda
5 el loro

3
1 las botas
2 el suéter
3 la bufanda
4 el saco
5 los guantes

4
1 la bañera
2 la taza de baño
3 el espejo
4 el estante
5 la regadera

Week 27

1
1 asustado
2 emocionada
3 amistosa
4 sediento
5 hambriento

2
1 el jabón
2 el lavabo
3 la pasta de dientes
4 el cepillo de dientes
5 el grifo

3
1 el proyecto
2 el rompecabezas
3 la imagen
4 la historia
5 la lección

4
1 el bosque
2 la montaña
3 el castillo
4 el lago
5 la barca

Week 28

1
1 A 2 B 3 B 4 A
5 B

2
1 con neblina
2 soleado
3 el clima
4 ventoso
5 nublado

3
1 el ratón
2 la impresora
3 la computadora
4 la pantalla
5 el teclado

4
1 el circo
2 la atracción
3 el helado
4 la feria
5 el payaso

Week 29

1
1 buscar
2 encontrar
3 unir
4 completar
5 intentar

2
1 el pez
2 la pesca
3 la caña de pescar
4 la red
5 el chaleco salvavidas

3
1 los dientes
2 la lengua
3 el diente
4 la sonrisa
5 la dentista

4
1 los frijoles
2 la carne
3 el arroz
4 la sopa
5 la tarta

Week 30

1
1 el pueblo
2 las lomas
3 el campo
4 el bosque
5 el mercado

2
1 la carta
2 la dirección
3 el sobre
4 la estampilla
5 el nombre

3
1 B 2 A 3 B 4 A
5 B

4
1 el techo
2 la ventana
3 la puerta
4 el piso
5 la llave

Week 31

1
1 B 2 B 3 B 4 A
5 A

2
1 la oficina
2 la biblioteca
3 el estadio
4 el gimnasio
5 el supermercado

3
1 la cocina
2 el basurero
3 el horno
4 el gabinete
5 el refrigerador

4
1 la roca
2 el cielo
3 la nube
4 el suelo
5 los insectos

Week 32

1
1 B 2 A 3 A 4 A
5 B

2
1. el menú
2. el restaurante
3. la cocinera
4. la comida
5. la mesera

3
1. jugar
2. saltar
3. girar
4. columpiarse
5. silbar

4
1. la carretera
2. la parada de autobús
3. el tráfico
4. el paso de cebra
5. el semáforo

Week 33

1
1. el plato
2. la botella
3. el vaso de vidrio
4. el plato hondo
5. la taza

2
1. A 2. B 3. A 4. A
5. B

3
1. el monedero
2. las compras
3. la canasta
4. el dinero
5. el carrito

4
1. el zoológico
2. la ciudad
3. el museo
4. la universidad
5. el rascacielos

Week 34

1
1. viajar
2. trabajar
3. hablar
4. encontrarse
5. mostrar

2
1. la astronauta
2. la Tierra
3. el sol
4. la luna
5. el cohete

3
1. el puente
2. el arroyo
3. el camino
4. el pícnic
5. la manta

4
1. la foto
2. la vista
3. la cámara
4. el recorrido
5. la tarjeta postal

Week 35

1
1. B 2. A 3. A 4. A
5. B

2
1. pequeña
2. abajo
3. en medio
4. alto
5. arriba

3
1. abrigado
2. seca
3. mojada
4. helada
5. acalorado

4
1. estudiar
2. susurrar
3. buscar
4. leer
5. tomar prestado

Week 36

1
1. el té
2. la galleta
3. el café
4. la leche
5. el azúcar

2
1. el oro
2. el ganador
3. la plata
4. el bronce
5. la carrera

3
1. despegar
2. aterrizar
3. darse prisa
4. bajar
5. subir

4
1. B 2. A 3. A 4. B
5. A

Week 37

1
1. gustar
2. no gustar
3. pagar
4. pedir
5. preparar

2
1. el peine
2. los lentes
3. el cepillo
4. el perfume
5. las joyas

3
1. el pingüino
2. el oso polar
3. la foca
4. el reno
5. la morsa

4
1. el pasto
2. la rana
3. el estanque
4. el cisne
5. el pato

Week 38

1
1. el piloto
2. el aeropuerto
3. la vacación
4. la maleta
5. el avión

2
1. traer
2. llegar
3. visitar
4. dar
5. saludar

3

1. castaño
2. rubio
3. pelirrojo
4. negro
5. gris

4

1. la ensalada
2. la lechuga
3. el tomate
4. el queso
5. las aceitunas

Week 39

1

1. el partido
2. la patada
3. el equipo
4. el marcador
5. el jugador

2

1. el escarabajo
2. la mosca
3. la mariposa
4. el caracol
5. la araña

3

1. valiente
2. con náuseas
3. dolorida
4. cansado
5. enfermo

4

1. B 2. A 3. B 4. B
5. A

Week 40

1

1. claro
2. despierto
3. oscuro
4. dormido
5. ruidoso

2

1. esconder
2. traer
3. alimentar
4. romper
5. cuidar

3

1. lejos
2. izquierda
3. detrás
4. derecha
5. delante

4

1. la boca
2. la barbilla
3. la ceja
4. el bigote
5. la barba

Week 41

1

1. el total
2. la esquina
3. la mitad
4. el centro
5. el cuarto

2

1. la piscina
2. el sombrero
3. el hotel
4. la silla reclinable
5. los lentes de sol

3

1. B 2. A 3. B 4. A
5. A

4

1. recoger
2. plantar
3. regar
4. crecer
5. cortar

Week 42

1

1. el reloj
2. el mediodía
3. el minuto
4. la medianoche
5. la hora

2

1. el fuego
2. la caravana
3. la tienda de campaña
4. la linterna
5. el humo

3

1. el verano
2. el invierno
3. el otoño
4. la primavera
5. las estaciones del año

4

1. el pegamento
2. la técnica
3. la caja de herramientas
4. las herramientas
5. la máquina

Week 43

1

1. pesar
2. comprar
3. dar
4. vender
5. llevar

2

1. el actor
2. el telón
3. el escenario
4. la cantante
5. el teatro

3

1. la bandera
2. la pelota de playa
3. la cubeta
4. la pala
5. el castillo de arena

4

1. el mes
2. la semana
3. el año
4. la agenda
5. el fin de semana

Week 44

1

1. arte
2. matemáticas
3. ciencias
4. lengua
5. el horario

2

1. construir
2. pintar
3. mezclar
4. arreglar
5. pegar

3

1. la mantequilla
2. la mermelada
3. el chocolate
4. la harina
5. la miel

4

1. peludo
2. lento
3. gordo
4. rápido
5. delgado

Week 45

1

1. la salida
2. el estacionamiento
3. las tiendas
4. la entrada
5. el centro comercial

2

1. el estudiante
2. el mapa
3. el ajedrez
4. el diccionario
5. el cuaderno

3

1. la medicina
2. la radiografía
3. el vendaje
4. la tirita
5. la mascarilla

4

1. quemar
2. reír
3. charlar
4. acampar
5. dormir

Week 46

1

1. el lobo
2. el búho
3. el ciervo
4. la ardilla
5. el zorro

2

1. el cangrejo
2. la concha
3. las rocas
4. las algas marinas
5. la estrella de mar

3

1. lleno
2. vacío
3. por la mitad
4. pocos
5. muchos

4

1. A 2. B 3. B 4. B
5. A

Week 47

1

1. geografía
2. diseño
3. historia
4. los idiomas
5. las materias

2

1. el nido
2. el pico
3. el ala
4. la garra
5. el águila

3

1. ruidoso
2. tranquila
3. desordenada
4. ordenada
5. aburrido

4

1. A 2. B 3. A 4. B
5. B

Week 48

1

1. la brújula
2. el norte
3. el oeste
4. el este
5. el sur

2

1. los trabajos
2. la diseñadora
3. el periodista
4. la artista
5. la fotógrafa

3

1. el anillo
2. la pulsera
3. el bolso
4. el collar
5. el reloj

4

1. el cometa
2. el espacio
3. el planeta
4. las estrellas
5. el telescopio

Week 49

1

1. B 2. A 3. B 4. A
5. B

2

1. el metal
2. la piedra
3. la madera
4. el plástico
5. la lana

3

1. los bigotes
2. la pata
3. la cola
4. el collar
5. el pelaje

4

1. inventar
2. pensar
3. explorar
4. actuar
5. diseñar

Week 50

1

1. jalar
2. sujetar
3. empujar
4. soltar
5. levantar

2

1. las rayas
2. caro
3. los lunares
4. el estampado
5. barato

3

1. primera
2. la competencia
3. el premio
4. segundo
5. tercera

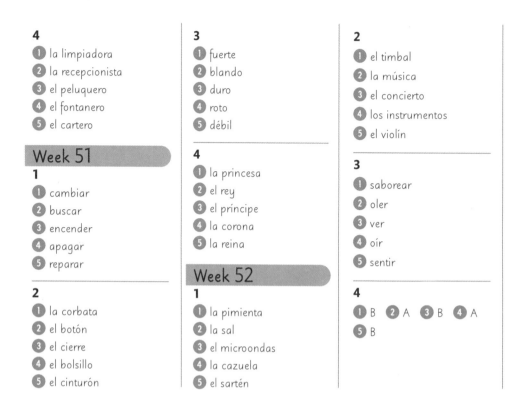

4

1. la limpiadora
2. la recepcionista
3. el peluquero
4. el fontanero
5. el cartero

Week 51

1

1. cambiar
2. buscar
3. encender
4. apagar
5. reparar

2

1. la corbata
2. el botón
3. el cierre
4. el bolsillo
5. el cinturón

3

1. fuerte
2. blando
3. duro
4. roto
5. débil

4

1. la princesa
2. el rey
3. el príncipe
4. la corona
5. la reina

Week 52

1

1. la pimienta
2. la sal
3. el microondas
4. la cazuela
5. el sartén

2

1. el timbal
2. la música
3. el concierto
4. los instrumentos
5. el violín

3

1. saborear
2. oler
3. ver
4. oír
5. sentir

4

1. B 2. A 3. B 4. A
5. B

Acknowledgments

The publisher would like to thank:

Adam Brackenbury for design and illustration assistance; Edwood Burn for illustration assistance; Ankita Awasthi Tröger and Andiamo! Language Services Ltd for proofreading; Abigail Ellis for indexing; Cristina Sanchez for translation assistance; ID Audio for audio recording and production; Christine Stroyan and Sophie Adam for audio recording management; and Rakesh Kumar, Priyanka Sharma, and Saloni Singh for jacket design assistance.

All images are copyright DK. For more information, please visit www.dkimages.com.